The Immigrant Heritage of America Series

Cecyle S. Neidle, *Editor*

Labor and Immigration in Industrial America

By Robert D. Parmet, 1938 -

York College of The City University of New York

TWAYNE PUBLISHERS

A DIVISION OF G. K. HALL & CO., BOSTON

Published in 1981 by Twayne Publishers,
A Division of G. K. Hall & Co.
All Rights Reserved

Printed on permanent/durable acid-free paper and bound
in the United States of America.
First Printing

Photo credit: "Steelworkers at Russian Boarding House,
Homestead, Pennsylvania 1907–08" by Lewis W. Hine,
Courtesy of the International Museum of Photography
at George Eastman House, Rochester, New York.

Library of Congress Cataloging in Publication Data

Parmet, Robert D., 1938–
Labor and immigration in industrial America.

(The Immigrant heritage of America series)
Bibliography: pp. 240–61
Includes index.
1. Alien labor—United States—History.
2. United States—Emigration and immigration—
History. 3. Trade-unions—United States—History.
4. Labor and laboring classes—United States—
History. I. Title. II. Series: Immigrant heritage
of America series.
HD8081.A5P37   331.6′2′0973   81–1438
ISBN 0–8057–8418–7   AACR2

To Andrew

Contents

About the Author

Robert D. Parmet was born in New York City and educated at The City College of New York and Columbia University, where he received a Ph.D. in History. He is now Professor of History at York College of The City University of New York, having previously taught at The City College and Newark State College.

A specialist in American history, his main interest is in immigration and labor. In 1971 he coauthored *American Nativism, 1830–1860*. A contributor to the *Encyclopedia of Southern History*, his articles have also appeared in such diverse publications as the *New-York Historical Society Quarterly*, *Journal of the Illinois State Historical Society*, *Connecticut Historical Society Bulletin*, and *Negro History Bulletin*. He is currently preparing a book on American patriotism.

Besides writing and teaching history, his interests include photography, travel, and music of the theater. He resides in Great Neck, New York, with his wife Joan and son Andrew.

Preface

They came from many lands. Asians as well as Europeans, they wanted to live and work in the United States. Some sought to stay only a short while before returning to their homelands, but others hoped to remain permanently in a country that offered greater freedom and opportunity than any known before.

Between the end of the American Civil War and the beginning of World War I, millions of such immigrants arrived in America. Immediately they took jobs in industry and agriculture, and began their pursuit of a better life. As they moved ahead, they encountered enemies.

Though employers usually welcomed immigrant workers, others in the labor force often resented them. American workers, native- or foreign-born, organized or independent, almost instinctively regarded late-arriving foreigners as threats to both jobs and wages. It was virtually axiomatic that immigrants accepted poorer conditions than old-timers. By working for lower pay and longer hours, and by coming in excessive numbers, the argument went, the newcomers' effect on industry was to reduce wages and increase unemployment.

That they created economic hardship did not surprise their critics. After all, these more recent immigrants differed considerably from their antebellum predecessors. The earlier immigrants had come mainly from the British Isles, Germany, and Scandinavia. Except for Irish and German Catholics, these people were predominantly Protestant. On the other hand, the late arrivals were natives of such places as Austria-Hungary, Russia, Poland, Italy, and the Balkans. They were mainly Roman Catholic and Jewish, and contrasted sharply in custom, dress, and language with the groups that had already become assimilated.

Chinese immigrants arrived in significant numbers even before the Eastern and Southern Europeans. Their growing presence on the Pacific Coast taught white American workers to hate and fear along racial lines hitherto associated primarily with blacks. In expressing their fears of the Chinese as economic competitors, Americans repeatedly injected racist concepts for purposes of reinforcement. That technique they afterward applied to Europeans and other Asians.

This pattern of fear and prejudice was a major characteristic of the American labor movement as it developed in the late nineteenth and early twentieth centuries and struggled to survive in a society increasingly dominated by industrial capitalism. The immigrant, a classic source of "cheap labor," thus emerged as second only to the capitalists themselves as the workers' enemies. Led by Samuel Gompers, most labor leaders strenuously promoted immigration restriction or exclusion—ostensibly to protect their members from this enemy.

This book examines labor's restrictionist attitudes and actions. It begins by introducing the question of native-foreign worker conflict, which it places within the context of American indusrialization through the Civil War. Then it discusses the anti-Chinese movement, tracing it from its origin as a California phenomenon to its elevation to the national level with organized labor's support. The discussion of the Chinese concludes with the enactment and enforcement of Chinese exclusion.

Turning to European immigrants, the book considers their changing character after 1865 and the question of imported contract labor, which reached a climax in 1885 with the passage of the Foran Act. To study the reception and performance of immigrants in industries in which they were concentrated, the book looks at three representative areas, iron and steel, coal, and clothing. The Italians, the most numerous of the new peoples, are then the subject of a chapter that discusses their activities in industries beyond those already covered.

In its last four chapters, this study returns to the legislative quest for restriction and exclusion. These chapters begin with the drive that led to the Literacy Test Act of 1917, then discuss the concurrent movement in California against the Japanese, and conclude with the making of the national origins system and its effect on the refugee crisis of the 1930s and World War II.

The author hopes that this account presents a clear picture of the often strained relationship between American and immigrant workers in the era of industrialization and mass immigration. This is its main purpose, rather than to take note of immigrant contributions to the labor movement and industrial growth. Unfortunately, it is not possible to cover the complete range of labor organizations or activities at the time. The book's emphasis is on ethnic relationships and their effect on labor unions and American immigration policy.

ROBERT D. PARMET

York College of
The City University of New York

Acknowledgments

This work has benefited from the advice, assistance, and encouragement of many persons. Joan B. Parmet, Herbert S. Parmet, and Beatrice Levy read the manuscript with care and affection. Israel Breslaw, Robert D. Cross, Thomas Curran, William R. McMillan, Joseph Schachter, and Herbert A. Strauss offered information, support, and advice. Lore Reich and Anne Dulka typed parts of the manuscript.

Numerous librarians and archivists provided courteous, professional assistance. At the York College Library, Gladys Jarrett, Benedetto Di Russo, Kevin Barry, and Shirley Geffner were particularly helpful. Elsewhere, at the Columbia University Libraries, New York Public Library, Paul Klapper Library of Queens College, Great Neck Library, Tamiment Library, YIVO Institute for Jewish Research, and the International Ladies' Garment Workers' Union Archives, the personnel were similarly gracious.

I was very fortunate to have had an editor, the late Cecyle S. Neidle, who really cared about my work. Her commitment to clear writing was evident each time she read my chapters. Critical but also considerate, she deserves special thanks.

Andrew Charles Parmet, to whom this book is dedicated, also contributed in his way to its successful completion. Through his patience and understanding, Andrew helped to ease the task of writing.

CHAPTER 1

Immigrants for Developing Industries

THE dream of upward economic mobility is characteristically American. As early as the era of Elizabeth I, Englishmen and other Europeans came to North America for economic reasons. Some settlers sought fortune, but most simply wanted relief from intolerable Old World conditions. America did not offer an easy life, but most of those who came became enthusiastic Americans.

The immigrants usually felt they had bettered themselves in their new land and closely identified with it. Grateful to America for their relative prosperity, they demonstrated intense loyalty to the new nation they were helping to create.

Though they acquired a new nationality, the foreign born did not necessarily sever their Old World ties. Conscience, kinsfolk, and other factors would not let them forget their places of origin, to which they retained strong emotional attachments and to which some expected to return some day. Moreover, to ensure that memories of the past be kept alive, the immigrants often took great care to transmit their cultural heritage across succeeding generations.

On the other hand, most newcomers could not ignore the reality that their future was in America. What was happening in America rather than in the old country affected their daily lives. Therefore, they were primarily interested in American conditions, such as jobs and wages. When an economic threat appeared, the source mattered little. Foreign-born workers instinctively defended their own interests, even against other, more recent, immigrants. Not surprisingly, they frequently supported anti-immigrant movements.[1]

Following the War of 1812, Americans moved west with confidence. With the second of two major wars with Great Britain having been satisfactorily concluded, the United States finally abandoned its preoccupation with foreign affairs and concentrated on internal development. Public as well as private funds went into significant improvements, particularly in transportation. By 1840, Americans traveled inland along numerous turnpikes, canals, and railroads, and sailed the seas on clipper ships. These innovations reduced shipping costs and helped to create a national market that supported a developing factory system.

Following several decades of slow growth, this system increased rapidly in the 1840s. As early as 1791, when Samuel Slater introduced the power loom to the United States, textile manufacturing experienced revolutionary change; the domestic or putting-out system of home manufacturing was disappearing. By 1830, the manufacture of cotton cloth woven by factory girls who resided in dormitories according to the "Waltham System" had already changed the face of Massachusetts, especially the towns of Lowell and Lawrence. By mid-century this system was successfully applied to woolens, and steam power was being substituted for water power. Concurrent with the use of power, standardization of parts in machine manufacturing and advances in the iron industry, notably the use of coal instead of charcoal, sent industrial production soaring.[2]

Aware that this revolution jeopardized their own interests more than those of any other group, skilled workers organized. The advent of factories and a national market for goods had created intense competition among manufacturers and compelled them to minimize costs. Lower unit cost through increased employee productivity was the simplest way to achieve it. Thus, it became desirable to reduce wages and to introduce longer hours and cheap labor, including the labor of children, convicts, and immigrants.

The skilled, relatively expensive journeyman worker who was likely to be replaced by an unskilled worker at the new machines was indeed in danger. His talents, which had previously commanded respect, now made him too expensive for employers intent on reducing costs while raising output in order to meet competition. In addition, the workplace had become large and impersonal. The time had clearly come for collective action.[3]

During the late 1820s and early 1830s worker combinations

became both citywide and political. In the face of employer opposition, public hostility, and legal obstacles, hitherto independent organizations formed central trade councils and Workingmen's parties. Most of these ventures were short-lived, but they served as precedents for future cooperation. In the 1850s several "national" craft unions came into existence.

The labor movement of the Jacksonian era encompassed middle-class reformers as well as workers. Transcending class lines, workers joined with reformers to expand public education, abolish debt imprisonment, and, in general, ease America's transition to a predominantly industrial society.

Because ideological as well as class differences could not be reconciled, this cooperation between trade union-oriented workers and reformers ultimately broke down, leaving the two sides in competition for the workingman's allegiance. The trade unions seemed to accept the industrial wage system as permanent. Reformers, however, looked forward to a day when workers themselves would control the means of production. Sharing the union point of view, the typographers, hat finishers, stone cutters, cigarmakers, iron molders, machinists, and blacksmiths all organized nationally before 1860. William Sylvis, a founder of the Iron Molders Union in 1859, would soon seek to place the various unions within one comprehensive organization.[4]

During the Civil War industrialists in the North respected military priorities above all others. Iron and steel went for weapons rather than for new railroads; power-operated sewing machines produced military uniforms; shoes and boots for the military received priority before civilian clothing. Under such restraints, industrial technology proceeded until peace and unchecked production were restored.[5]

While industry made its adjustments, labor suffered. Wage earners had several legitimate grievances, including discriminatory military conscription, heavy taxation, and steep inflation. In addition, workers feared the effects on industrial wages resulting from competition with emancipated blacks. Nonetheless, workers in general remained loyal to the Union cause.[6]

The draft, along with a sharp drop in immigrant arrivals, reduced the labor supply. Since 1840, immigrants had come in good numbers during prosperous periods. Now, when they were needed for wartime production, they were scarce. Skilled labor had to be found. Toward that end, two companies were established. A group of industrialists representing textile, transportation and iron interests formed a Foreign Emigrant Aid Society while independent entrepreneurs organized an American Emigrant Company, both to recruit European labor.

In 1864, Congress came to their assistance. In response to the concern of both industry and President Lincoln, Congress legalized contract labor agreements providing for repayment of passage costs for periods up to one year. Furthermore, it appropriated $25,000 to establish a commissioner of immigration in the State Department and an Immigrant Office at the Port of New York. With this new machinery, the federal government helped to distribute immigrants by placing them in jobs. Not until 1907 would the government again provide such assistance.[7]

As business and government sought craftsmen from abroad, labor leaders attempted to form a comprehensive organization of wage earners. In 1861, the International Union of Machinists and Blacksmiths tried to join with other trade unions in forming "a National Trades Assembly." However, by 1864 it was evident that those efforts had failed.[8] Two years later success was achieved under different auspices. The National Labor Union was founded at Philadelphia with William Sylvis of the Ironmolders playing a prominent role. A loosely structured organization, containing both trade unionists and nonunion reformers, it grew until it had approximately 400,000 members by 1869. Unfortunately, in that year President Sylvis died, and without his leadership the union faltered. Politically minded elements gained strength in the organization, causing trade unions to withdraw.[9] By 1872, the National Labor Union had collapsed, unable any longer to function as a political or economic force. It could not even find a presidential candidate for a new party it had formed.[10]

Before they lost control of the National Labor Union, the trade unionists had promoted the idea of an eight-hour day.[11] It was their most pressing demand; another was to ban contract labor. In cooperating with other iron workers, notably puddlers and boilers, to found the National Labor Union, Sylvis's iron molders had hoped to keep British steelworkers from competing with them. In 1868, following a campaign by the union, Congress repealed the Contract Labor Act of 1864.[12]

However, by 1870 foreign-born laborers were to be found throughout American industry. As in the past, their number increased in prosperous times, for example, between 1865 and 1873, and declined during depressions, as in the middle of both the 1870s and 1890s. The attraction of jobs in America was apparent. Eager for employment and often inexperienced in dealing with industrialists, they were willing to do the difficult, unpleasant work. Cornish miners extracted copper deposits in Michigan's upper peninsula, while others from Scotland, Wales, and northern England took the anthracite and bituminous coal from the pits of Pennsylvania.[13] Until Slavs and Southern Europeans began to supplant them in the 1870s, Scotsmen, Welshmen, and Englishmen were the foundation of the labor force in Schuylkill County's anthracite region.[14] In New York City, British miners dug a passageway under Broadway in 1869.[15] Of the 152,107 miners in the United States by 1870, no fewer than 63.3 percent were foreign born, 22.6 percent having come from Great Britain and 15.0 percent from Ireland. Of the entire labor force, 21.6 percent were foreign born, three fourths of whom came from Ireland, Germany, and Great Britain.[16]

At about the same time as the National Labor Union expired, another comprehensive labor group arose to cope with the problems of industrialization and immigration. They were the Noble Order of the Knights of Labor, organized in Philadelphia in December 1869. Initially a secret organization of trade unions, it was founded by Uriah S. Stephens and eight garment cutters,[17] and soon admitted virtually all people who called themselves "workers" regardless of class, with the exception of such "enemies" as liquor dealers, lawyers, and bankers. Structurally, the Knights had a system of representative assemblies, which became national in scope by 1878. Created in that year, the General Assembly also became the annual national convention, which chose the officers.

In 1879, the Knights came under the command of the colorful Terence V. Powderly. A machinist and mayor of Scranton, Pennsylvania, Powderly succeeded Stephens as chief executive with the title of Grand Master Workman. Under his leadership

the Order gained considerable membership, especially in 1885–
1886, following two successful strikes against railroad lines run
by Jay Gould. By the middle of 1886 the total reached 700,000,
the highest number of any nineteenth-century labor
organization.[18]

The Knights' growth occurred after the disastrous depression
of the 1870s, which was otherwise ruinous to organized labor.
This collapse began on September 18, 1873, when the prestigious
Jay Cooke & Co. failed following unsuccessful attempts to finance
the Northern Pacific Railroad.[19] Economic conditions in 1873
were bad, as the usually optimistic economist, Henry C. Carey,
had noted even earlier in the year. "In the present order of
things," he observed, "hands compete with hands for work;
wages are inadequate, and actual suffering and ... destitution
are experienced, to the disgrace of Christendom, and to the be-
wilderment of its philosophers."[20] In 1878, when recovery finally
came, the nation was in a state of shock.

With an estimated three million unemployed during the depression, violence was always imminent. In Pennsylvania, a
secret society of miners known as "Molly Maguires" terrorized
employer sympathizers, resulting in the execution of ten members
for murder. As the nation celebrated its centennial in July 1876,
Marxian socialists in Chicago formed a Workingmen's Party of
the United States, which frightened many people because they
advocated the nationalization of railroad and telegraph lines.
Also in July, socialists in St. Louis called a general strike which
lasted two and a half weeks and resulted in near revolution and
considerable violence. Finally, a year later the United States experienced its first nationwide strike. Beginning as a protest
against a B & O Railroad wage cut, workers struck in Maryland,
West Virginia, Pennsylvania, and New York. Civil insurrection
threatened as President Hayes summoned federal troops to sup-
press the strikers. Before the strike ended much blood had been
shed and the entire Pittsburgh railway depot lay in ruins, destroyed by fire. To many observers, these events demonstrated
conclusively that American labor was influenced by socialists and
communists and was thus dangerously radical.[21]

Less dramatic than the strikes, but also significant, was the
impact on the trades. Many skilled workers, concluding that

their emigration to the United States had been a mistake, returned home. Natives of Sheffield, England, went back when they heard that conditions there had improved. Some workers, who discovered that they had been brought to America as strike-breakers, also went back, occasionally aided by the union on strike.[22]

Numerous unions did not survive, including the Knights of St. Crispin. This combination of shoemakers, which had been the largest predepression trade union, failed, but was taken over by the Knights of Labor in 1878 when the latter organized their General Assembly.[23] Fewer than a third of the thirty national trade unions in existence in 1873 were still alive by 1877, including the Cigar Makers International and International Typographical Unions. However, even those two unions survived, though each suffered membership losses of at least fifty percent.[24]

Outward appearances to the contrary, the socialists who emerged from the depression were hardly a united group. Though they had been active in the United States since the 1850s, American socialists remained relatively quiescent until 1872, when Karl Marx's International Workingmen's Association shifted its headquarters from Geneva to New York. With that move ideological warfare broke out between the two major socialist camps, the disciples of Marx and those of the German social democrat, Ferdinand Lasalle. Marxists saw the trade union as the vital worker instrument in the class struggle with capitalism, while Lasalleans believed political action to be the way to achieve worker dominance. Temporarily setting aside their differences in 1876, the two sides united to form the Workingmen's party, which in 1877 became the Socialist Labor party. As such it would remain the chief agency for American socialism for the next two decades.[25]

Samuel Gompers was among those in the Marxist camp. Of Dutch-Jewish ancestry, Gompers emigrated to the United States in 1863 at age thirteen. A cigarmaker's son, journeying with his family from London's East Side to New York's East Side, Gompers's transition "was an experience involving little more than geographic relocation, a process that abused human sensibilities only incidentally."[26] As he later recalled, "emigration to America promised relief" from economic hardship in London.

Moreover, that relief was facilitated by money from a fund maintained by the Cigarmakers' Society of England which regarded emigration as a suitable alternative to unemployment.[27]

Gompers took pride in his ancestry, especially the Dutch side. He did not deny that he was a Jew, but nonetheless felt it necessary to make clear that he was a superior type. His parents, "both Hollanders born in Amsterdam," had "preserved many of the customs of the Dutch community" in their home in London. At age six he had attended a Jewish free school where he was taught "reading, writing, arithmetic, geography, and history." Afterward, in a night school, he studied the Talmud, which he considered valuable for developing the mind, and "Hebrew— not the mongrel language spoken by many Jews of the present age—but that honorable language that unlocked a literature of wonderful beauty and wisdom."[28] Though his parents were fairly orthodox Jews, he claimed and boasted of his nonconformity. "I believe that restrictions dwarf personality and that largest usefulness comes through greatest personal freedom."[29] These are interesting words from a person identified by the time they were written with immigration restriction—affecting millions of Yiddish-speaking Jews—and conformity within the American labor movement.

By 1873, Samuel Gompers was active in New York City's cigarmakers' union. He was reading socialist authors and receiving tutoring in Marxism from a Swedish co-worker, Karl Ferdinand Laurrell. With Laurrell and Adolph Strasser, Gompers strove to strengthen his union.[30]

As his understanding of an commitment to trade unionism deepened, so did that of many members of the Socialist Labor party. Economic prosperity after 1879 resulted in membership defections to traditional party loyalties and led to an influx of divisive German revolutionaries. Politically, the SLP seemed to be going nowhere. As a consequence, trade unionism loomed as an attractive alternative, even to numerous political activists among the membership.[31]

Exploiting the anticapitalist momentum generated by the railway strike of 1877 and the weakness of the Lasalleans, Gompers's cigarmakers led a movement for union amalgamation. Joined by the iron and steel workers, typographers, and car-

penters and joiners, they urged the creation of a national federation of trade unions. P. J. McGuire, founder of the United
Brotherhood of Carpenters and Joiners in 1881, shared the
spotlight with Gompers in this mobilization. The outcome was
a meeting set for Pittsburgh on November 15, 1881.[32]

At Pittsburgh the Federation of Organized Trades and Labor
Unions of the United States and Canada came into being. However, immediate prospects were not bright, as the Federation
faced stiff competition from the Knights of Labor, whose
period of rapid growth had already begun. Most unions remained with the Knights. In 1882, after a dispute over the protective tariff, the Iron and Steel Workers left the Federation
and resumed relations with the Knights.

It took until 1886 for the federationists to regroup their forces.
Finding the Knights' competition ever more threatening, even
to his own cigarmakers' union, Gompers urged a reorganization
of the Federation. In a final gesture of peace, McGuire sought
to reach a settlement with Powderly's people. When that effort
failed, the reorganization became imperative. Consequently, in
December 1886, at Columbus, Ohio, the trade unionists created
a new American Federation of Labor and elected Gompers as
its first president.[33]

Born out of fear of the Knights, the union federation emerged
as the defender of craft organizations. Success came quickly, as
the Knights began to slip badly. After 1886, a combination consisting of competition from the American Federation of Labor,
the effect of strikes that had been lost, loose structure, and the
disastrous Haymarket Affair spelled the demise of the Knights
of Labor.[34]

It followed the Haymarket Affair which occurred in Chicago
in May 1886. As policemen attempted to break up an anarchist-
led meeting in Haymarket Square, a bomb was thrown into
their midst, killing seven. Subsequently, eight anarchists were
tried and convicted of murder though the identity of the actual
bomb thrower was not known. Seven were sentenced to death,
including a member of the Knights, Albert Parsons. In the
panic-filled atmosphere, the Knights refused to help Parsons
or the other defendants. Instead, the Order repudiated and condemned them and their philosophy. "The Order of Knights

of Labor has no desire to see the reign of anarchy in this country," declared their official journal as it meekly suggested mercy on the basis of "insufficient testimony" and a "prejudiced jury" at the trial. This position satisfied nobody, neither workers nor the general public.[35]

As the American worker discovered the merits and possibilities of organization, he and others kept a critical eye on those who were entering the labor market from abroad. After 1820 numerous Protestant Americans of all social classes increasingly saw their world endangered by the coming of millions of immigrants from Ireland and Germany. Afraid of Roman Catholicism, which they regarded as an alien religion controlled by the pope, a foreign potentate intent on conquering the globe, native-born Protestants had begun to mobilize by the 1830s. Their movement, which took fraternal, political, and even violent form, was also directed against immigrants as the hapless pawns of both pope and political bossism. The newcomers, it was charged, were easily exploited for purposes of political corruption, especially by urban Democrats in such places as New York and New England. By the middle of the 1850s, coinciding with the growing national tension over the slavery issue which was destroying the two-party system, a nativistic American party arose. Because they denied knowledge of any aspects of their party, even its very existence, members were termed "Know-Nothings" by their opponents. As an anti-Catholic, anti-immigrant party, draped in patriotism, it appealed to people seeking an easy solution to the nation's problems. However, by 1856 it was already on the decline, itself a victim of the sectional struggle over slavery.[36]

Cutting across class lines, this nativism reached national proportions but disappeared soon. Yet at mid-century there was a second nativist movement, one which almost exclusively involved workingmen, and which continued through and beyond the Civil War. This movement originated in California during the Gold Rush days of 1849 and 1850 and intensified during the railroad-building era of the 1860s. It turned worker against worker and set the stage for organized labor's later crusade against the foreign born.

The gold discovered on Johann Sutter's property in 1848 attracted too many people to California. The rush for riches during the following year came when mining enterprise was marked by rampant individualism and government was unable to control or regulate the new residents. Newcomers came, not only from the East, but also from the Pacific, which made for competition and jealousy.[37] Coming from Mexico, Chile, Peru, Australia, and elsewhere, the Pacific immigrants were skilled and experienced. Most of them were faster and thus more productive diggers than the Americans.

As early as 1849, hostility to these competitors began to manifest itself in San Francisco. White thugs attacked and beat dark-skinned Hispanics, whose tents and shacks were looted and burned. In 1850, California enacted a twenty-dollar per month tax on foreigners who worked in the mines.[38] Objections to that tax led to a summer of violence, forcible collections, and expulsions.[39]

When twenty thousand Chinese arrived in 1852, they supplanted the Hispanics as the primary foes. The suddenness of their coming must have electrified the Americans. Victimized by the already existing antiforeign sentiment, the Chinese were often kept by force from working in or near mining camps. Opposed by whites, especially independent miners, and obliged to pay the foreign miners' tax, they moved into farming, gardening, laundry, and domestic work where their labor was needed.[40]

As Gunther Barth has written, the vast majority of Chinese arriving in California in the 1850s and 1860s did not intend to remain permanently. They came "with a vision; they would make money to return to China with their savings for a life of ease, surrounded and honored by the families which their toil had sustained." They were "merely sojourners and they shaped the initial encounter with Americans," who resented their "limited goal" and accordingly excluded them from "the privileges and obligations of other immigrants." In other words, it was unfair for them to take their earnings and run back home.[41]

As symbols of docile, unskilled workers, the Chinese were called "coolie" laborers. "Coolie," originally a Bengalese or Tamil word for "burden bearer," was also a two-word Chinese phrase meaning, idiomatically, "hired unskilled laborer." By the middle to the nineteenth century it was generally applied by outsiders to Chinese common laborers.[42]

The immigration of these laborers was a well-organized business. Arriving in groups, they went immediately to San Francisco's Six Companies, controlled by local Chinese merchants, which provided food, shelter, and employment. Under contract to repay their passage costs, the laborers were under "strict internal discipline." The Six Companies did their own enforcing. They hired policemen and lawyers, and even gave final clearance to shipping companies for any Chinese leaving California.[43]

Expelled from the mines, the Chinese found much employment after 1863 in railroad construction. In 1863 Congress authorized railroad construction between Nebraska and California by the Union Pacific and Central Pacific railroads. Aided by generous grants of land, the Union Pacific was to build west as the Central Pacific built east, the two meeting in Utah. Charles Crocker and Company was the Central Pacific's construction company. With white laborers frequently leaving to seek gold, Crocker turned to the Chinese, who had previously been used as strikebreakers. By 1867, Central Pacific agents were offering Chinese laborers thirty-one dollars per month, which was five to six dollars above their prevailing wage rate. No other California employer paid above the existing rate. In June 1867, following a strike by an estimated five to seven thousand Chinese for a forty-dollar month and an eight-hour day, the rate was raised to thirty-five dollars. Though the strike was considered a failure, the increase was granted afterward perhaps to avert a future walkout. In 1868, when the Central Pacific's labor force reached its maximum size, it included between eight and ten thousand Chinese.[44]

In the city, the Chinese seemed to excel at cigarmaking, into which they moved before 1859. It led to the first urban opposition to them. In November 1859, a People's Protective Union was launched to boycott Chinese-made goods in San Francisco. Much noise was made and pressure applied to drive the Chinese from the cigar trade, but it failed. By 1866, about 1,800 of the 2,000 employees in cigarmaking were Chinese. Four years later, 2,800 were Chinese. In addition, they had set up their own businesses, by 1866 comprising "at least one-half of the total number of proprietors of cigar factories in San Francisco."[45]

Further reaction to the Asians was swift and ugly. In January 1866, following the dismissal of Irish land reclamation laborers and their replacement with Chinese at half the previous wage, "a party of nearly three hundred hoodlums" set upon the latter "with stones, bricks and clubs." "Kill them! kill them!" the on-looking crowd shouted. The casualties included fifteen badly beaten and one killed. In addition, their shanties were given the torch.[46] In February 1867, there was another riot. This one was in opposition to Chinese employment in grading some San Francisco property. It led to prison sentences for eleven whites. In protest, whites formed anticoolie clubs. The Pacific Coast Anti-Coolie Association, formed in March, soon had branches throughout the city and elsewhere in the state. On March 29, a Workingmen's Convention in San Francisco came out against Chinese immigration as did a state convention of the clubs held in May.[47]

Almost unbelievably, as though nothing had been happening in California, the United States and China entered into a treaty in 1868. Negotiated by Anson Burlingame, minister to China since 1863, the document opened the door to Chinese immigrants. They now had the same rights in the United States as had other foreigners. Moreover, Americans were expressly forbidden to discriminate against them. Commercial groups and those interested in the uplift of colored peoples, both strong in the northeast, welcomed this treaty. On the other hand, for the anti-Chinese movement it meant a major new target in a wider war.[48] With California's labor force in 1870 being forty percent native born, twenty-five percent Chinese, and fifteen percent Irish, and the remaining twenty percent foreign born from Germany, England, and elsewhere, the elements were present for additional bitter and prolonged conflict.[49]

CHAPTER 2

The Chinese: A Threat to the American Worker

THE coming of the Chinese provided a perfect issue for those who spoke for the American workingman. White workers reacted almost instinctively to what they felt was an Asian menace in their midst. From California to Massachusetts they understood the meaning of cheap labor competition and supported those politicians and labor leaders who vowed to eliminate it. The combination of racial and economic fears, exploited by the sincere and demagogic alike, spurred white labor's organization and helped to cause the nation's shift to a policy of immigration restriction.

Numbers were not necessarily the determining factor. Labor leaders regarded the Chinese as responsible for the attempt to depress wages. Though these foreigners were already numerous on the West Coast, it was not yet the case in the East. There "the threat was ... more potential than actual, but quite real for labor leaders nonetheless."[1]

By 1869 it was clear that the Chinese problem extended well beyond California. The completion of the Central Pacific Railroad that year, coupled with an economic depression, "brought the Chinese into sudden and conspicuous disfavor with the working classes" of other states and territories, most immediately, Nevada and Washington.[2] "Of the three to five thousand released by the Central Pacific, many remained in Nevada."[3] The initial result was conflict. Objecting to the engagement of Chinese laborers to do roadbed grading for the Virginia and Truckee Railroad then under construction, the miners' unions of Virginia City and Gold Hill resorted to force. In September 1869, 350 miners marched on the Chinese camp and compelled the foreigners to flee to the hills. By agreement afterward, the Chinese could complete their job, but not be employed within the confines of Gold Hill and Virginia City.[4]

The Chicago *Workingman's Advocate*, which reflected the views of the National Labor Union, recognized the danger inhering in the Western situation and anticipated the eastward migration. "We warn," said the *Advocate* in February 1869, that "just as soon as the Pacific railroad is completed, . . . these Chinese will begin to swarm through the rocky [*sic*] mountains, like devouring locusts and spread out over the country this side."[5] In April, the Mechanics' State Council of California issued a circular to alert laborers outside the state that "fifty thousand Chinamen" were displacing white workers on the Pacific Coast. Published in the *Advocate,* the warning was obvious.[6] Soon afterward, editor A. C. Cameron announced that, as predicted, the Chinese blight had spread. Chinese, he wrote, had been observed "in the streets of St. Louis, Chicago and Philadelphia." They would come by the thousands until they "fill the land in every direction." Sought after by employers in Boston, New York, New Jersey, and Pennsylvania to provide "cheap labor," Cameron continued, "these Pagan rat-eaters" must be kept out of the country. The Burlingame Treaty of 1868 with its provision for unrestricted immigration of Chinese "must be abrogated."[7]

A development in Memphis brought the situation to a head. Seeking a substitute for black slave labor, a group of southern white planters in convention at Memphis seized upon the idea of coolie labor. The National Labor Union, hearing of these intentions, became incensed. "At present we are unconditionally opposed, *under any circumstances,* to the project of peopling the Western or Southern states with the scum of the Chinese empire." Those in favor, the *Advocate* charged, wish to "degrade the American workman to the level of the slave."[8] The claim was that neither slave labor nor Chinese labor could bring prosperity to the South.[9]

That August, at its own convention in Philadelphia, the National Labor Union responded formally to the southern attempt "to revive the infamous Coolie trade." President William H. Sylvis having died suddenly on July 27,[10] the organization's new leadership denounced the Memphis scheme. Afterward, the convention adopted resolutions calling for "rigid enforcement" of the 1862 federal legislation prohibiting the importation of coolie labor and stating "*Resolved,* That we are unalterably opposed to the importation of a servile race for the sole and only purpose of pauperizing the labor of the American workingman."[11]

Lest anyone doubt that the nature of the Chinese threat was of national import, events the next year in Massachusetts served to sound a fresh alarm. Calvin F. Sampson of North Adams imported seventy-five Chinese laborers from California to break a strike called by the shoemakers' union, the Knights of St. Crispin.[12] Hired to work at one third the rate paid native craftsmen,[13] these foreigners, shoe industry spokesmen argued, benefited the community as they lowered production costs.[14] On the other hand, the Massachusetts Bureau of Labor Statistics declared in 1871 that this kind of cheap labor, if extended to the Commonwealth's woolen and cotton mills, cutlery works, furniture, hat and boot factories, would ruin them all.[15] Evidently the North Adams experiment with the Chinese did not succeed, for by 1880 they were gone except for some laundrymen.[16] Similarly, Chinese strikebreakers brought into the Beaver Falls, Pennsylvania, cutlery works in 1872 initially displaced white workers, but, along with the firm which hired them, vanished by 1889. Again, their only continuing employment was in laundry work.[17]

As eastern labor learned to despise the Chinese, Californians reached new peaks of frenzy. In 1870 there were "spectacular demonstrations" and an anti-Chinese convention. Activity began in the spring, with many meetings of unemployed whites, especially members of the Knights of St. Crispin. Cooperating with plumbers and carpenters, they held a mass meeting preceded by a parade in San Francisco. At that demonstration, a convention was planned "to oppose the immigration of Chinese laborers, and cultivate public opinion up to the abrogation of the treaty with China." Held in August, the convention approved resolutions condemning the coolie system, asked an end to the treaty and coolie immigration, and opposed employment of Chinese by public officials and "subsidized steamer lines importing Chinese.' In addition, the Californians repudiated anti-Chinese violence and asked the nation's laborers to endorse their positions.[18]

Responding to pressure, the California legislature and San Francisco Board of Supervisors came forth with a new batch of anti-Chinese measures. In March 1870, the legislature made it unlawful to bring Asiatics into the state without prior presentation of evidence of good character. Designed to exclude immoral women, this act was declared unconstitutional by federal courts after being upheld in California. In 1876 and 1878, the legislature barred Chinese from construction projects related to irrigation and reclamation. Throughout the 1870s it sought, above all, to abrogate the Burlingame Treaty of 1868.[19]

The San Francisco Board of Supervisors tried harassment to rid the city of Chinese. One ordinance outlawed walking on a sidewalk while carrying a pole with baskets at each end on the shoulders. Another, the "Cubic Air" law of 1870, made it illegal to rent rooms where people would sleep if five hundred cubic feet of air per person were not provided. A third law required a one-inch haircut for all persons in custody of the county sheriff, which, to the Chinese, meant the loss of the queue, a sign of disgrace. Finally, the supervisors imposed a much higher tax on laundries using no horses for deliveries than on similar establishments using one or two horses. The Chinese, of course, made hand deliveries. That ordinance, passed in 1873, was declared unconstitutional in 1874. In 1876 the same kind of law was passed, but was voided by the courts.[20]

The movement for such legislation had racial, religious, and economic overtones. As historian Alexander Saxton has noted, the antebellum heritage of the Democratic party was antiblack and proslavery. Irish immigrant laborers, finding the Democratic party hospitable to them, supported it and shared its prejudices because clearly they feared black competition. When it suited them, they used violence, for example, against abolitionists in the New York City Draft Riots of 1863, and against management when organizing the Pennsylvania coalfields. Both the animosity to nonwhite labor and the will to violence moved west with the Irish and were directed at the Chinese.[21]

While the severest critics of the Chinese were the labor unions and Irish Catholic workingmen, their primary defenders were the businessmen and the Protestant clergy. The latter, active in California since 1853, argued that it was God's will that the Asians had come to California where they would become Christians. Hopefully, upon their return home across the Pacific these converts would proselytize in their homeland.[22]

Welcome or not, the Chinese were apparently established in all trades. After an investigation in 1876, a special congressional committee concluded that the Chinese contributed to the rapid development of the Pacific Coast's resources. Moreover, in several trades they had become dominant. They virtually monopolized the laundry, cigarmaking, and needle trades industries, and drove whites out of fruit picking, gardening, silk and woolen manufacturing, and other activities.[23] Henryk Sienkiewicz, a Polish writer in California at this time, said that one word, "everything," described the work done by the Chinese.[24]

These laborers were part of an immigrant population whose size is difficult to determine. Sources vary considerably. According to the United States census, in 1870, 49,277 Chinese were in California and 63,199 in the country. For 1880, the figures were 75,132 and 105,465, respectively. On the other hand, the Chinese Six Companies, which covered the entire Pacific Coast, reported that they had 58,300 members in 1866 and 148,600 in 1876. Regardless of which estimates are accurate, most of the Chinese were males of working age who made up perhaps twenty-five percent of California's work force by 1870. In San Francisco, there were possibly as many Chinese as white unskilled and semi-skilled workers.[25]

California's economy was shaky in 1876, and the large number of Chinese made the situation potentially dangerous. The national depression, begun in 1873, had extended to the West. Some ten thousand men were unemployed in San Francisco alone by the winter of 1876–1877. Partially reflecting industrial disturbances elsewhere in the country, the working classes of the city soon started a rebellion.[26]

Dennis Kearney, an Irish-born drayman, was ready to exploit their discontent. A sailor who had arrived in San Francisco in 1872, Kearney soon purchased a carting firm and made good. Having taught himself to read, write, and speak in public at the

Lyceum of Self-Culture and the Public Library, he declared war against several enemies. He began by attacking the working class for laziness, extravagance, and their affinity for liquor and tobacco. In addition, he had denounced religion, including his own Catholic faith. On the other hand, in these early days, he did not attack business or the Chinese. When disputing with labor, he invariably sided with management, and as for the Oriental immigration, it was defensible in that it depressed excessively high American wages.[27]

Suddenly this defender of labor's enemies reversed himself. In 1877 Kearney helped to organize a "Workingmen's Trade and Labor Union" to elect honest public officials. On the eve of the election, some members of the union in vain demanded the return of campaign funds collected and held by their president J. G. Day, and secretary, Kearney. Perhaps one to two thousand dollars had been raised, but no election ticket had even been printed. Following this dispute, Kearney appeared at the Lyceum of Self-Culture and astounded his listeners, whose own pro-working class views he had previously denounced, by announcing that he would demand "bread or blood" and organized a new, significant party.[28]

In effecting this transformation, Kearney had also gone from peace-keeper to rabble-rouser. In July 1877, he had been a member of a committee of public safety, known as the "pick handle brigade," which had ended five days of anticoolie rioting and violence in San Francisco.[29] Then, by September and October this new friend of the workingman "sky-rocketed to fame as the orator of the sandlots," the speakers' site in front of City Hall. Borrowing the name of the Socialist Workingmen's party of the United States, founded in the East the previous year, Kearney launched a new organization which was avowedly antipolitician, antirich, and anti-Chinese.[30] Taking for his own the words of H. L. Knight, the party's secretary, Kearney shouted, "The Chinese must go." This became the regular Sunday afternoon cry of the sandlots and the motto of the Workingmen's party of California.[31]

Kearney's rhetoric was both incendiary and demagogic. In one speech, alluding to the burning of Moscow in 1812, he threatened San Francisco with the same fate if the situation

of the working classes were not improved. In another, he denounced the rich and said that "Judge Lynch is the judge wanted
by the working man. I advise you all to own a musket and a
hundred rounds of ammunition."[32] Though Kearney personally
delivered his speeches, in preparing them he had the assistance
of a local newspaperman whose reputation for truthfulness was
anything but good.[33]

As economic historian Ping Chiu has noted, this anti-Chinese
movement was primarily composed of "Irish nonindustrial labor."
Moreover, Kearney's "own Draymen and Teamsters' Union was
singularly immune against Chinese competition." Yet his personality sparked the imagination of California workers, who, skilled
and unskilled, combined with small businessmen, farmers and
politicians to "form a common front" focused essentially on one
issue. In their defense against this tide, employers could only
"resort to arguments of economic necessity and economic growth;
neither of these was an effective vote-getter."[34]

Among those who joined the Workingmen's party of California
at this time was Frank Roney, who would prove to be one of
Kearney's severest critics. Roney, a young Irish revolutionist who
had fled his homeland, had arrived in San Francisco a short time
ago. It was he, rather than Kearney, who organized the party's
first statewide convention in January 1878. Though this gathering in San Francisco adopted a platform which denounced the
Chinese, Roney, according to his autobiography, accepted that
"superficial" grievance in order to be able to pursue more important objectives, namely, the cause of trade unionism.[35]

Beginning with the election of a state senator in Alameda
County in January 1878, the Workingmen's party gained influence in California politics. Despite scandal and dissension, the
party remained powerful until 1880, when factionalism proved
fatal. Its main achievement came in September 1878, at the
California Constitutional Convention. Having elected fifty of
the 149 delegates, the Workingmen's party succeeded in putting
anti-Chinese measures into a new state constitution. Article
Nineteen provided for state regulation of aliens detrimental to
the common welfare, which represented a prohibition on Chinese
employment in public works, and discouragement on the part
of the legislature toward the immigration of aliens ineligible for

citizenship. This article was secured, but its provisions would later be nullified as they conflicted with the Burlingame Treaty and the Fourteenth Amendment to the United States Constitution.[36]

The Workingmen's party had organized and acted allegedly in the interests of labor. Whether it actually did represent the workingman is another question. Certainly Frank Roney did not think so. The party's "staunchest members," he wrote, "were the small property holders." "Real estate values," he continued, "were supposed to have . . . decreased because of the presence of the Chinese, when as a matter of fact they . . . were increasing." The propertyless were "not considered." Alexander Saxton points out that at the Workingmen's Thanksgiving Day parade in 1877, "only six of seventeen groups" identifiable among the marchers "could be classified as labor organizations, and of these three (Shoemakers, Tailors, Cigarmakers) were probably associations of journeymen and small proprietors rather than trade unions. The remainder were neighborhood or language-association anti-coolie clubs." In other words, most marchers were not trade unionists. What Kearney sought, Saxton says, was political power by gaining control of the local Democratic clubs.[37]

Regardless of the composition of the anti-Chinese movement in California, it had national repercussions. Federal action against the Burlingame Treaty was swift in coming. As early as 1876, both the Democrats and Republicans made anti-"Mongolian" planks part of their national party platforms.[38] In that year Congress formed the commission to investigate conditions in California, and then, in 1879, enacted a fifteen-passenger limit on vessels bearing Chinese immigrants. President Hayes, despite considerable sentiment in favor of the measure, vetoed it. In a lengthy message to Congress he acknowledged that "the very grave discontents of the people if the Pacific States" deserved the nation's "most serious attention," but also noted that the bill abrogated part of the treaty of 1868.[39] A few months later, irate Californians responded to Hayes with a near-unanimous, 154,638 to 883 vote for complete Chinese exclusion.[40] In August 1880, a committee of San Francisco workingmen addressed an appeal "To the Friends of Labor Everywhere." They were "cursed," they complained, "with Chinese competition"

which degraded "the white Christian laboring-classes." Furthermore, they claimed the presence of the Chinese promoted pa-
ganism, heathenism, prostitution, and filth. In response, the
General Executive Board of the Knights of Labor called upon
members to refrain from voting for congressmen before determining their position on abrogation of the Burlingame Treaty.
In support of this action, the Knights' General Assembly then
overwhelmingly defeated a point of order that would have paved
the way for Chinese membership in the organization and urged
that Chinese firms or those who employed Chinese be boycotted.
Finally, members were to apply pressure on their congressmen
to seek an end to the treaty.[41]

As the anti-Chinese forces remained active and strong, immigration restriction became inevitable. In November 1880, following President Hayes's appointment of a commission to journey
to Peking, a new treaty was arranged. This document gave the
United States government the right to "regulate, limit, or suspend" the "coming or residence" of Chinese laborers, "but . . . not
absolutely prohibit it."[42]

Thus the corner was turned and the United States could
restrict the flow of Chinese. The next step would be legislation
to that effect, which organized labor ardently supported. If
anything, following the signing of the treaty of 1880, American
workingmen were more anxious than ever to exclude their Asian
competitors. Though only fourteen Chinese lepers were deported
from San Francisco in late 1880, the sight of their departure
was described as being "most hideous and revolting.[43] To American labor all Chinese were considered diseased.

Chinese labor appeared to be worse than leprosy. It was a
malady that could destroy American civilization, according to
views expressed at Pittsburgh's Turner Hall in November 1881.
There, at a meeting forging the Federation of Organized Trades
and Labor Unions of the United States and Canada, the Asians
were again condemned. In addition to agreeing upon a name
for their organization, the 108 delegates, fifty-eight of whom
represented central labor councils and trade unions, and fifty
the Knights of Labor, adopted a thirteen-point platform. They
urged the passage of legislation covering numerous problem
areas, from trade union and labor organization incorporation to

child labor, apprenticeship, the length of the workday, and labor competition. The employment of child labor under age fourteen should be prohibited along with "convict or prison labor," and laws should be adopted to provide "every American industry" with total tariff "protection from the cheap labor of foreign countries." Furthermore, the platform demanded "the passage of a law by the United States Congress to prevent the importation of foreign laborers under contract."[44]

Charles F. Burgman of San Francisco offered a supplementary resolution on Chinese labor. A cigarmaker from the Representative Assembly of the Pacific Coast Trades and Labor Unions, Burgman presented the following:

1. WHEREAS, The experience of the last thirty years in California and on the Pacific Coast having proved conclusively that the presence of Chinese, and their competition with free white labor, is one of the greatest evils with which any country can be afflicted; therefore be it

Resolved, That we use our best efforts to get rid of this monstrous evil (which threatens, unless checked, to extend to other parts of the Union) by the dissemination of information respecting its character, and by urging upon our representatives in the United States Congress the absolute necessity of passing laws prohibiting the immigration of Chinese into the United States.[45]

Sherman Cummin of Typographical Union no. 13, Boston, responded to Burgman's resolution, and defended the Chinese. He did not think they "would swallow up our civilization," though theirs was much older than ours.. Besides, our nation's constitution "guaranteed them the hospitality of our shores"; "they should have the same rights as other foreigners."

"The gentleman does not represent the views of Massachusetts workmen when he makes such statements," retorted Michael J. Byrne of the Operative Plasterers' Union of Buffalo, New York. "Let the Chinese be civilized in China," he added.

Without success Cummin attempted to amend the resolution by substituting "regulating" for "prohibiting." The unamended resolution was then adopted with but one voice, probably Cummin's, in dissent.[46]

By spring, Congress obliged with restrictive legislation. An initial bill, suspending Chinese laborers for twenty years, was vetoed on April 4, 1882, as an unreasonable suspension of immigration which thereby violated the recent treaty with China. However, on May 6, President Arthur approved a modified version which provided for a ten-year ban on such immigrants "from any port or place." Chinese illegally in the United States were subject to deportation, and none was eligible for American citizenship.[47]

As could be expected, organized labor claimed credit for passage of the Exclusion Act. Terence Powderly, who had lobbied in Washington on behalf of the Knights of Labor, felt that he had sufficiently convinced congressmen of the Chinese menace.[48] Samuel Gompers of the Federation of Organized Trades and Labor Unions, pointed with pride at his own efforts. "Numerous monster demonstrations" by the membership and "agitation" by his Legislative Committee, he reported to his brethren, had called attention to "the unrestricted importation of Chinese Coolie slaves." "The act as passed is by no means as satisfactory a remedy for the Mongolian curse as the working people had a right to expect," he added, "but without vigorous agitation we are satisfied the whole question would have been ignored."[49]

Gompers could not ignore the Chinese in 1882, and would not do so until his death, more than forty years later. In his posthumously published autobiography he explained the initial skirmishes of his anti-Asian war. In his own trade, cigarmaking, "at least" a quarter of those employed on the Pacific Coast in 1878 were Chinese. White cigarmakers, independently organized, protected themselves against the low-wage foreigners by "using a white label to distinguish white men's work done under white men's standards." However, as neither organized labor nor California could exclude the Chinese, "Federal law was needed." Furthermore, as eastern employers were then threatening "to import Chinese strike breakers," the cigarmakers gave "early and hearty endorsement to the movement for a national organization of labor unions, for the help of all wage-earners was needed in support of Chinese exclusion." Gompers, in brief, attributed the creation of what soon became the American Federation of Labor directly to the Chinese threat.[50]

Denying to the end that he harbored prejudice against the

Chinese, Gompers contended that he understood their history and philosophy and had "profound respect" for their nation. His opposition to their coming, he claimed, related to "the effect of Chinese standards of life and work" and to the fact that racial problems were "created when Chinese and white workers were brought into the close contact of living and working side by side."[51]

Unfortunately, it is impossible in retrospect to set Gompers apart from his rank and file in the matter of racism. Asian workers were not permitted membership in Federation affiliates. Gompers denied them union charters and even kept local organizations from according them representation. Though in principle he opposed separate ethnic unions as inherently divisive, he would tolerate them when formed by Jewish, German, and Italian immigrants, but not among Asians.[52] Therefore, the latter could receive no assistance in organizing and raising their standard of living.

Few observers were willing to await the results of the 1882 legislation. After its enactment, "Chinese immigration came to a standstill,"[53] but American Sinophobia continued. "Their touch is pollution," said the Knights' *Journal of United Labor* of the Chinese, quoting traveler and author Bayard Taylor.[54] In San Francisco, there were other complaints. The Chinese had already caused the unemployment of many young, white workers and were currently driving out native farmers by underselling them in every line.[55]

As early as February 1884, the Knights demanded additional restrictive federal legislation.[56] Congress and the president were remarkably responsive. On July 5, 1884, an act of Congress amended the 1882 law to prohibit the entry of laborers "from any foreign port or place," not only China. Second, it tightened the identification procedure for the admission of nonlaborers. So strictly was this legislation enforced that it caused hardship for many Chinese and provoked a protest in 1886 by the Chinese government.[57]

Even the new restrictions on the Chinese could not keep the rank and file of the Knights from resorting to violence against them. In September 1885, resentment of Chinese coal miners at Rock Springs, Wyoming Territory, produced a massacre.

Rampaging whites took twenty-eight Chinese lives, wounded fifteen, and destroyed much property. Most of the assailants were Knights, of which Terence Powderly was made aware. Privately he suspected that his anti-Chinese campaign had sparked the assault. However, publicly he blamed the bloodshed on congressional indifference to the plight of the white miners.[58]

Rock Springs was only the beginning of widespread anti-Chinese violence in the West. The Asians were either expelled, forced out of their dwellings by arson, or subjected to new ordinances in more than two dozen places in California.[59] On November 3, 1885, the Chinese population of Tacoma, Washington Territory, was expelled from the city. In a driving rain, "about 200 Chinese and their movable property" were marched nine miles out of town to a railroad station where they waited over night for a train to remove them from the vicinity.[60] Obviously inspired by Tacoma, and with the participation of local Knights of Labor, the leaders of Seattle, Washington, expelled 150 Chinese during November 4 to 6.[61] In 1886 the outrages extended northward to Alaska. "At Douglas Island near Juneau, ... about 100 Chinese were attacked and set adrift in the ocean." Total Chinese losses from these riots of 1885–1886 amounted to "fifty lives and $250,000,000" in property damage.[62]

While taking care not to condone the lawlessness, organized labor deftly glossed over the outbreaks and reiterated its anti-Chinese indictment. At its December 1885 meeting, the Federation of Organized Trades and Labor Unions declared itself "in full accord with the workingmen of the Pacific coast in the fierce struggle for existence to which they are subjected by reason of competition with the Chinese."[63] Arguing against Chinese slave labor, a spokesman for the Knights said, "We claim the right to a living compensation for labor done."[64] Meanwhile, other Knights were complaining that "white labor" labels were being placed on products actually manufactured by Chinese.[65] Pleading with their General Assembly for "action" to free the white "race from the want and degradation being put upon it by the blighting effects of Chinese labor and the frightful results of Chinese presence," a committee of California Knights called the time an "hour of peril."[66]

By the end of 1886, when the Trades Federation became the

American Federation of Labor, the old sentiments were echoed. At its final convention, the FOTLU termed the 1882 law "worthless . . . when not enforced by men in full sympathy therewith," and at its first convention the new organization approved a Chinese immigration resolution very similar to its predecessor's of the previous year.[67]

In the late eighties and nineties, Congress continued to cooperate with the exclusionists. In 1888, following China's rejection of an unfavorable immigration treaty proposed by the United States, Congress prohibited by law the return of previously departed Chinese laborers. In May 1892, the Geary Act extended the 1882 legislation for ten more years. In addition, it required all Chinese laborers, within the United States to register with the government or face deportation.[68] Terence Powderly, delivering what proved to be his final report of the General Executive Board of the Knights, called this law imperfect. Yet he said it had to be defended against the missionary interests who aimed at "the entire abolition" of the exclusion laws. Missionaries, he said, feared antagonizing the Chinese government which could "interfere" with their work in China.[69]

In the matter of a treaty, China reopened negotiations and another was concluded by March 1894. Its terms virtually duplicated existing legislation, even to the extent of prohibiting laborers for ten years. However, the 1888 ban on laborers returning to the United States was rescinded.[70]

This treaty was agreed upon while the United States was feeling the effect of its second major depression in two decades. The economy had collapsed in 1893, leaving three to four million workers unemployed. It was a grim job situation even without a heavy Chinese influx.

In Cuba, conditions were worse. There the depression and American tariff barriers had battered the sugar and tobacco economy. Reflecting the distress, a revolt broke out against Spanish rule. Instinctively, workers in the United States showed compassion for their counterparts on the island, many of whom were skilled and had been employed at times in this country. Furthermore, Cuba's fight for freedom from a European power was redolent of the spirit of the American War for Independence.[71] Since 1893, when sugar interests on Hawaii had overthrown the native monarchy and established a new government, annexation had been an issue. Blocked by President Grover Cleveland, a Democrat, the acquisition of Hawaii was supported by William McKinley, a Republican, when he became president in 1897. McKinley submitted a treaty of annexation,, which the Senate refused to ratify.

West Coast unions, the American Federation of Labor, and the Knights of Labor vehemently opposed the campaign to take Hawaii. They called annexation a threat to American labor standards and traditions of foreign policy isolationism. To Samuel Gompers, Hawaiian labor was unskilled, nonunion, tied to a contract system, and largely of Chinese origin. Annexation would provide easy access for these Asians to the North American mainland.[72]

The cries of Gompers and other anti-imperialists were overwhelmed by the sounds of trumpets and cannons. By April 1898, the United States went to war with Spain over Cuba. Three months later, with the Spaniards having been easily defeated, Hawaii was annexed by joint congressional resolution. By December, with the momentum of victory still strong, the United States acquired even more territory. Through the Treaty of Paris, Spain ceded Puerto Rico and Guam and sold the Philippines for twenty million dollars.

Gompers was again steadfastly opposed, calling annexation of the Philippines an "unpardonable mistake."[73] "If the Philippines are annexed," he asked a Chicago audience, "what is to prevent the Chinese, the Negritos and the Malays [from] coming to our country? How can we prevent the Chinese coolies from coming to the Philippines and from there swarming into the United States engulfing our people and our civilization?"[74]

For more than a month the Senate debated the Treaty of Paris. Finally, on February 6, 1899, it was confirmed, but by a margin of only one vote more than the two thirds necessary to ratify.[75]

Hawaii had been annexed in 1898, during the war, as Congress simultaneously outlawed Chinese immigration either to the islands or from them to the United States mainland. In 1900, the Geary Act's registration provisions were applied to that acquisition.[76]

Despite these steps, there was still reason for insecurity. In

1900, both the Knights and Federationists looked to May 5, 1902, the expiration date of the Chinese Exclusion Act. The Knights urged that the law be reenacted, but Gompers wanted more than a mere extension; he asked that the period of exclusion be "made unlimited." The A.F. of L.'s annual convention concurred.[77]

So intense was labor's anti-Chinese campaign that even the otherwise tolerant could not easily resist it. In convention for only the second time, even the immigrant-led International Ladies' Garment Workers' Union yielded to pressure from its West Coast membership. The Cloak Makers' Union no. 8 of San Francisco, in June 1901, asked that "all ASIATICS (Chinese or Japanese) be barred from membership, either honorary or active, in all locals of the I.L.G.W.U., and that no charter be granted by the I.L.G.W.U. to any organization of cloak makers being composed either partly or wholly of Japs, Chinese or other Asiatics." In response, the convention adopted a compromise resolution. Thus the garment workers recommended to their locals that they admit all persons who applied for membership. "But that no charter shall be issued to an organization composed wholly of Chinese or Japanese." Repeated in 1902, the pressure from San Francisco achieved the desired result: "all Asiatics" were barred from membership.[78]

As hysteria in the West kept mounting, it actually became impossible for the national labor organization to do anything but lend support. Citing "the railroad and other combines" as foes of the exclusion law "in their greed for cheap servile labor," the Knights reiterated their call for reenactment.[79] A week later, on November 21, 1901, a California Chinese Exclusion Convention met in San Francisco. Present were delegates representing 148 California labor organizations.[80] The assembled Sinophobes unanimously condemned Chinese labor and "further immigration of this yellow peril."[81]

To buttress his campaign, Gompers collaborated with Herman Gutstadt, a San Francisco unionist and white labor agitator, on a pamphlet, entitled *Some Reasons for Chinese Exclusion: Meat vs. Rice*, which was issued by the A.F. of L. and republished as a United States Senate document in 1902. It was, simply, a racist indictment of the allegedly cheap living and working Chinese.[82]

Gompers was supported by Terence V. Powderly. Displaced in 1893 as head of the Knights by J. R. Sovereign of Iowa,[83] Powderly afterward turned to law and civil service. In 1896, he campaigned for McKinley over William Jennings Bryan in the presidential contest. That choice angered organized labor, but obviously pleased the victorious McKinley. The Republican president responded favorably when Powderly, in March 1897, applied for appointment as commissioner-general of immigration in the Treasury Department.[84]

In the Senate, McKinley's recommendation for appointment ran into opposition, but it was finally approved by March 1898.[85] Then, as commissioner-general, Powderly was staunchly exclusionist; "the spirit of Dennis Kearney took over" the immigration bureau.[86]

Pressing their drive for a new law, labor organizations from across the country flooded Congress with memorials, resolutions, and petitions. With the A.F. of L. as "ringleader," John Mitchell of the United Mine Workers Union raised his voice in support. So did other leaders, including those of the Railroad Brotherhoods and the Western Labor Union. In the campaign, "the most active unions were the cigarmakers, typographical workers, and miners." In general, as indicated by the petitions, "throughout the ranks of labor [there was] an unusual display of unity and intense feeling."[87]

The unionists found a strong ally in President Theodore Roosevelt, who, in December 1901, endorsed continued, strengthened exclusion in his annual message.[88] Following his address, Congress moved swiftly. Seventeen bills were introduced. The strictest, which Powderly drafted, was submitted by Representative Julius Kahn of California. Eventually called the Mitchell-Kahn bill, owing to its sponsorship, this measure proposed the indefinite exclusion of Chinese laborers from the United States mainland as well as insular possessions. In April 1902, it became law. In 1904, Chinese exclusion became permanent.[89]

Concurrently, as if to justify constant vigilance, a new menace was surfacing in the Pacific. It came from the Japanese. The American workingman and Western civilization would again require defense against Asian immigrants.

CHAPTER 3

"New" Europeans, New Conflicts

BEFORE the Civil War immigrants entered the United States virtually without restriction. Aware of the need for increased population to develop the nation, and of the Old World origins of most Americans, Congress raised no barriers. The only regulations on immigration were those imposed by a few states, which assumed they had jurisdiction in this area. New York and Massachusetts, each with a major port of entry, enacted head taxes. Undeterred by these minimal measures, Europeans came in great numbers; more than five million arrived between 1820 and 1860.

Antebellum nativists reacted to these immigrants with calls for proscriptive legislation. Significantly, though they did propose keeping out paupers and criminals, their primary focus was not on restriction or exclusion. It was really on the evil influence, especially political, of resident aliens, naturalized citizens, and the Roman Catholic Church. By subduing the forces of "foreignism" and upholding those of "Americanism," most of the nation's problems could be solved, including that of saving the Union which was being divided over slavery.

Anti-Chinese sentiment shifted the focus of the nativists from those foreigners who were already in the United States to those who had not yet come. Racially and culturally different, and politically powerless, the Asians were barred. With sufficient provocation, Congress could take similar steps against Europeans. Not all Europeans were vulnerable: only those who did not look, act, speak or worship like the millions who had preceded them since the seventeenth century. Conscience might preclude exclusion, but certainly not restriction. With arguments remarkably similar to those arrayed against the Chinese, the

45

economic, cultural, and even moral disqualification of some Europeans for admission could be demonstrated. To many leaders of organized labor, it would matter little whether these "new Chinese" came from Italy, Austria-Hungary, or Russia. What would be important was the assumption that they were, like the Asians, a threat to wages and jobs.

With the era of Reconstruction long since ended and Civil War issues fading, the United States plunged into the 1880s with a renewed spirit of nationalism. The growing population was spreading across the continent and swelling cities were made attractive by prospective industrial employment. Opportunity, spokesman for the successful claimed, was available to all who applied themselves.

Of those who sought to share in this apparent bonanza many were nonnative. Among the 50,262,000 Americans in 1880, 6,679,943, or 13.3 percent, were of foreign birth.[1] Of the latter, ten years of age and over, almost a fifth were engaged in mining and manufacturing, while an eighth were in agriculture. However, as part of the nation's total work force the foreign born constituted almost a third of those in industry and slightly more than a tenth of the farmers. Analyzing this distribution of immigrant labor, the commissioner of the United States Bureau of Labor saw cause for concern. Carroll D. Wright noted that the immigrants tended "to assimilate with our mechanical industries. This increases the supply of labor in comparison to the demand, lowers wages, contributes to whatever over production exists, and cripples temporarily the consuming power of the whole."[2]

This ominous analysis had enormous significance. Coming from the nation's leading labor statistician, it lent authority to the position which organized labor would soon adopt. Moreover, it pertained to the period preceding the onset of genuinely heavy European immigration. Clearly a warning, it reduced the immigrant to a commodity by placing him into a supply and demand context, without reference to human considerations. Doubtless influenced by rising anti-immigrant sentiment since 1880, Wright thus helped to shape a negative consensus.

Before the 1880s, the primary source of immigration were Northern and Western Europe. From 1820 through 1874 annual arrivals from there always exceeded three quarters of all new aliens, usually surpassing ninety percent. On the other hand, those from Southern and Eastern Europe usually made up less than two percent of the total. But during the last quarter of the nineteenth century, changes, gradual but nonetheless dramatic became apparent. In 1875, for the first time, the latter group constituted ten percent. They would slip slightly below that figure the next year, and again in 1880 and 1881, but afterward they would soar above and far beyond it. Finally, by 1896 they would constitute a majority of the immigrants entering the United States.[3]

The great change came about primarily because of deteriorating European economic conditions. As historian Maldwyn Allen Jones has written, a variety of complex factors shifted the sources of heaviest emigration away from the British Isles, Germany, and Scandinavia. For three decades after 1860 those regions suffered from an agricultural crisis brought about by a drastic drop in grain prices. Industrial depression, too, contributed to the exodus, especially from Germany in the eighties. However, by the nineties agriculture stabilized, industrialization created jobs, birthrates declined, and governments devised new social policies, all of which served to reduce levels of emigration.[4]

As that emigration peaked and then declined, another exodus occurred. In Austria-Hungary and Italy the land systems displaced hundreds of thousands of peasants. Permitted since the 1860s to divide their lands, peasants within the empire of the Habsburgs did so too fast. Their speedy subdivision resulted in plots too small to sustain the numbers of people living on them. Fearing a fall to the position of day laborers from the loss of their property, peasants chose to emigrate. Initially a movement of Bohemians and Moravians, the departing tide soon included Jews, Poles, Ruthenians, Magyars, Slovaks, Rumanians, Slovenes, Serbs, Croats, and Dalmatians. Each of these areas from which these people fled had specific economic problems, but on the whole they were "displaced peasants and agricultural workers" at the mercy of "more widespread and permanent economic influences."[5]

For the Italian peasants the difficulty was similar, but the "social forms and values" making for emigration were different.

To be sure, southern Italy had its share of surplus population, low agricultural prices, high taxes, and deficient land. Yet, as Rudolph J. Vecoli has pointed out, these peasants, or "*contadini,* both as cultivators and emigrants, acted on the principle of economic individualism pursuing family and self-interest." Anxious not to engage in the degradation, as they saw it, of manual labor, these peasants sought economic opportunities which did not bind them to the soil. To better themselves, south Italian peasants seized the chance to become shopkeepers, artisans, priests, or emigrants. They "viewed a sojourn in America as a means to acquire capital with which to purchase land, provide dowries for their daughters, and assist their sons to enter business or the professions."[6] Beginning with the 12,354 immigrants who entered the United States in 1880, more than twice the figure for 1879, these Italians came in ever-increasing numbers. By 1900 they reached the 100,000 per year mark, which was annually surpassed until 1915, when Italy's participation in World War I severely reduced the number.[7]

Russia was a third major additional source of immigrants. There the chief factors were religious and political. On March 1, 1881, revolutionaries assassinated Czar Alexander II, which prompted a government-inspired wave of pogroms, or riots, against Jews throughout the land. By the summer of 1881 an exodus of Jewish refugees began, just before a second round of terror the next spring. The May Laws of 1882 forbade Jewish mobility within their already limited geographical area, the Pale of Settlement. Furthermore they ended Jewish land ownership in rural areas and Jewish employment on estates as managers or stewards.

Added to this economic assault was a cultural one, the denial of educational opportunity. The "percentage rule" of 1886 and 1887 limited Jews to ten percent of the total number of students admitted by secondary high schools and universities within the Pale. Outside the Pale, the proportions were lower, and Jews were entirely barred from some institutions. Thus violated, vilified, humiliated, and detached from economic and cultural life, the Jews began to depart. "In the thirty-three years between the assassination of Alexander II and the outbreak of the First World War, approximately one third of the East European Jews left their homelands." Beween 1881 and 1910 more than 1.1 million Russian Jews came to the United States.[8]

Though culturally different from earlier immigrants, those from Eastern and Southern Europe were in several respects quite similar to the older arrivals. Jews were not the first to flee to America to escape religious persecution; English settlers had long ago established a precedent for that. Similarly, the quest for a good life did not originate with Italians or Slavs; Irish refugees from the potato famine were familiar with hunger and poverty. Then, too, America had not traditionally attracted the rich and well-born; the bulk of newcomers during the colonial period and then between the War for Independence and American Civil War were to a great extent lower and lower-middle classes.[9] Finally, as economist Joseph Schachter has recently demonstrated, "the new immigration was actually more skilled than the old immigration. Comparing immigrants of the 1870–1880 decade with those of 1880 to 1910, Schachter finds a higher level of skills in the latter group, but, on the other hand, lower socioeconomic status. The relatively unskilled farmers of the "old immigration" enjoyed a "higher socioeconomic position" than the skilled and clerical workers who came later. In other words, though their skills were greater, the "new immigrants" belonged to a lower socioeconomic class which made it very easy for people to assume that they were also less skilled.[10]

Though they came in modest numbers, the vanguard of the Eastern and Southern European immigrants encountered immediate hostility. Arriving in the Pennsylvania coal fields, an area of widespread labor disorder since the end of the Civil War, they came to the worst place at the worst possible time—the depression of the 1870s. Some of the Italian and Hungarian immigrants were imported under contract by employers seeking to blunt the militancy of native labor with the docility of newly arrived foreigners. Few actually were imported, but all became instant objects of suspicion as mindless, employer-controlled creatures brought for the purpose of reducing conditions to still lower levels. There were no more than seven thousand of these immigrants in Pennsylvania before 1880, but those who were there were subjected to public and private abuse of the vilest sort. Physical attacks, fines and prison sentences on minor pretexts, wages taken by cheating, and over-crowded barns and shanties to sleep in, were all part of the pattern.[11]

The identification of Italians as "troublemakers" was made in 1874. South of Pittsburgh, bituminous coal miners struck for higher wages. To break the strike, the operators thought first of bringing in Swedes. However, when employed recently to break an Illinois strike of coal diggers, Swedes and other Scandinavians had not succeeded. Three operators eventually went to New York City where they contracted with the New York Italian Labor Company for strikebreakers. On September 23, "about two hundred Italians" arrived in the bituminous country. Angry at the foreigners, who were also armed, the local citizenry took violent action. On Sunday, November 29, a battle between the natives and newcomers along the Allegheny River resulted in three dead among the latter. The remaining Italians soon left the area; they were gone within four months.[12]

Despite this failure, the idea of importing labor under contract remained alive. In 1875, Franklin B. Gowen, president of the Reading Railroad and anthracite operator, broke a bitter strike and the organization behind it, the Workingmen's Benevolent Association. Gowen's cost, he estimated, was at least four million dollars, but henceforth, under a new policy he could substantially reduce his railroad and mine labor costs in Schuylkill County by importing contract labor.[13]

With the immigrant population rapidly increasing in the eighties, the contract labor issue became prominent. As John Higham says, "relatively few" immigrants actually came under contract with employers. "But corporate power seemed so great and menacing to American workers that they [the Americans] attributed a captive status to the new nationalities." Each arriving carload of Eastern European strikebreakers seemed to confirm this impression. Apparently imported to serve American industrial masters, these people were regarded by American labor as a "servile class." During the nineties, organized labor would regard contract laborers as pawns of the capitalists. In brief, contract laborers were made to appear a menace to American workers.[14]

As the contract labor question grew, Congress considered the "new" immigrants in the context of an even older problem.

Traditionally the reception of incoming aliens had been left by the federal government to the seaboard states. In turn, the states let charity volunteers administer their regulations and welcome the immigrants. This system was supposed to impart order to the admissions process, provide assistance to the temporarily handicapped, and discourage the coming of the permanently disabled to prevent them from becoming public charges. In 1876, however, the Supreme Court declared that state regulations violated the exclusive right of Congress to manage foreign commerce. Appalled that immigration assistance funds would now have to come solely from voluntary sources, New York's public and private agencies joined with those in other eastern seaboard states in appealing for a federal law to regulate the immigrant flow. They sought legislation to relieve the financial burden of having to care for people whom they suspected, according to social Darwinist theories of becoming paupers and criminals. Moreover, they urged the levying of a head tax on each immigrant to cover administrative and relief costs and the absolute exclusion of those liable to require public support.[15]

By 1882 the fact that immigration had indeed become heavier was gaining attention. While not yet urging action to reduce it, the Knights' *Journal of United Labor* nonetheless suggested "at least hasty examination" into its causes. That inquiry would, of course, include the Italians whom "the average American is disposed [to regard with] . . . loathing and contempt," but also those who have not troubled us to any great extent in the past."[16] However, the *New York Times* was more representative of prevailing opinions because it endorsed restrictive legislation pending in Congress "to prevent the wholesale landing of criminals paupers, and helpless persons."[17]

In 1875, Congress had barred prostitutes and convicts, and now, in August, 1882, a general immigration law was at last approved. Six years of opposition by business elements was overcome by pressure from New York's political and charitable interests, and the realization that the Castle Garden immigration depot was in chaos. The legislation placed a fifty-cent head tax on each entering alien and excluded "any convict, lunatic, idiot or any person unable to take care of himself or herself without becoming a public charge."[18]

The Immigration Act of 1882 was not passed at the request of the American workingman, nor was it designed to benefit him. The slight head tax was for revenue purposes while the exclusion was directed at those who were deemed unable to compete in the labor market. Clearly it was indicative of antiforeign feeling, with racial connotations, on the part of a broad cross-section of society.

For the moment, organized labor concentrated on banning the importation of those foreigners who did not offer competition, as in the Pennsylvania mines. The *Times,* while rejecting the idea of keeping out able-bodied, voluntary immigrants, saw "a good deal of justice" in the argument against imported labor in industries with tariff protection. It was "obviously unfair," the newspaper argued, for employers to seek a price advantage through protection "on the plea that this will enable them to pay higher wages to American labor, and then to import the foreign labor in order to avoid paying higher wages."[19]

As historian Charlotte Erickson has demonstrated, the pressure for a law to prohibit contract labor "was begun and organized by a group of craft unionists," some of whom were affiliated with the Knights of Labor. Agitation over this issue by the craft unions began in 1881, two years before the Knights' General Assembly took it up. The Federation of Organized Trades and Labor Unions, when it was founded, made a ban on contract labor one of its guiding principles, and, four months later, advised trade unions of the problem. Behind the Knights' action was the Window Glass Workers Association, which had taken part in the founding Federation convention. A member of that organization of skilled craftsmen drafted a bill to be submitted to Congress. At their 1883 convention, the Knights cited the evil of contract labor. Afterward, they organized petitions and mass meetings against it.

Finally, in January 1884, Martin Foran of Ohio, former president of the Coopers International Union, introduced a bill in the House of Representatives. In committee hearings, Powderly and other Knights offered "remarkably weak" testimony on the incidence of contract labor. Only the Window Glass Workers made a strong presentation, bringing certified copies of contracts and the testimony of glassworkers who had once been contract laborers. The Amalgamated Association of Iron and Steel Workers sent their representative to testify.

In June 1884, when the House debated the bill, its proponents used a "new immigration" argument. Foran and others largely ignored the few hundred skilled craftsmen who were the actual targets of the legislation in favor of a lurid, racist diatribe against Italians and Hungarians who were allegedly being imported in great numbers by capitalists.

The scare technique succeeded, especially in the House, which, in June 1884, approved the bill with three amendments. Those changes effectively weakened the document. They included exemptions for new industries, people aiding relatives, and those entering into contracts after arrival in the United States. By not covering contracts made by aliens after they landed, the bill overlooked most of the hiring that was done by steamship lines and other private employment agencies.[20]

Favorable committee action did not speed passage by the Senate. There the bill was held over to the second session of the Forty-eighth Congress. As it awaited consideration by that body, both the trade unions and the Knights continued their agitation. Powderly and his organization persisted in describing contract laborers as unskilled, taking special delight in denouncing the "slave labor" working conditions of Hungarians in Pennsylvania.[21] Amply publicizing the fact, the General Master Workman then wrote to key senators urging quick approval.[22] By convention resolution and personal appeals, the Federation of Organized Trades and Labor Unions maintained its pressure.[23]

While organized labor waged war, industry remained silent, and thus tacitly accepted the Foran Bill. There simply was no need for opposition as industry was not importing significant quantities of European labor "and was certainly not importing unskilled workers on contract in any numbers, if at all." Furthermore, many industry sources, anxious for labor support for protective tariffs, acknowledged labor's right to secure its own comparable form of protection.[24] Business also recognized one basic truth, namely, that the measure would probably be ineffective. Along with exemptions added in the House, the bill clearly permitted the importation of skilled workers where needed. Such need, it was understood, would not be difficult to demonstrate.[25]

Unopposed by industry, in February 1885 the bill cleared the Senate and was then signed into law by President Arthur. Organized labor naturally claimed credit for its passage but was itself under no illusions about its probable effect. While calling it a "step in the right direction," Gabriel Edmonston, secretary of the legislative committee of the Federation of Organized Trades and Labor Unions, also admitted that it "may not affect a very large number of immigrants, or may be evaded."[26] Regarding the latter, there were already complaints that contract labor was being employed on a federal improvements project at Galveston, Texas. As for the law itself, it allegedly required amendment to be made more effective.[27] Powderly viewed enforcement as "difficult, if not impossible." His complaint was that the law did not provide financial compensation for workers or associations who incurred expenses in bringing suit against violators. "We should go to Congress," he said, "and see that an amendment is added to the bill which will make it of some service to the country."[28]

The objections raised to this rather inept legislation were indeed valid, but the contract labor debate more effectively served the purpose of expressing antiforeign attitudes than establishing the existence of a threat to workingmen. It was an easily exploited, respectable issue designed to attack foreign-born elements to whom it actually did not relate. Unchallenged, the strident verbal assault on Hungarians and Italians would soon expand into a full-fledged war on the "new immigration."

Powderly simply did not want foreigners to compete for American jobs. He was unprepared, by the fall of 1885, to demand the prohibition of immigration. Such a request, he said, "would be un-American." Yet he could still suggest that immigrant labor entering the tight American job market would wind up unemployed. Clearly they would be better off not coming in the first place.[29] Similarly abandoning the pretense of opposing only contract labor, other Knights condemned the entry of "paupers, criminals, or persons devoid of reason, as a gross injustice." District Assembly 47 of Cleveland sought to end "the influx of moneyless laborers from foreign countries" until American economic conditions improved.[30]

Across the country attitudes were much the same. In a poll

by the Wisconsin Bureau of Labor, employers and American
workers generally evidenced a common belief that immigration
should be restricted. Said one employer: "Keep away all impure
blood from the American shores. Make a limit and not flood the
country with foreigners and anti-American people." A tanner
from Milwaukee said, "we do not want any more European labor
at present," and immigration in general should be stopped or
restricted. Wisconsin did, indeed, experience an influx of Italian
railway workers in 1885 and 1886. However, when the Labor
Bureau investigated complaints that they were contract laborers
imported from Italy, the objections were thrown out. They did
come under contract, but from other states. American workers
contemptuously viewed them as virtual slaves of those who
brought and employed them.[31]

In Washington, too, the concern was not about contract labor
as much as too much immigration. Issued in March 1886, the
commissioner of labor's first annual report observed that the
recently enacted law was "practically inoperative, because no
desire exists to break its provisions." Bureau of Labor agents
"were not able to learn of a widespread importation of labor
under contract." Instances uncovered were local in nature and
did not involve entire industries." The real problem was the
"rapid immigration."[32] Drawing his own conclusions from the
government's findings, one observer charged that America was
"becoming a dumping ground for the refuse of Central Europe."
Moreover, argued S. M. Jelley, American workingmen have become aware of the "great evil . . . in the tide of immigration" and
are demanding its "effective restriction."[33]

As anticipated, the Foran Act was easily evaded. In addition
to the law's generous exemptions, even the provision for inspectors at ports of entry was omitted. In 1887, Congress authorized
the secretary of the treasury to contract with the states for their
officials to inspect, but appropriated no funds for that purpose.
Immigration superintendents were confined to asking individuals
if they came under contract. The next year some money was
appropriated for inspection. Additionally, at the behest of the
A.F. of L., provision was made to deport contract laborers at
the expense of the importer or steamship company. Initially
deportation could occur within a year of entry, but the Federa-

tion sought to double the period. In 1907 it was lengthened to three years.[34]

Contract labor was a convenient demon of little actual substance. Although organized labor continued to complain about it and secure Foran Act amendments, as indicated above, the workers' fears were more emotional than rational, and racist than economic.

Ironically, the Knights of Labor, the one genuine haven for black and unskilled American workers, was the loudest among labor groups against the "new" immigrants. The reason for this apparent contradiction is clear: Powderly. Essentially a person of limited outlook, the General Master Workman focused on what was closest and most meaningful to his own experience. The invasion, as he saw it, of his Pennsylvania by Hungarians and Italians ignited an incredible volley of verbal abuse aimed at driving them out and preventing others from entering.

In 1887 Powderly and the *Journal of United Labor* awoke to the danger of the immigrant poor. In their view America could no longer afford to welcome the oppressed of Europe, which now consisted of "an overwhelming tide of ignorant and irresponsible humanity," ignorant of democracy and in racial conflict with each other.[35] The United States was importing anarchists, dynamiters, ballot-box stuffers, and repeaters, and other elements of an "undigested mass" of Europeans. "It is THE CHINESE CASE OVER AGAIN," noted an educator, providing "unfair and killing competition for our own labor."[36] "Has not immigration been too much of a good thing?" asked the *Journal*.[37] Attacking two villains simultaneously, Powderly likened the monopolist to the anarchist, the latter presumably being foreign born. They were "twin evils," both of which cared "nothing for American institutions."[38] "STOP PAUPER IMMIGRATION," the *Journal* finally urged;[39] even Great Britain was trying to unload its paupers upon the United States.[40]

At last the Knights' publication identified Pennsylvania as a place where such a problem actually existed. American coal and railroad workers there were competing with "foreigners, notably Hungarians and Italians." That competition was "a growing evil not to be ignored."[41] In other words, Pennsylvania's as well as the nation's workers needed help. To keep the paupers of Europe from being added to those of America, the *Journal* urged the enactment of restrictive federal immigration legislation.[42]

The Knights remained on a rampage through 1888, virtually oblivious of the contract labor question. The new immigrants, it was reported, threatened even Texas with "anarchy, distress and pauperism."[43] Of course, as Powderly never tired of insisting, these "semi-barbarous" people came not of their own accord, but through "undue influence . . . by agents of American employers."[44] The nation's "corporate system," he claimed, with its wild speculation since the Civil War, utilized unrestricted immigration as a means to maximize profits.[45] Ever mindful of the coal miners, Powderly produced a four-part exposé of the working conditions of Hungarians and Italians in his hometown of Scranton, Pennsylvania.[46] Referring to that state, another Knight reported to the General Assembly that "many parts'" were "known as the Europe of America by the products of its cheap labor."[47]

While the Knights waged their war, the leadership of the American Federation of Labor remained calm. For the former, on the decline since the disastrous events of 1886, little was lost but possibly something could be gained by flailing the foreign born. For Gompers and the Federation, the considerations were different. His relatively young organization included many foreign-born members who were not yet ready to urge the restriction of European immigrants other than contract laborers. Then, too, the membership was not ideologically heterogenous and the role of socialism and socialists still unclear. Why chance disruption for uncertain gain?

Instead, Gompers pursued the safe, dual course of Chinese and contract labor exclusion. He personally served as a clearing-house for reports of Foran Act violations, which he received and forwarded to immigration authorities.[48] In convention, the A.F. of L. endorsed strengthening the law,[49] but was unprepared to accept the idea of general restriction.[50]

Though led by Powderly in the 1880s, the movement by organized labor against the "new" immigration would intensify and gain significant additional support in the next decade; and, as the crusade gained momentum, the likelihood of success increased. Occurring at a point in American history when theories of racial superiority and inferiority were questioned by few, it was not difficult to persuade Congress and the public that Eastern and Southern Europeans were, like the Chinese, a threat to the livelihood and civilization of organized labor.

CHAPTER 4

Strangers in the Steel Mills

THE Slavic and Hungarian "new" immigrants brought an agricultural heritage to America, but quickly demonstrated that they could adapt themselves to the needs of an industrial society. Employed in iron and steel mills and anthracite and bituminous coal mines, they were at the center of the nation's economic development. They contributed much to the rise of industry as they pursued the goal of creating a better future for themselves.

Contrary to the fears of labor leaders and the more solidly entrenched type of workers, the newcomers were not inherently indifferent or hostile to the idea of trade unionism. At Homestead, McKees Rocks, and elsewhere, they readily revealed a job and class consciousness worthy of any of their predecessors in America. Sometimes their organizational or strike efforts succeeded; more often than not, especially in iron and steel, they failed. In either case, if the test of "Americanism" was fighting for a decent living, there is ample evidence that the Eastern European immigrants passed admirably.

The Slovaks, Poles, Croatians, Lithuanians, and others who arrived after 1880 were mainly victims of economic misfortune who hoped for a better future in the New World. Primarily peasants who lived on heavily mortgaged property which was usually too small to provide an adequate income, they migrated in search of a better chance. Some sought seasonal work in Germany; others chose America, from which they hoped eventually to return with savings sufficient to satisfy mortgage demands or purchase new properties. Many found jobs in American iron and steel mills.[1] In other words, these people were not aimless, ignorant peasants; they were "on the whole intelligent, and they well knew why they were leaving and where they were headed."[2]

59

When they reached the United States, they entered the steel industry which then was undergoing unionization. Under the leadership of English-speaking workers, they were drawn to various organizations beginning as early as 1861, when the boilers and puddlers' Sons of Vulcan was formed with 3,331 members.[3] Fifteen years later, that union merged with smaller organizations to create the Amalgamated Association of Iron and Steel Workers. In 1887 they affiliated with the American Federation of Labor. With a membership of 25,000 by 1892, the Amalgamated Association would participate in the bitter Homestead strike.[4]

From 1882 to 1886, the Knights of Labor were also active in the steel industry. During these prime years Terence Powderly's people organized, among others, the unskilled as well as skilled laborers of Allegheny County, Pennsylvania. With its appeal to those workers ignored by the craft-oriented Amalgamated Association, the Knights offered competition which was beneficial mainly to management.[5]

The influx of "new" immigrants during this era of evolving industrial relations dramatically divided the work force into mutually antagonistic camps. The workers who predominated in the steel plants, and who came form Western Europe, found the newcomers repugnant. Calling them "Huns" or "Hunkies," meaning Hungarians, the old stock workers separated themselves from the immigrants.[6]

There was something about the non-English-speaking newcomers that was reminiscent of the immigrants from China. "The feeling against them," Henry George observed in 1886, "has been like that which exists among the laboring population of the Pacific coast against the Chinese." These Europeans were not heathens or lepers, but there was "much in their manner of living" that was suggestive of the Asians.[7]

As historian David Brody claims, there was "an unbridgable gulf" separating the two sides. "They don't seem like men to me hardly. They can't talk United States," complained one old stock worker. Furthermore, the newcomers were allegedly lazy; Rumanian stokers at the Fort Wayne Rolling Mill fell asleep when the night boss turned his back.

These complaints and others contributed to the feeling that the immigrants were an inferior class of people whose presence depressed labor standards and displaced native workers. But despite their complaints, the English-speaking steelworkers had no personal reason to resent them, for by moving onto the bottom rungs of the steel industry ladder, their presence as well as continuing economic growth served to push the old stock upward into skilled and supervisory positions.

Simply stated, many felt it demeaning to work alongside Eastern Europeans. They saw some jobs as suitable only for "Hunkies," because those tasks were "too damn dirty and too damn hot for a 'white' man." The immediate consequence of this attitude was that it limited the jobs open to the "white" men. In fact, the aversion to on-the-job contact or competition with Slavs and Hungarians reduced the supply of natives even for skilled workers; Americans wanted higher status "pencil jobs."

Anxious to remain apart, the English-speaking element ignored the immigrants outside the mill. Contemptuous of the foreigners, the Americans psychologically came to identify with other components of the community, such as artisans and shopkeepers. In addition, they admired their employers, whom they regarded as models. "As much for social as for economic reasons," Brody explains, "the citizenry of the mill towns aligned with the steel companies."[8]

The social tension and economic competition between American and foreigner was clearly evident in Steelton, situated south of Harrisburg, Pennsylvania. The site of the Pennsylvania Steel Company, Steelton was incorporated in 1880, when it was already attracting a wide variety of workers from both America and Europe. Blacks came from Maryland and Virginia, Germans from neighboring Pennsylvania towns, Irishmen from the British Isles, and Slavs and Italians from Southern Europe. Arriving mainly after 1880, the Slavic immigrants were for the most part Bulgarians, Croatians, Serbians, and Slovenes.[9]

Though the old stock did not attempt to exclude the newcomers from the Steelton mill, they did exercise social control. Assuming an elitist attitude, they claimed the right to instruct the immigrants and to criticize their behavior. Hopefully, the new stock would blend into the community, but on a social level below that of their predecessors.[10]

The black migrants were far easier to control than the foreigners. Native whites objected to their shanty houses and social conduct, which included dancing, drinking, and fighting. The remedy was segregation of neighborhoods and elementary schools. Significantly, though the blacks were subjected to this kind of discrimination, they escaped the massive ridicule heaped upon the white immigrants.[11]

The latter felt the full force of old stock condescension and contempt. Holders of the most menial mill jobs, these Slavs nonetheless had regular weekly amounts deducted from their pay checks to support Steelton's Irish-controlled St. James Church. Those Slavs who actually attended that church were victims of a system of pew rentals that enabled the wealthy Irish to sit up front while they stood in the rear.[12] Such treatment seemed appropriate for people who were rumored to eat stray dogs. However, the more complete indictment against them included charges that they lived cheaply, drank heavily (especially on Sunday), behaved rowdily, maintained unsanitary boardinghouses, and aimed to take American money with them back to Europe. Potential returnees did not become naturalized citizens, which also stirred criticism.[13]

Many of the foreigners did indeed return, especially as a result of the hardship brought about by the depression of 1907–1908. Steelton then lost more than a third of its Croats, Serbs, and Italians, and most of its Bulgarians, its most recent immigrants.[14]

These peoples were very mobile, perhaps more so than American workers. As Michael Weber has demonstrated, such was clearly the case for labor in Pittsburgh. Of a sample of 354 foreign-born workers there in 1880, only one could be found in 1920.[15] As the return flow to Europe intensified with downturns in the business cycle, it is probably correct to say, as Gabriel Kolko does, that it constituted a "reverse safety valve" for surplus labor.[16]

The immigrants' mobility was occupational as well as geographical. Regarding themselves as transients, many could not commit themselves to unions.[17] Similarly, their frequent job changes made them difficult to organize. At Steelton, a Croatian socialist newspaper blamed immigrant coolness to unions on that situation.[18]

Organized by skilled, old stock workers in 1890, the Steelton local of the Amalgamated Association went on strike in 1891.

After having first been locked out by the Pennsylvania Steel Company in response to wage and union recognition demands, the local struck, but was easily defeated. Protected by Pinkerton detectives, and supported by the community press, the company ran the mills with the assistance of southern black strikebreakers. In this the union local could not get the support of its national leadership nor win over Steelton's black workers because of their resentment against past discrimination. Amalgamated president William Wiehe declared the strike to be unauthorized because the national headquqarters of the Amalgamated Association had not approved the local's wage demands.[19] Homestead, Pennsylvania, near Pittsburgh, was the site of a plant of the Carnegie Steel Company. Of the 7,911 residents of Homestead in 1890, thirty-one percent were foreign born and sixty-two percent were of foreign parentage. Of the laborers at the plant, the skilled were mainly American, but two thirds of the unskilled were immigrants.[20]

The skilled workers, members of the Amalgamated Association, suddenly found themselves in conflict with the company. Insistent on securing wage cuts, Henry Clay Frick, the company manager, without notice terminated negotiations and locked out his employees behind a barbed wire fence. Then, when he attempted to import a private army of three hundred Pinkerton agents to enforce his actions, the workers opened fire on them as they came up the Monongahela River on barges. Routed by the enraged workers, the Pinkertons retreated to Pittsburgh. Order was finally restored by eight thousand state militiamen after six days of fighting. Protected by the troops, Frick hired new employees. Then anarchist Alexander Berkman tried unsuccessfully to assassinate Frick, which further upset a public already appalled at the labor violence. By November the strike was officially over. The present employees now consisted of two thousand strikebreakers and only eight hundred of the plant's original total of almost four thousand workers.[21]

The Homestead affair crippled the cause of steel unionism and taught the immigrants a lesson. Why organize and by so doing jeopardize one's opportunity to have money for a return to one's homeland? The dream of a new farm or family security in Europe could be readily destroyed by another defeat.[22]

Yet Homestead continued to attract the immigrants, whom the company, of course, hired.[23] Mainly single men, they came, lived in barrack-type boardinghouses, and dreamed of returning home. All had to be thrifty. Turn-of-the-century earnings, during prosperous times, were $9.90 per week; those who labored more than ten hours per day plus Sunday could reach $12.00. Expenses for single men averaged $11.00 per month.

With their surpluses, some Slavs saved for purposes other than emigration. Some saved to send for their families, help aged parents, or even to purchase homes in America. In 1907, more than two dozen Slavs bought homes in Homestead.[24]

Reluctant to incur the wrath of management by unionizing, Slavic and Hungarian immigrants turned their collective instincts toward fraternal organizations. Normally the members of a few boardinghouse groups would take the initiative and create such organizations to provide sickness and accident insurance. According to Margaret Byington, Homestead had a minimum of twenty-six lodges with 2,108 members.[25] Unfortunately, these enterprises often failed because they could not keep up with the mounting expenses generated by an ever-increasing accident rate.[26]

After 1900, the steel industry's labor force was unorganized, mainly Eastern European,[67] and seething with internal discord. At Steelton, the company and old stock workers found ways to antagonize the foreigners. In 1904, fifteen Slavs began a brief strike when their pay was shifted from an hourly to a piece work basis. Rather than heed their protests, the company ousted them. The dismissed strikers then bought steamship tickets and returned to Europe. A year later the Slavs were the object of a resolution passed by the local branch of the Order of United American Mechanics, an old stock white organization. That group demanded federal legislation to protect the American laborer "against direct competition in our country by the incoming of the COMPETITIVE ALIEN—the foreign pauper laborers themselves." Finally, natives resorted to social discrimination. On patriotic occasions they usually paraded, but without the Slavs and blacks, who had to form their own parades. At the mill, native whites tried not to work with the immigrants, and even preferred being laid off to accepting jobs normally handled by immigrants. In 1913, a foreman was arrested for selling jobs to immigrants for fifty dollars. The result of these attitudes and practices was disunity as well as disquiet.[28]

At Homestead there was similar division. There the social separation between Slavs and old stock natives was even greater than that between whites and blacks. There was no mingling in churches, lodges, or residences, and almost none in schools.[29]

The ethnic divisions within the steel industry's work force were vertical as well as horizontal. Horizontally, the separation, as the workingmen regarded it, was between the "English-speaking" or "white men," and the "Hunkies" or "Guineas" who were also called "foreigners." To qualify as "English-speaking," an individual had only to be born "somewhere west of the Russian Empire or north of Austria-Hungary." His actual linguistic ability was irrelevant. "Hunkies" were Slavs as well as Hungarians, while "Guineas" were "Hunkies" plus Italians.

Though the most obvious division was between those groups, the vertical cause for friction was also very clear. Among the "English-speaking" workers, the native Americans and English disliked the Welsh, while among the "foreigners" there was even greater dissension. Magyars clashed with Slavs, while Finns, Poles, Slovaks, and Lithuanians had their respective "sectional differences." Finally, there were religious conflicts. Greek Orthodox Christians distrusted Roman Catholics, while both had little use for Protestants.[30]

With the steel workers so divided, it was not surprising for Margaret Byington to observe about Homestead in 1910 "that trade unionism belonged to an earlier generation." "A generation of boys," she added, "has now grown up and entered the mills without knowing by personal experience what unionism is, or, except by hearsay, what the great strike of 1892 was about."[31]

In its study of trade union affiliation in iron and steel the United States Immigration Commission confirmed Byington's observation. Of 4,185 males twenty-one years of age or over and working for wages, only 1.6 percent were organized.[32] Studying the Pittsburgh district, the commission found only 1 of 678 workers, 633 of whom were foreign born, to be union affiliated. Thus, it concluded that "there is practically no active interest in union matters either among the foreign or the native born in this community."[33] It should also be noted, as the commission did,

"Whenever it is found out that an employee is a member of a union he is promptly discharged."[34]

As the Pressed Steel Car Company of McKees Rocks, Pennsylvania, south of Pittsburgh, discovered, enraged workers did not have to be unionized to strike, and the foreign born were not docile. In July 1909, the company announced a change in its wage system. Each worker's wages would henceforth be dependent upon the productivity of his "gang," and no new rates would be posted. Forty men then formed an ad hoc committee to request an explanation and the posting of the wage rates. Pressed Steel responded by dismissing the committee members, thereby precipitating a strike.[35]

At war with management was a work force consisting "of about 1,200 skilled English speaking mechanics and 3,500 semi-skilled and unskilled immigrants." The less-skilled foreigners began the strike, and were joined by the more highly skilled Americans. To one observer, "it was simply a united claim on the part of unskilled, ignorant 'Hunkies' for justice, and the Americans stood with them." A meeting of the strikers "was addressed in thirteen languages," which were translated by several interpreters.[36] Americans and Europeans acted together supported by Pittsburgh's steel district public opinion.[37]

The Industrial Workers of the World also sided with the strikers. Founded in Chicago in 1905 to offer the working class a radical, socialist alternative to the American Federation of Labor, this organization was anxious to enlist immigrants. Its leaders included William D. Haywood of the Western Federation of Miners, Daniel DeLeon of the Socialist Labor party, and William E. Trautmann of the Brewery Workers' Union in Massachusetts. DeLeon, an advocate of political involvement by unions, was expelled in 1908 when "direct action" tacticians assumed control of it. In August 1909, General Organizer Trautmann came to McKees Rocks, met openly with the strikers, and started a local.

When Trautmann arrived, he found the atmosphere explosive. Rioting had already taken the life of one striker. A week after Trautmann's appearance immigrants incensed at the company's increasing use of strikebreakers resorted to additional violence. The result was a battle between strikers and state troopers which took eleven more lives. The "Cossacks," as the angry Slavs called the troopers, used their horses to drag arrested strikers through the streets.[38]

The walkout ended in September. Facing a united group of strikers whose cause had won the public's sympathy, the company relented and the workers appeared to have won a great victory.[39]

What they actually won was a return to prestrike conditions. Worker unity throughout the conflict had been more apparent than real. The skilled American workers, unhappy with the close relationship that developed between the Industrial Workers of the World and the semi- and unskilled immigrants, were eager to have the status quo restored. Acting in concert, C. A. Wise of the skilled workers and the Pressed Steel Car Company had Trautmann jailed and then broke a brief second strike backed by the I.W.W.

Thus, the immigrants had struck twice, the first time without any union leadership. They had been militant and had responded positively to the I.W.W.'s organizational effort. Yet they were ultimately defeated because their colleagues, the Americans, despised both them and their radical friends. The native workers preferred collaboration with management to solidarity.[40]

The phenomenon of a walkout without a union extended even to Steelton. In 1912, cranemen and yard crews there stopped working and demanded a pay increase. Pennsylvania Steel then fired the strikers, which only prompted more men to lay down their tools. Eventually company officials listened to demands presented by a worker committee, but chose to ignore them. As most of the striking immigrants could not afford to go indefinitely without pay, many simply left Steelton for firms in Pittsburgh and Williamsport.[41] In this confrontation, management again emerged victorious, but it was the mobility of the immigrants and their willingness to search elsewhere, not docility or ignorance of issues, that determined the outcome.

Five years later Steelton was the scene of yet another unsuccessful strike. However, this walkout was not called by immigrants. It was action taken by a native group affiliated with the American Federation of Labor with no black, Slavic, or Italian representation on its policy committee. Consequently, less than half the work force answered the strike call, and the plant, owned by Bethlehem Steel since 1918, never closed entirely. On the verge of defeat, the local union called a meeting at Croatian Hall and appealed to the immigrants for support. As John Bodnar says, "many foreigners simply returned to work." Ethnic division again proved a cumbersome obstacle in the path of worker success.[42]

At Gary, Indiana, in 1919, the ethnic question was at the heart of a strike against the nation's largest steel producer, United States Steel. Despite general wage and price inflation generated by the recently concluded World War, steel industry wages lagged behind. Most workers still worked six days a week, twelve hours a day. The weekly average was almost sixty-nine hours.[43]

In September 1919, representatives of some twenty-four steel industry unions with 100,000 members sought to negotiate a change in these conditions. They wanted an eight-hour day and a wage increase, but board chairman Elbert H. Gary refused to bargain with them. That refusal led to a strike which quickly included 350,000 workers in nine states.[44]

This strike lasted almost four months, supported most staunchly by the immigrants. During the war, the Amalgamated Association and, for the first time, the American Federation of Labor, had recruited significant numbers of Slavs. By identifying trade unionism with democracy, the unions tapped the foreigners' idealistic instincts. Native whites also joined but with less enthusiasm. Blacks, mindful of union prejudice and interested in more immediate gains than membership could offer, generally stayed away.[45]

The foreigners were tenacious strikers, unlike the Americans, who often seemed indifferent. That indifference stemmed from an unwillingness, fostered by conservative propaganda, to associate with the mainly Slavic strikers. Regularly the promanagement press charged that the walkout was radical and unpatriotic, inspired by Bolshevism which had conquered Russia in 1917. Thus, it was an alien undertaking to be avoided by loyal Americans. Around Pittsburgh, most American steelworkers did indeed consider the strike a "Hunky" operation.[46]

Studying the strike in person, labor expert David Saposs confirmed its predominantly "new" immigrant and Slavic character. He found Serbs, Croatians, Slovaks, Russian and Austrian Poles,

Hungarians, Rumanians, Greeks, Italians, Lithuanians, and "a dozen other nationalities" from Eastern and Southern Europe. "This horde of immigrants," he observed, "reached America entirely unacquainted with modern industry and practically ignorant of the existence of labor organizations." Yet, except for those looking to return to Europe the next spring or summer, or those who could not be organized for lingusitic reasons, they struck. Moreover, according to Saposs, "the immigrants who worked during the strike were the ones least interested in the welfare of this country; *those who struck were the ones who have their homes and families here and who intend to remain and make this their permanent home."*

So intense was the commitment of these workers that they even acted against the counsel of many of their own priests, clan leaders, and editors who opposed the strike. That leadership group was either sensitive to the charge of "Bolshevism," friendly with Steel Corporation executives, or compromised by company donations to ethnic charities. Some leaders even urged their people to be more concerned about the return to the European fatherland than the strike, which could deplete savings and make the trip unfeasible.[47]

Though the foreigners stayed off the job, the Americans led a return to work. Many feared the loss of good positions, or admired their bosses. Others ran out of money. Still others were weary and susceptible to the loyalty argument and continuing company pressure, which included the use of strikebreakers. Finally, winter was arriving. The collapse was gradual, beginning in Chicago in December, and complete by early January 1920.[48] "Go back to work!" Uncle Sam ordered in seven languages on a United States Steel poster, and that is what the workers did.[49]

It would be many years before Eastern Europe iron and steel workers would win their struggle for social and economic acceptance. In the four decades before 1920 they disproved much of what was said about them out of prejudice and fear. Despite their agrarian origins, they proved to be the sturdiest soldiers in the fight for improved conditions in the mills.

CHAPTER 5

The Coal Miners

UNLIKE their fellow workers in the steel industry, Eastern European immigrants in coal mining had the benefit of a relatively strong union. Defeated and distracted in the wake of Homestead, steel unionism languished, because attempts at revival were repulsed by the industry. As a consequence, the largely foreign-born work force was left without protection. On the other hand, in coal mining there emerged a labor organization with sufficient intelligence and strength to prevent management from successfully manipulating ethnic differences. Brought together by the United Mine Workers of America, the supposedly ignorant and indifferent foreigners demonstrated that they, too, were aware of what was worth fighting for.

The organization of American coal-mine workers into a national union had Old World origins. In 1861, a group of British miners from Staffordshire who had settled in Belleville, Illinois, organized the American Miners' Association. Daniel Weaver, who, with Thomas Lloyd, led the movement, issued a call for American miners to unite for "mutual protection, and improvement and education." When coal miners' representatives from Illinois and Missouri then met in St. Louis in January 1861 and founded the A.M.A., Lloyd became president and Weaver secretary.[1]

The primary aim of this union was mine safety legislation in the coal-producing states. Throughout the 1860s the need for such miner protection was dramatized by several colliery disasters in England, Germany, and the United States. By maintaining close contact with English unionists, the Americans were kept abreast of the European accidents and the measures taken by Parliament to prevent recurrences in England. The fact that

Parliament had enacted statutes as early as 1860 and 1862[2] made all the more galling the loss of 109 miners in Luzerne County, Pennsylvania in 1869 when a fire sealed a single escape shaft.[3]

In 1872 the miners finally achieved victory in America. The Illinois General Assembly enacted the nation's first regulation of the entire mine labor force, prohibiting the employment of all females and boys under age fourteen. Moreover, the law greatly expanded the authority of county mine inspectors by giving them hitherto nonexistent regulatory powers. It was a clear consequence of English examples and influences.[4]

By then the Irish made a considerable impact. Their emigration since the 1840s was a product of agrarian disillusionment or landlessness. Once in America they settled in the anthracite region of Pennsylvania as well as in urban centers such as Boston, Chicago, and New York. By 1870, four anthracite counties contained 44,122 Irish immigrants.

They came to Pennsylvania, but were not welcome. Native Americans were indifferent, or openly hostile, to Irish economic and social problems. The newcomers became synonymous with low pay, child labor, and alcoholism. The drinking habit was suspected of weakening families and contributing to many arrests for disorderly conduct. Neither did Irish Catholicism endear itself to Protestants, who regarded it as a foreign faith. Occasionally, "no Irish need apply" signs appeared in the coal area. Similarly, even when they were employed, they sometimes found themselves dismissed by native English and Welsh mine bosses who wanted to make openings for their own kind.[5]

That many Irishmen sought revenge for their mistreatment was not surprising, but the means they used were often terrifying. Named after a legendary figure from Ireland who drove off tax collectors with pistols strapped to her thighs beneath her petticoat, the Molly Maguires ran rampant in the anthracite region. Violent to the point of murder, these miners intimidated or assaulted those who sympathized with management or opposed coal unionism. Operating with impunity, especially in Schuylkill County, they were finally brought down by the testimony of James McParlan, a Pinkerton detective who infiltrated their ranks, which resulted in two dozen convictions for murder. By 1877 the organization was shattered.[6]

On balance, the contribution made by immigrants from the British Isles to the mining industry, indeed, to the labor movement as a whole, were overwhelmingly positive. As historian Clifton K. Yearley, Jr., notes, American miners' unions, which by 1901 would have 226,000 members, "each sprang from organizations established by British and Irish immigrants." In addition, these immigrants "figured prominently" in the development "of twenty-four great national and internatinal unions and in more than forty additional state and local trade unions, trades assemblies, or labor-reform bodies." The leadership of the National Labor Union, Knights of Labor, and American Federation of Labor came primarily from the same sources. The Irish were "The Organizers."[7]

Into their midst came the "new" immigrants. During the Civil War, when they made their appearance in the anthracite fields, Poles in Shamokin, Pennsylvania, organized a benefit society. From southern parts of the state the Slavs shifted northward to the Wyoming region by 1868. Italians came during the 1870s, establishing a community in the Lehigh area. In the 1870s Slavs and Italians together made up 6.44 percent of the anthracite work force as opposed to 57.46 percent for Britons and Germans.[8]

Immediately there was ethnic tension and fragmentation. Fearing the loss of jobs, natives and "old" immigrants sought protection. Some means were nonviolent, including the organization of such anti-Catholic societies as the Junior Order of American Mechanics and the Patriotic Order of the Sons of America. Others were not. Two Hungarians were "beaten and kicked in a shameful manner" by a drunkard as they walked before a railroad depot, "and a crowd stood by and laughed."

Though the conflict seemed to be between "old" and "new" peoples, there was considerable ethnic division within each side which prevented a united stand. The ethnocentrism of the situation was reflected in numerous foreign-language newspapers, fraternal orders, paramilitary groups, beneficial societies, churches, and holidays. "In 1902 the anthracite regions supported 142 Catholic churches, of which 62 were Irish, 19 Polish, 18 Greek, 15 Slovak, 12 Lithuanian, 10 German, and 6 Italian." To win the votes of this diverse population, local politicians had to balance their tickets with representatives of the various groups.[9]

The dream of an organization for all miners continued beyond the American Miners' Association, which was gone by the seventies. It was sustained, initially, by John Siney of Schuylkill County. Siney first organized his region's anthracite workers, and then turned to forming a second national miners' union. The result was the Miners' National Association, founded at Youngstown, Ohio, in October 1873. Then came the Depression of 1873, and down went wages and Siney. Though he counseled against violence and futile strikes as the downturn deepened, Siney wound up being prosecuted for criminal conspiracy in Pennsylvania. He was acquitted, but not his codefendant, organizer Xingo Parks, who received a one-year penitentiary sentence, which was subsequently commuted by the governor. As for their association, it could not be salvaged. The continuing depression and a depleted treasury destroyed rescue attempts.[10]

The unionists' defeat seemed complete. Even Siney's original union, the Workingmen's Benevolent Association, died by June 1875. On strike for five months, Schuylkill County anthracite miners—on the verge of starvation—capitulated before Franklin B. Gowen, mine operator and president of the Reading Railroad.[11]

The setbacks of the seventies were followed by new approaches in the eighties. Christopher Evans introduced miners in Ohio to the Knights of Labor, which enjoyed some growth following the return of prosperity in 1879. In 1885, after objecting to continuing secrecy by the Knights, Evans broke with them and helped found the National Federation of Miners and Mine Laborers. A year later, that organization held a joint convention of miners and operators at Columbus, Ohio. That meeting produced an unprecedented twelve-member arbitration and conciliation board to help settle national or interstate disputes. In 1889, John McBride, another Ohioan, organized the secret National Progressive Union.[12]

As the Knights of Labor's assemblies in coal regions admitted nonminers, many miners avoided them. Instead, those miners established separate organizations. In 1883, bituminous miners formed the Amalgamated Association of Miners of the United

States; two years later it was succeeded by the American Miners' Federation, affiliated with the American Federation of Labor. Its offshoot and counterpart in anthracite, founded in 1884, was known as the Miners and Laborers Amalgamated Association.[13]

Perseverance soon produced labor unity. In September 1887, twenty thousand anthracite workers in the Lehigh region struck against independent operators who refused to negotiate with them over their demand for a fifteen percent wage increase. Significantly, the strike was co-sponsored by the Miners and Laborers' Amalgamated Association and the Knights' National Trade Assembly 135.

To end the strike, the operators decided to run the mines with "new" immigrant labor. Strikers who remained off the job could starve. However, when the Slavs and Italians were asked to work, they surprisingly refused. Rather than side with management, a number of immigrants chose to quit the Lehigh region. Undaunted, the operators found nonresident immigrants. On September 11, Calvin Pardee imported Italian strikebreakers, who were contemptuously called "black legs" as well as "scabs."

The use of "scabs" led to violence. At one colliery, Hungarian strikers fought with Hungarian strikebreakers. In addition, two strikebreakers were shot and three coal breakers burned down.

Public opinion, too, was hostile to the use of strikebreakers. In December 1887, it was rumored that Belgians were on their way to the mines. Republican-Greenback congressman Charles N. Brumm, reacting swiftly, asked via a resolution that President Grover Cleveland enforce the Contract Labor Act of 1885. Alerted by the Treasury Department to prevent the entry of Belgian miners, customs officials at Philadelphia detained a dozen of them.

The strike was broken in six months. Unable to halt the flow of strikebreakers, sustain small business support, or gain the backing of local Protestant and Catholic clergymen, the strike fell apart. Striker violence was effectively checked by Coal and Iron Police. In early March 1888, the unions finally surrendered.[14]

In the aftermath of defeat there were doubtless some who laid the blame on the immigrants.[15] Yet, as Victor Greene has demonstrated, they were the scapegoats, not the cause. Their loyalty to the strike clearly exceeded that of the old stock workers, and they could not be held responsible for such factors as inept and divided union leadership, mine operator tenacity, and continuining coal production while they struck. "The Slavs," notes Greene, "were found in the front ranks of the demonstrators, and they sacrificed much for labor unity." Sadly, their own unions did not recognize their valor.[16]

What the mine labor movement did recognize was the need to reorganize if it hoped to survive this defeat. Reorganization of its diverse, disheartened elements involved compromise and concession. Otherwise, the emerging industry pattern of lost strikes, reduced wages, and dismissed dissident employees would continue unabated. In 1888, some members of the Miners' National Trade Assembly joined the American Miners' Federation to create a Miners' National Progressive Union. Here was a merger of the Knights of Labor and the American Federation of Labor affiliates. By 1890, when the remaining Knights of the National Trade Assembly resolved their differences with the new body and signed up, the fusion was completed and the product renamed. It was now known as the United Mine Workers of America, and was headed by John Rae, who had been president of the Progressive Union.[17]

The infant U.M.W. was a weak union. As John Brophy recalled, the merger that formed it "was largely on paper"; Pennsylvania locals remained interested in the Knights of Labor. Then came yet another depression, beginning in the coal industry in 1892, which again reduced wages and employment.[18] The timing of this downturn was terrible, for it occurred during a period of expansion of the coal-producing area made possible by railroad extension. New laborers, largely immigrant, were streaming into the industry, only to find part-time employment at low wages. The number of bituminous workers jumped by 52,000 between 1890 and 1894.[19]

Too much coal was being produced for economically depressed Americans to consume. To boost wages by making coal scarce and thus more expensive, leaders of the mine workers agreed to suspend work. An English tactic, it would remain in effect until the abundant coal supply was exhausted. The strike began April 1, 1894. After eight weeks, the United Mine Workers claimed that 180,000 were idle.

By the end of July the walkout ended in failure. The strike had not injured the operators because they still had plenty of coal on hand. As the public had continued to underconsume coal, and as production in fields where the union was ineffective or nonexistent had remained level or even increased, little, if any, pressure had been put on management. Discredited by this defeat, the union almost disappeared.[20]

Once again there is the question of the immigrants' part in a lost strike. John Brophy, whose father and uncle had participated in the strike, remembered that "a few recent immigrants from central Europe were brought in as strikebreakers," but that most "scabs" "were native Americans from the backcountry, known as 'buckwheaters,' because their little patches would grow buckwheat, but not much else." In addition, the strikers "held together very well" despite attempts by operators to divide them along nationality lines. Antiunion newspapers, using nativism to prejudice the public, denounced the strike as the product of foreign conspirators, that is, British immigrant union leaders.[21]

By resolutely maintaining their strike, the Eastern Europeans refuted their critics. They made it that much more difficult for it to be said that they were in America "for just one purpose—to hoard every dollar they can lay their hands on."[27]

Nonetheless, their detractors persisted in perceiving them as enemies of the coal labor force. Despite occasionally pleasant old stock–new stock social relations,[23] the picture that remained was of intense friction between the two sides. Furthermore, it became clear before long that the old stock was abandoning the industry. The United States Bureau of Labor put it this way: the new workers displaced the old, lowered the living standard, and contributed "a disproportionate amount of crime." In addition, they were accident-prone owing to inability to comprehend English-language instructions and regulations, and were difficult to organize for the purpose of seeking improved conditions.[24] According to Commissioner-General of Immigration Terence V. Powderly, they took the jobs of others and were "draining our country of a vast amount of money" by sending it to Europe.[25] Labor economist John R. Commons agreed that they did contribute to oversupply and underemployment, as did new machinery used for cutting bituminous coal.[26]

The negative consensus on the impact of the newcomers

seemed to point in a single direction. According to a Welsh-born miner and United Mine Workers official, the English-speaking community in the anthracite region agreed on "one point." Though most of them were foreign born, they shared the sentiment "that there should be some restriction on immigration."[27]

Mine operators were not necessarily more anxious than union officials to deal with people with whom it was often difficult to communicate. Concerned with their own competition and production, owners and supervisors resented miners who could not speak English and who understood little of contracts and job procedures. According to Herman Justi, a coal industry spokesman, the immigrants entering the mines had to "be educated" when they arrived. He and other relatively forward-looking operators even admitted that unionism could serve an educational function.[28]

No doubt management did have such problems, but, as Dr. Peter Roberts noted in 1901, the Eastern European immigrants had been introduced into the anthracite fields to serve the operators' purpose of subverting the stubborn Anglo-Saxon employees. Furthermore, though the newcomers left the leadership of miners' organizations in the hands of the old stock, they quickly formed a huge proportion of the work force. A survey of 150 shafts in 1897 revealed that 38 percent of the workers were alien. In some locales the Slavic population pushed past 70 percent before 1900.[29] By 1905, foreign-born Slavs and Hungarians in Pennsylvania comprised 39 percent of both anthracite and bituminous labor, while English immigrants made up only 2.7 and 5.0 percent of each, respectively.[30]

When provoked, the growing numbers of newcomers continued to act with spontaneity and unity. Such was again the case in the Lehigh region, where they struck for six weeks during the fall of 1897. They began their protest at the Lehigh and Wilkes-Barre Company, which wanted mule drivers to provide additional work at no increase in pay. Then, at the Van Wickle Company, they struck over discriminatory pay. Soon the walkout spread to other firms in the Hazleton area, which was brought to a standstill by the beginning of September. Amazingly, Slavs, Hungarians, and Italians were acting on their own without any union leadership.

Then tragedy occurred. On September 10, at Lattimer, sheriff's deputies fired directly into an army of unarmed, marching strikers, killing nineteen and wounding about forty. The fallen were Poles, Slovaks, and Lithuanians.

The immediate effect of the "Lattimer Massacre" was to pull more men out of the mines. By September 15, some 11,000 were on strike. Eventually they won pay increases, but the killings went unpunished. Defenders of the deputies attempted to justify the shootings by noting that all of the slain were foreigners. In 1898, a jury failed to convict the lawmen.[31]

Spontaneous action sometimes wins battles, but rarely wins wars. To achieve durable, long-run victories, the anthracite miners needed organization, which the United Mine Workers offered. In 1894, the bituminous-based union sent three organizers into the anthracite region. Of the trio, John Rinn, Phil Penna, and John Fahy—the latter in particular—moved the miners toward membership. Handsome, masculine, articulate, and experienced in recruiting people of diverse ethnic backgrounds, Fahy succeeded brilliantly. The Slavic communities responded immediately, forming foreign-language locals in such places as Shenandoah, Mount Carmel, Mahanoy City, and Hazleton.[32]

The United Mine Workers union reached the foreign born largely because of its willingness to address them in their own languages. Repeating past procedures, the union published its *Journal* in foreign languages and used immigrant speakers at rallies.[33] In 1898, its annual convention resolved to publish "our proceedings in two or three different languages" because some of the "many different nationalities in our mines . . . can not read English."[34] Later that year, Patrick Dolan, president of District 5, Pittsburgh, was delighted to find an organizer who could "talk four or five dierent languages,"[35] Dolan was also sensitive to complaints that "the foreign language printed in our Journal is not the Slavish [*sic*] language, but the Bohemian, and . . . the Slavish [*sic*] miners do not thoroughly understand it."[36] In sending out meeting notices for union locals, Dolan arranged to have them in "English, Italian, Slavish [*sic*], Hungarian and Polish." In addition, they were posted at mines and appeared in daily newspapers. Unfortunately, many miners did not turn out. "We cannot do anything with those people," he explained, "unless we surprise them in the morning with a body of men and a band."[37]

To reach Slavs, two pages of the *United Mine Workers' Journal* were printed "in one of the Slavonic languages." The "experiment," as President John Mitchell termed it, lasted three years. In 1901, Mitchell explained why it was a failure: "It has not only proven a large financial loss, but has also engendered jealousies and ill feeling in the ranks of the non-English speaking members of our union." The United Mine Workers sold only 850 copies per year to foreign-language subscribers while employing a special editor for them at $1,040 a year. Furthermore, advertisers claimed that the foreign language made the journal less attractive for their purposes. As for the other languages in the union, Mitchell said that every nationality wanted to be represented. Therefore, following his presidential recommendation, in the name of impartiality and fiscal soundness, the journal was again printed only in English.[38]

Ostensibly, the United Mine Workers was among the most tolerant unions of its day. Like other unions, it required an initiation fee from new members, but it refused to exclude members on the basis of race, color, or national origin.[39] Similarly, it insisted that members not "be debarred or hindered from obtaining work on account of race, creed or nationality."[40]

On the other hand, toleration had its limits and often tested the patience of the union leadership. The newcomers were often exasperating. Transplanted peasants who learned the mining craft in America, they were different from their British forerunners.[41] That difference also included unionism. "Imagine a community of back-woodsmen who never heard of a Labor Union before," one local union official wrote to John Mitchell, complaining of "lack of interest in organization." Many miners, he reported, "seem to be entirely devoid of understanding."[42]

The temptation to transmute anti-immigrant attitudes into action even appealed to John Fahy. Following his initial success in organizing the anthracite miners, Fahy discovered that the union was short of funds. With "fewer than ten thousand paid members between 1894 and 1897," the United Mine Workers could not properly maintain its organization in the anthracite area. Finding traditional recruitment methods expensive, Fahy now turned to the less costly tactic of legislative lobbying. Possibly influenced by nativist unionists, he urged the Pennsylvania legislature to pass the Campbell Act, which taxed companies with alien male workers three cents per day for each person. This law, which was later declared unconstitutional by the courts, was a major source of immigrant discontent in 1897.[43]

To the U.M.W. leadership, the Eastern Europeans seemed inferior even when they struck successfully. They appeared erratic and unsophisticated. Beginning on September 17, 1900, 130,000 Pennsylvania anthracite miners went on strike. Their six-week walkout eventually won, among other improvements, a ten percent wage increase.[44] Yet, as the strike developed, President Mitchell expressed reservations about the workers who were winning it. They reminded him "very much of a drove of cattle, ready to stampede when least expected." In union meetings, he noticed, they were "so impressionable" that they were "swayed from one side to the other in accordance with the force or eloquence of the speaker."[45]

Another official, Vice-President T. L. Lewis, could not abide the continuation of long-standing ethnic tensions. The Pittsburgh district miners and mine laborers, seventy percent of whom were non-English-speaking, according to Lewis in January 1901, harbored "a variety of the most intense prejudices." Most of these people, he said supported the union, but many were strongly inclined "to add fuel to the jealousy and discord among the miners, unmindful of the fact that it was suicidal to our craft to keep our forces divided." Lewis concluded that much of the unnecessary bitterness was "created by men who seemed to have no real conception of the objects of the United Mine Workers."[46]

Yet the survival of the union depended on its ability to organize the heterogeneous miners. The unorganized could be black as well as foreign born.[47] Blacks were welcome even though they, too, were imported by management to break strikes.[48] However, to win over the main body of the unorganized, the foreigners, required basic education in unionism.[49] By 1905, toward that end, the United Mine Workers employed "more than sixty-five . . . organizers and field workers," in addition to its national executive board, all members of which doubled as organizers.[50] Union membership, which had been 32,902 in 1898, jumped to 115,521 in 1900, and 267,331 by 1905.[51]

Though the immigrants were enrolled, conflict between Slav

and Anglo-Saxon persisted. The foreign-born membership constituted a physical threat to the American community, including union officials, which was evident in the Lehigh region in the 1900 anthracite strike.

In late September, Slavic women led assaults on nonstrikers. The climax came when a boardinghouse allegedly full of nonstriking Poles was dynamited. In response, the U.M.W. leadership issued a public notice to the effect that this kind of violence by "ignorant foreign strikers" gave "President Mitchell and labor leaders some uneasiness." In brief, the union was opposed to such a display of irresponsibility. Nevertheless, a week later, in the hamlets of Sheppton and Oneida, near Hazleton, Slavic men and women used stones and clubs to attack both nonstrikers and coal company officials. Before peace was restored, five hundred strikers fought twenty Coal and Iron Policemen, which left one person dead and wounded thirteen.[52]

The wage increase won in 1900 was fine, but it was not accompanied by an agreement with the coal industry on a formula for deciding future working conditions, which dissatisfied the leadership of the United Mine Workers. Union officers repeatedly pressed the mine operators to accept a joint conference plan for resolving differences. The effort lasted eighteen months, and failed. Management would neither agree to such a plan or even formally recognize the union. Finally, in May 1902, another strike was called when the operators not only rejected additional union demands, but also insisted that they would have nothing to do with the U.M.W. Some 150,000 workers walked off the job. They would not return until five months had elapsed.[53]

At the helm of the United Mine Workers during this strike was the same extraordinary figure who had directed the victory at Spring Valley. Rising through union ranks in Illinois, he a coal miner's son who had worked in the mines since age twelve.[54] In 1888, he had witnessed, and as a consequence admired, Slavs, Hungarians, and Italians on strike near his home at Spring Valley. Rising through union ranks in Illinois, he became a U.M.W national organizer by 1897. The next year he was first elected the union's national vice-president, and then, upon the resignation of Michael D. Ratchford, he was voted into the presidency.[55]

As president, Mitchell insisted on union recognition backed

by a membership exultant over the 1900 victory. To keep alive the memory of that strike, the miners called October 29, the day it ended, "Mitchell Day."[56]

When the men stopped working in 1902, they were solidly behind their president. "The coal you dig isn't Slavish or Polish or Irish coal—it's just coal," Mitchell had said. Furthermore, he now warned old stock diggers against speaking of newcomers as "Hunks and Dagoes." In the company of their clerical leaders, he told Hungarians and Italians that their democratic union was offering them a better life. The miners, who had great confidence in him, placed his picture next to those of their saints. "Johnny da Mitch will win," they said.[57]

Owing to several factors the union president prevailed. First, there was the obstinate attitude of the mine operators. George F. Baer, chief spokesman and president of the Philadelphia Railroad Company, expressed views so arrogant and insensitive as to offend even antiunion observers. Three days before the stoppage began, Mitchell suggested submitting the dispute to arbitration by a five-person group selected by the National Civic Federation or by "a committee composed of Archbishop Ireland, Bishop Potter, and one other person whom these two may select." "Anthracite mining is a business, and not a religious, sentimental, or academic proposition," Baer immediately replied.[58] On the other hand, in a letter to a railroad stockholder two months later, the president said the following:

I beg of you not to be discouraged. The rights and interest of the laboring men will be protected and cared for—not by the labor agitators, but by the Christian gentlemen to whom God has given control of the property rights of the country and upon the successful management of which so much depends. Do not be discouraged. Pray earnestly that the right may triumph, always remembering that the Lord God Omnipotent still reigns and that His reign is one of law and not of violence and crime.[59]

Another factor was the intervention of President Theodore Roosevelt. Breaking with a tradition of government partiality toward business in labor disputes, Roosevelt summoned both sides to a conference in Washington. What he heard at that meeting in October 1902, disturbed him. Baer, speaking for the operators, castigated not only Mitchell and the mineworkers, but Roosevelt as well. The unionists, he charged, were anarchistic and criminal, and the president was remiss in not having dealt with them as such. Mitchell, in sharp contrast, spoke quietly and reasonably, and established an instant rapport with Roosevelt. Motivated by social and political considerations in addition to his distaste for the operators, Roosevelt moved to compel management to acquiesce to arbitration by threatening federal seizure of the mines.

The final factors contributing to the success were Mitchell and his membership. By maintaining his composure in the face of extreme provocation, he showed a statesmanlike quality that won the president's sympathy. The miners remained united. Though many could have returned to work under the protection of the Pennsylvania militia, which had been called out by the governor to maintain order, they did not. That demonstration of tenacity and unity proved that the walkout was not a compulsory action controlled by the union leadership.

Under the force of Roosevelt's threat, both sides accepted the creation of an arbitration commission. The report of the commission awarded the miners a ten percent wage increase, but did not call for formal union recognition. The recognition the union received was tacit, as labor was granted a place on a conciliation board to settle future disputes.[60]

Thus, John Mitchell triumphed and became a virtual saint to his foreign-born followers. He could not fully understand their reverence for him, which was nonetheless genuine. During the strike, while speaking at a town home mainly to immigrants, foreign-born workers had appeared with weapons ready for use lest the police attempt to injure him. That night the foreigners stationed a guard around his hotel for further protection.

Then, on October 26, 1902, after the strike, the immigrants honored him with a testimonial at the Hotel Hart in Wilkes-Barre. There he was eulogized as "a second Napoleon of labor" by a "committee representing the anthracite coal region, of Polish, Ruthenian, Lithuanian and Slavic descent." Afterward, organizer Paul Pulaski presented him with an expensive gold watch and a gold medallion with "J. M." in diamonds. However, when a speaker told Mitchel that the sum of one hundred

thousand dollars would be raised for him from Lithuanians and
Poles, he asked that it not be done. Such a gift, he explained,
would create a gap between himself and the membership.

The adulation heaped on him reached its peak on October 29,
"Mitchell Day," when they "went wild with enthusiasm." About
ninety percent of them stayed off the job as "some stores and
schools closed ... and most communities held parades."[61]

In sustaining his image as champion of the foreign born,
Mitchell received some valuable assistance. Always ready to
help him in his relations with Pennsylvania political leaders
as well as with the Slavic community was Louis N. Hammerling.
Hammerling, who figured prominently at the Wilkes-Barre testimonial, was an editor of foreign-language newspapers, the
general manager of the Lithuanian-Polish Club of Luzerne
County, and a general agent for the *United Mine Workers'
Journal*. In short, he was a man with many connections. To
Terence V. Powderly, Mitchell introduced Hammerling as "an
active energetic worker in the labor cause" whose Luzerne
County organization had "several thousand members in the
anthracite field."[62]

Hammerling was more to Mitchell and the United Mine
Workers than a medium of communication with the foreign born.
During the 1902 strike, he was an emissary to Republican senator
Boise Penrose of Pennsylvania, who in turn served as an inter-
mediary between the miners and operators. Mitchell passed
worker demands to George Baer indirectly through Hammerling
and Penrose.[63] Active in Republican politics, Hammerling was
also a conduit to President Roosevelt.[64]

In return for his services, this political operator asked Mitchell's
help in getting government jobs for himself. He aspired to such
plums as superintendent of public printing for Pennsylvania,
assistant postmaster-general of the United States, collector of
internal revenue for Scranton, or, as he put it to Mitchell, "Assistant Secretary of any of the other Departments, which is the
same thing." Unfortunately for him, the union president could
not secure any of these positions.[65]

A final, curious aspect of the relationship between Hammerling
and Mitchell likewise concerned favors. Unceasingly anxious to
ingratiate himself with Mitchell, Hammerling offered him several

secret, money-making schemes. Among these opportunities were a $50,000 speaking tour, a ten percent share in houses to be built for anthracite miners, a portion of the stock of a chain of correspondence schools, and stock in the Lubricating Grease company, in which Hammerling was a stockholder.[66] Mitchell declined the latter opportunity, claiming to be short of funds, but he did at least indicate interest in the lecture and construction deals.[67] It is entirely possible that beneath the surface of John Mitchell lay a massive vein of corruption.[68]

To the general public, unaware of his nefarious dealings with Hammerling, Mitchell in the afterglow of 1902 was a statesman of labor who took pride in his achievements. At a conference of the National Civic Federation, he noted that in America "more than elsewhere . . . racial differences and jealousies are played upon in order to crush the unions and defeat strikes." Though "racial jealousies have been fanned by employers to the point of deadly outbreak," he added, his own union had "demonstrated that with proper organization and patient education" those problems could be lessened and the "non-unionist" worker "at least to a certain extent, eliminated."[69]

While Mitchell on one hand described how problems could be solved, on the other he suggested a way to avert them altogether. In a book, *Organized Labor,* he called for "not prohibition, but regulation" of immigration. Following what by now had become the direction of the American Federation of Labor, he explained his purpose. "The trade union," Mitchell wrote, wanted regulated immigration "partly in order to prevent the temporary glutting of the market, but to a much greater extent to raise the character of the men who enter." Therefore, regulation would aid both the worker and society, but, he cautioned, "it should not be directed by racial animosity or religious prejudice."[70]

In 1906, Mitchell again urged regulation while trying to sound unbiased. In January, in a report to the United Mine Workers, he extolled the union as "liberal and tolerant in its administration," and said it offered "equal protection" to miners of different backgrounds.[71] Yet before the Civic Federation, in September, he sounded another note. Now he spoke of the unfairness of recent immigrants' taking the jobs of American workmen, and urged "educational qualifications" for admission to the country. He advocated such restriction despite his own warning to avoid "even the suspicion of seeking to keep immigrants from landing here because of national or religious prejudices."[72]

Under criticism from within the United Mine Workers for the loss of strikes in Alabama, Tennessee, and Pennsylvania, and in ill health, Mitchell retired in 1908.[73] However, even in retirement he urged immigration regulation without prejudice. He kept to that theme despite his contention, which he stated more forcefully than before, that there were too many of the foreign born in the country.[74]

What Mitchell refused to concede was that the immigrants were the foot soldiers of the U.M.W. They were in the front lines of the union's organizing campaigns, strikes, and occasional defeats—and they would continue in that role, especially in 1914.

During his presidency Mitchell failed to organize Wyoming and southern Colorado. The militant organizer Mary "Mother" Jones reported to the United Mine Workers in 1905 that Rock Springs, Wyoming, was an impossible place. The Union Pacific Railroad owned virtually all the property there, and the population of six thousand included "representatives of forty-three nationalities." As for the Trinidad district of Colorado, it was controlled by Rockefeller interests. A strike there in 1903–1904 failed, according to Mitchell's critics, because of "an unholy deal" between him and management.[75]

In 1913–1914, the United Mine Workers again tried to organize that section of Colorado. This time it encountered tragedy as well as defeat. In a strike against John D. Rockefeller, Jr.'s Colorado Fuel and Iron Company, a union of English, Eastern European, and Mexican workers demanded recognition and a pay increase. Instead, they became the victims of violence, first at the hands of hired guards, and then from a detachment of the state militia. In April 1914, troops attacked the tent village of the strikers. They captured it and burned it to the ground. A day later, two women and eleven children were found smothered to death in a cave in which they had sought escape.

This "Ludlow Massacre" converted the miners into avengers. For the next week they destroyed mine properties and attacked guards and militia. Southern Colorado was at war, which was ended only by federal troops sent by President Woodrow Wilson.[76]

As in the past—1887, 1897, 1900, and 1902—the immigrant miners had stood firm. They had once more demonstrated devotion to the union cause. The United Mine Workers' achievement in organizing them was indeed considerable.

CHAPTER 6

The Garment Workers:
Organizational Beginnings

NOWHERE did immigrants more dramatically demonstrate
their commitment to trade unionism than in the garment industry. As was the case in the coal and steel industries, Eastern
Europeans in the needle trades took the places of native- or foreign-born Americans of Western European ancestry. However,
unlike the immigrant workers in the mines and mills, the immigrants at the sewing machines founded and directed their own
unions and often rose to the level of employers.

Led mainly by Russian Jewish socialists, these unions fought
for survival on two fronts. Their primary contest, of course, was
with management, over such matters as working conditions and
union recognition. In that fight a combination of union militancy
and tragedy eventually brought acceptance at the bargaining
table.

There was also the struggle against the initially conservative
leadership of the American labor movement. Committed both to
capitalism and immigration restriction by 1897, the American
Federation of Labor and its nativist member unions looked with
suspicion upon the recently arrived immigrants. To the Amalgamated Clothing Workers of America, which was founded in 1914
by dissenters from an A.F. of L. union, the United Garment Workers of America, Samuel Gompers, and his associates stood in
outright opposition.

The garment industry developed in the nineteenth century as
a mainly urban phenomenon. Cities such as New York, Chicago,
Rochester, Philadelphia, and Baltimore all became significant
clothing centers. New York, the port of entry for most immigrants,
where a great many of them settled, emerged as the foremost

center, especially for women's clothing. Yet everywhere, as immigrants came and worked for wages below those accepted by older workers, displacement and group tension ensued.[1]

The men's clothing industry of New York City had been in existence more than a half century before the arrival of the Eastern European Jews. Begun during the 1820s, the industry grew steadily throughout the next decade, and by 1840 was of some significance to the city's economy.[2]

Its rapid growth resulted primarily from the low price of its products. Ready-made coats and suits cost only half as much as custom-made garments. Such price competition was possible because labor, too, was paid well below the usual rate. During the slow season, journeymen tailors worked in shops and their own homes on the inexpensive goods. These workers were largely English, Scotch, and American.

Then came the Irish and Germans. Victims of famine, the former arrived in great numbers in the 1840s. By 1850, the Irish were joined by the Germans, who brought from Europe a tradition of home industries. The latter began the practice of taking clothes home and having family members put the garments together.[3] As they were less expensive than shop workers, the German home workers forced Irish and American factory girls out of their jobs.[4]

Aided by the introduction of Elias Howe's sewing machine about 1850, the clothing industry expanded rapidly. By 1860, it included 4,014 manufacturing shops and it employed 114,800 workers.[5] Also by this time, Germans had become the city's dominant ethnic group in tailoring. Fifty-five percent of all the tailors living in New York City were German born, while thirty-four percent had come from Ireland.[6]

Though many of the German tailors were Jewish, and Jewish immigrants increasingly entered the garment trades before 1860,[7] Jews did not as yet play a conspicuous role in the industry. They tended to be concentrated in the relatively unattractive secondhand clothing trade along Chatham Street rather than in the Bowery or on lower Broadway, where the major clothiers conducted their businesses. The secondhand neighborhood, known also as "Jerusalem," was regarded with "contempt and ridicule" by outsiders.[8]

At mid-century most of the workers in the ready-made men's clothing industry were women, who traditionally received even lower wages than men. However, in the custom trade, skilled men were preferred. In the next few decades, a combination of progress in technology and growth of immigration displaced both the women and skilled men. The introduction of the sewing machine and cutting machine pushed aside both groups.

As unskilled immigrants could quickly learn to operate sewing machines, highly skilled custom workers lost their primary market advantage. Moreover, because men could more readily use the foot-power sewing machine, women lost additional advantage. Though women predominated in the industry as late as 1850, they were in the minority ten years later. By the 1870s, Jews from Germany, Austria, and Hungary entered the industry. They immediately accepted both the sewing machine and an even newer invention, the heavy cutting knife. Requiring greater strength than conventional shears, the cutting knife was unmanageable for some women, who thus left their craft. The Jewish men took their jobs at below standard wages.[9]

The newcomers to America, who turned to the ready-made clothing industry, actually worked in three distinct types of factories. First, there was the "inside" shop, which a manufacturer ran with his own labor. Second, workers took goods with them to the "home-shop," where wives and children assisted. Finally, the "outside" shop was operated by a contractor who received work from a manufacturer and then assigned it to home workers or workers on his own premises.[10] With many American girls working in the factories, contractors often found it easier to give out the work to immigrants at home than to antagonize the natives by taking in the newcomers.[11]

Though the German immigrants introduced the "home-shop," they did not monopolize it. The ranks of the homeworkers also included Americans, Irish, and Jews, living and laboring in unsanitary surroundings unregulated by the city. Observing the tenement houses on Mulberry, Mott, and Baxter Streets, one tailor noted: "From 1875 to 1880 these were inhabited largely by Jews engaged in making clothing. Each family employed from one to two hands, all living and working in the same rooms. There was no water in the building, and toilets were situated in the back yard."[12]

Able to operate with the cheapest labor and lowest overhead, the contractor quickly became a dominant figure in the industry. With shrewdness, intelligence, and as little as fifty dollars to purchase material to be converted into finished products, any individual could set himself up as a contractor. The working conditions in which his unorganized, largely immigrant employees labored, as well as the filthy conditions, long hours, and low wages, constituted what was known as the "sweatshop."[13] As historian Abraham Menes notes, the sweatshop system did not begin with the heavy Jewish immigration of the 1880s, but the Jewish workers offered little resistance to it. *"The workers themselves wished to work longer hours and thus to earn a little more, so as to hasten the day when they could bring their families to America."*[14] Furthermore, as immigrant editor Abraham Cahan recalled, "the average Jewish immigrant felt that in comparison with what he had suffered in the old country, America was paradise. The worker ate better and was better clothed than in the old country."[15]

Immigrant competition for sweatshop jobs was often a disguised blessing. The abler Irish and Germans who lost their positions found themselves upwardly displaced. The Irish moved higher in the industry while the Germans tended to go into other lines of work. The latter remained in Manhattan's clothing industry until 1892, but afterward shifted to Brooklyn, where there was presumably less competition. Rather than compete by accepting very low wages, German and American girls found employment elsewhere, such as in offices and department stores.[16]

For the Jewish immigrants of the eighties and nineties to have flooded the garment industry was a perfectly natural development. In historian Joel Seidman's words, these people were "the tailors of eastern Europe" who came to America, found other Jews already working in the needle trades, and then made their own entry.[17]

They came from a social background different from that of other "new" immigrants. Unlike the others from Eastern Europe, the Jews were largely townspeople rather than peasants.[18] Those who came from Russia in the immediate aftermath of the assassination of Czar Alexander II to 1881 were also mainly *luftmenschen*, or people without trades or occupations. Only later, beginning around 1900, would skilled artisans, artisan-merchants, professional, and intellectuals become the most characteristic Jewish migrants.[19]

Once in America, regardless of prior occupation, the Eastern European Jews underwent reclassification and social demotion to proletarian status. They became low living standard wage earners in various productive trades. The small sweatshop accurately reflected their new, reduced status.[70]

This transformation of the Jews was similar to what had already happened to many of them in Europe. In Russia, following the emancipation of the serfs in 1861, Jews were displaced by Gentiles in peasant- and estate-related occupations, and were thus compelled to move to large cities, where they found employment in urban trades. Those who left their homelands for such countries as England and France likewise found jobs in metropolitan areas.[21] In England, the Jewish workers also pioneered in garment industry unionism.[22]

Also unlike some "new" immigrants, such as the Slavs and Italians, almost all the Jews came to America intending to make it their home. Instead of aspiring to short-run economic gain, they emigrated to avoid persecution, and, without a homeland to welcome them back, more than ninety-five percent remained in America. Moreover, they came with a much higher percentage of women and children than other Eastern Europeans, which made finding a stable job and earning a livelihood matters of the utmost urgency. To support the family required hard work and long hours.[23]

Owing to linguistic and religious factors, the Jews sometimes had difficulty finding jobs in America. Unlike the Jewish immigrants from Germany, whose ability to speak German actually opened many commercial opportunities to them, these people spoke Yiddish. Industry, which fortunately for them was expanding rapidly, was the only sector of the economy to absorb them. It did so with reluctance. Suspecting, with obvious justification, that they were low-wage competition, many organized and skilled workers kept them out of their trades.

On the other hand, the Jews often remained apart from work places where non-Jews predominated. They preferred places where they could observe their sabbath and *kashruth*, or dietary laws.[24] In search of their own kind, the Jews thus gravitated toward and developed certain "Jewish trades" where almost all employers as well as workers were Jewish.[25]

This search for a congenial environment and for a trade where they would be comfortable among their own kind led inevitably to a Jewish concentration in the garment industry. The post-1880 Jewish immigrants found many Jews—employers and employees— already in it, and plenty of opportunities because it was still in its early stages of development. There were opportunities for both wage earners and the self-employed. Thus they moved to it increasingly in the eighties. As early as 1890, a census taken in the three most densely settled Jewish districts of New York's East Side revealed that approximately sixty percent of the gainfully employed were in the needle trades.[26] Eventually the garment trades provided employment for two thirds of all Jewish wage workers.[27]

By the beginning of the twentieth century it was clear that the Jews were in control of the garment industry, which their labor had developed over the previous two decades. Somewhat resentfully, the popular journalist Burton J. Hendrick described some of the social consequences of their dominance. Hendrick said that Fifth Avenue, between Fourteenth and Twenty-third Streets, had ceased being fashionable. Jewish merchants and manufacturers had torn down the brownstone houses formerly occupied by the old aristocracy and replaced them with marble and granite loft buildings from sixteen to twenty stories high. Furthermore, at noon time the once elegant promenade now featured "one impassable mass of Jewish workers."[28]

As a people recently removed from oppression, the Eastern European Jews had extremely negative attitudes toward church and state. In Europe, the church had supported political despotism which had denied rights to all, but especially to the Jews. Even the synagogue, at the center of the Jewish community, often had legal advantages over the common people. Swiftly transported from European ghetto to American industry, the immigrant brought with him a distrust of both secular and religious authority. In America his antiauthoritarianism made it relatively easy for Jewish labor leaders to persuade his comrades to recognize the benefits and virtues of socialism.[29]

Other factors, too, furthered the development of unionism among the Jews. The fact of proletarianization was in itself significant. Compelled to enter industry and new trades after their arrival in the United States, the immigrants felt a sense of grievance. Called "Columbus tailors" in the garment industry,[30] these new wage earners were responsive to leaders who stressed labor's dignity and the working class's significance in society.[31]

After 1900, a "second wave" of Eastern European Jewish immigration brought people with a tradition of working class values. They were more skilled than the *luftmenschen* of the "first wave" who had preceded them. Since 1897 a Jewish labor movement, the *Bund*, had sprung up in Russia which offered some hope for relief from czarist oppression. Following government sanctioned pogroms at Kishinev in 1903 and elsewhere in 1905, Bundists fled the country. In fact, "immigration to America became almost a mass flight." In America, the radical Jews made war on the sweatshop to attract other immigrants to their own brand of socialist unionism. Under their leadership, as historian Melvyn Dubofsky observes, "what politics accomplished for the Irish, trade-unionism promised New York's Jews."[32]

As the Eastern European Jews moved into the needle trades in the eighties, they were joined by newly arrived Italian immigrants. Only a few of the latter came during that decade, but a huge influx followed after 1890. By 1900, the Italians made up fifteen percent of New York City's garment industry work force.[33]

The Italians entered the needle trades for different reasons than the Jews. To Italian men, many of whose wives and daughters became garment workers, such an occupation was consistent with women's ways of earning a living. It was normal for women to work at sewing machines to make clothes for their children and themselves. The girl who chose dressmaking to earn money was also learning how to sew clothes for herself.[34]

Actually, "four groups" of Italians turned to the garment industries, two each of men and women. The men included those with and those without previous garment industry experience abroad. In America, the experienced tailors found work in urban custom tailoring shops, and were the first Italians to organize into unions, which some of them came to lead. Those without European experience were usually young when they entered the industry, and often became pressers and operators on coats and suits. From their ranks eventually came the most noted Italian-American leaders in the garment trade.

The Italian workers included married women who were experienced in finishing goods at home, and single girls and younger marrieds who normally worked away from home. The older marrieds were forced to work because of economic circumstances, and were generally illiterate and very poorly poid. Their day work usually ran from 8:00 A.M to 6:00 P.M., with interruptions. They received four to five cents per hour. "The Italian woman," historian Mabel Willett observed in 1902, "holds her own against all other finishers ... because she does the same amount of work for lower wages." Therefore, it is not surprising that by 1900 these women made up "practically all the home finishers in New York." In the meantime, the poorly educated younger women, who had learned some sewing in Italy, worker at factory jobs that did not require much training.[35]

One reason why women worked at home was because most Italians, not unlike many Americans, believed that women should not work outside the shelter of their homes. In 1905, a study of Italian families indicated that fewer than five percent had working wives. Among Jews the aversion to factory work was even greater. Conditioned by their upbringing in their Old World *shtetl*, or small town, and by fears that immorality often resulted from working alongside men in the factory, Jewish women usually stopped working when they married. They did homework in the early years of the clothing industry in America, but after 1900 it often became unacceptable to their husbands even if they had been shop girls when single. Factory jobs that opened were often turned down by married Jewish women.[36]

As a later wave of immigrants than the Russian Jews, the Italians quickly became attractive to employers. The number of

Italian shops proliferated in the 1890s, numbering in the "hundreds" in contrast to scarcely any in 1889. As pressers and operators in the mid-nineties in shops with minutely subdivided labor, they were both inexpensive and unorganized. In contrast, Jewish labor was more expensive, and Jews were moving into better paying industrial areas. So swiftly did the Italians advance in the garment industry that by 1905 there was a reasonable expectation that if the trend continued the Italians would "become the dominant race." Indeed, by 1910 Italians constituted fifteen percent of New York's cloak makers, and, by 1913, more than a third of the city's women dress and waist workers. By 1930, owing to immigration restriction and the unwillingness of Jewish children to follow their parents into the needle trades, the Italians became "the most numerous single ethnic group among the industry's workers."[37]

Such competition inevitably created friction between Italian and Jewish workers. Unfortunately, cultural and ideological differences made that friction difficult to eliminate. As a group, the Italians were more status conscious and tied to family and custom. Consequently, they were much involved with local or provincial societies. On the other hand, the Jews were more cosmopolitan in their outlook, and had a wider range or interests which made it easier to drop some of their customs. As they had a greater appreciation for education, than the Italians, they more readily developed a leadership group both within the working class and outside of it.[38]

To the Italians security meant close ties with family rather than church, trade union, or political organization. Bound to "intense family ties and village loyalties," they found it difficult to develop solid community organizations and move socially and economically upward. Lamenting the little that Italian organizations did for the Italian people. Father Bassi of St. Lucy's Church remarked, "We should all unite as the Jewish people do." However, as the great majority of the Italian male immigrants came to America without their families, their basic concern was themselves. They wanted to save enough money to bring their relatives to America or to help them in Italy. Accordingly, they endured low pay, long work days, and cheap living accommodations, and spent very little on food, clothing, and recreation.[39]

Few Italian immigrants arrived in America convinced socialists. Most had lived in southern Italy rather than in the northern industrial sections where socialism was strong among literate mine and factory workers. As many of the immigrants were illiterate and considered their residence in America as temporary, social revolution was not of primary concern to some of them. Neither was unionism.[40]

Even in New York City, which had a very strong sense of unionism by 1913, Italian immigrants seemed indifferent to unions. A study of forty-eight Lower Westside Italian families revealed that "only five" among them included unionists, who "were inclined to be rather inactive." Social worker Louise Odencrantz explained this phenomenon by saying that the Italian was "an individualist at bottom" who was unconcerned about his fellow workers as long as he did well.[41]

Italian women wage earners seemed particularly difficult to organize. Of 1,095 studied by Odencrantz, 1,027 were factory workers, and only 110 belonged to a union. "Seventeen per cent, or 43 of the 259 shops in which they worked, were organized."[42]

Though organizing these women was not easy, it did have its rewards. As Odencrantz noted, during the strike in the men's clothing industry in 1910 "women who could not speak a word of English stuck loyally to the strike to the end, even at great personal sacrifice." On another occasion, an Italian woman already on strike for six weeks said, "I will not betray my patria," when her employer "offered her lodging with Italian board and $2.00 a day if she would return."[43]

Immigrants played a bigger part in the needle trades than in any other industry in America. In 1880, foreigners comprised sixty-one percent of tailors, not including operators.[44] In 1890, the foreign-born percentage of the custom trade was seventy-one, a figure which was probably matched, or exceeded by the ready-made trade.[45] In addition to producing garments, these immigrants created a labor movement, but one divided by ethnic and ideological differences.

The first organizations of garment workers were formed long before the Civil War. In the men's clothing industry, they were present by 1824 and significant, at least in New York City, by

1850, when a major strike occurred. Led by the Journeymen Tailors Society, a custom tailors' union, tailors struck for the first time. Also in 1850, they were called upon in a general strike by the Industrial Congress, which included all unions in the city. Tailors, who were divided into German and English groups, were the most numerous strikers. The Germans were especially active. Thirty-nine of them were arrested and fined for preventing a contractor from continuing the work at his home with "scab" labor.[46]

Though this strike activity coincided with the origins of the sweatshop system,[47] the tailors did not remain organized. During the depressed 1870s, the organized cutters fought for an eight- or nine-hour day. With assistance from the Knights of Labor, they achieved a nine-hour day.[48]

Between 1876 and 1882, as the Russian Jews entered the garment industry, working conditions worsened considerably with the introduction of the "task system." Regarded with contempt as "Columbus tailors," the newcomers were excluded from tailors' organizations and relegated to working at low-quality clothing in sweatshops where they performed "tasks" for contractors. The system involved a team or "set" of workers, each with a distinct function, who did a specified daily amount of work and was paid by the week. In the absence of a union, contractors regularly added to the day's task, or workload, which had to be completed before the next day's work could be begun. What began as a nine-coat day was extended to ten, twelve, fourteen, eighteen, and then twenty, which required fifteen to eighteen hour days. Work begun one day might not be completed until noon the next. Thus, at the end of the six-day week, a man could be paid for three and a half to four days' work.[49]

As poor as conditions were, the eighties brought a plentiful supply of Jewish immigrants willing to accept them. 193,000 came during that decade, to be followed by 393,000 in the next and 976,000 in the third to 1910. Of the new arrivals in the latter decade, 396,000, or thirty-seven percent, were tailors, and 39,000, or four percent, were dressmakers or seamstresses. In addition, the tide brought cap and hat makers, furriers and milliners. Altogether, the skilled needle workers who entered the United States at that time comprised about half of all Jewish immigrants.[50]

The newcomers fueled a vast expansion of both the men's and women's garment industries. Between 1880 and 1890 the number of men's clothing establishments increased by 226.2 percent; in women's clothing it rose by 117.8 percent. The work force in the men's and women's trades jumped by 85.8 and 66.8 percent, respectively.[51]

Increasingly the labor these immigrants provided became organized. Almost from the moment of their arrival in America in the eighties to the turn of the century they constructed an extraordinary framework of unions. Within the following two decades there was growth and internal conflict, which eventually brought essential recognition by management and a sense of permanence.

Before 1888, the Jewish needle workers did attempt unionism, but little came of their efforts. In July 1883, striking immigrant men and women formed a Dress and Cloak Makers' Union, which affiliated itself with the Knights of Labor as a local assembly. The strike was a success, but not the union. The workers neglected their organization, which then disappeared. As it did, wages dropped to prestrike levels.[52] One of the founders of that union, editor Abraham Cahan, later assessed it as "a great deal of soul without a body," which could not survive is successes.[53] By 1901 it was very clear that the tendency to organize a union to win a strike and then neglect that union after victory was achieved, was characteristic of Jewish workers.[54]

Similarly, tailors and shirtmakers in the eighties first organized and then disintegrated. In 1884, Hungarians and Galicians (Austrians) founded a Tailors' Union, which consisted primarily of piece workers, but also included task or "goal" workers. The semiskilled latter were not very interested in unionism. Consequently, manufacturers lengthened their work day. Unable to prevent this exploitation, the union lost support and became impotent.[55] The Shirt Makers' Union that was formed at this time included contractors who "worked as hard as their employees" and workers who "were constantly becoming contractors." By the end of 1886, almost all shirtmaking shops in

New York were organized, but afterward, following the usual pattern, the union fell apart.[56]

In the capmaking industry, the situation was slightly different. In that line manufacturers manipulated four groups—native Americans, Irish, Germans, and Russian Jews—to destroy unionism. In 1886, a union was nonetheless organized, but it disintegrated within a year following an unsuccessful strike.[57]

German and Hungarian Jews, who wanted to keep themselves apart from the newer immigrants, dominated the work force of the cap industry. Besides cultural, denominational, linguistic, and economic differences between the two groups, there was an ideological division. The German Jews were traditional, practical unionists, while the others had a tendency toward revolutionary idealism. In 1888, when German Jewish cap operators founded the Cloth and Cap Operators' Union no. 1, they kept aloof from the United Hebrew Trades, also organized in that year, but by Eastern European Jews.

Shunned by the German Jews, the newer immigrant cap-makers created their own club with a socialist orientation. Shortly thereafter, though, the two organizations merged under the auspices of the United Hebrew Trades formed in 1888. In 1889, following some strikes, one of which was lost, the Cap Operators' Union became conciliatory and agreed to join the U.H.T. That move led directly to the creation of a healthy Cap-makers' Union.

The problems in capmaking were like those throughout industry in the eighties where German and Eastern European Jews faced each other. One worker noted that "A Russian was heartily disliked, while a Russian Jew was violently hated. We suffered far more from the workers themselves than from the foremen."[58]

The feelings of the German Jewish workers were evidently not shared by German socialists. While the Jewish unions were struggling to stay alive, German unions operated with stability under the auspices of a federated United German Trades. In October 1888, representatives of the U.G.T., the Socialist Labor party, which Lasallean socialists had begun in 1877, and three Jewish unions founded the United Hebrew Trades on the model of the German organization. The founders accepted a "Declaration of Principles" drafted by two of the group, Morris Hillquit, a socialist shirtmaker, and Bernard Weinstein, an immigrant from Odessa who had once worked in the same cigarmaking factory as Samuel Gompers. Their document stressed the Marxist view of history and the class struggle, and also called for reform of industrial working conditions.[59] "The United Hebrew Trades," Hillquit observed forty years later, marked "the starting point of systematic and uninterrupted organization among the Jewish workers in New York. It was the nursery of the whole Jewish labor movement of America."[60]

The establishment of the United Hebrew Trades was brought about also with the "direct assistance of Samuel Gompers." The president of the American Federation of Labor did not think workers should be organized according to religion, but he did understand that "to organize Hebrew trade unions was the first step in getting those immigrants into the American labor movement." In the case of the Jewish trades, more than religion tied them together; there were linguistic, cultural, communal, and structural factors. In 1892, faced with the question of whether the United Hebrew Trades should consist of "Jewish" or "mixed" unions, the Jewish socialist leadership chose to let member unions decide for themselves. Unfortunately, the hostility Jewish workers faced when they tried to join older unions made that decision an easy one. They formed Jewish unions, and on that basis Jewish workers became part of the American labor movement.[61]

Before the United Hebrew Trades could become a force within organized labor, the matter of Daniel DeLeon had to be resolved. DeLeon, a brilliant socialist theoretician, was an important member of both the Socialist Labor party and the Knights of Labor. In 1893 and 1894 he succeeded in inducing some socialist garment workers to join the Knights' District Assembly 49, which thereby came under his political and ideological control.[62]

The Curaçao-born DeLeon believed that socialist-thinking Russian Jews were his natural allies in building a labor movement under his leadership. Consequently, he moved ahead and won the backing of the U.H.T. for a new organization, the Socialist Trade and Labor Alliance, which he founded in 1895.[63]

This venture, which emphasized worker uplift specifically through political rather than economic action, badly split Jewish labor in New York. In April 1897, Abraham Cahan and fifty-four other anti-DeLeon socialists founded a newspaper, the *Jewish Daily Forward,* to oppose the transformed United Hebrew Trades. In addition, the Cahan group helped organize a Federated Hebrew Trades as an opposition body.

Cahan's actions proved effective. They drew many unionists away from DeLeon and his supporters.[64] In 1901, Cahan led most Jewish socialists out of the Socialist Labor party and into a new Socialist party of America. The United Hebrew Trades, which had withdrawn from the American Federation of Labor under DeLeon's direction, returned. Finally, the Socialist Trade and Labor Alliance lasted until 1905, when DeLeon merged it with the Industrial Workers of the World at that organization's birth.[65] With calm restored, an era of amity emerged among four elements, the Jewish garment unions, the U.H.T., the Socialist party, and the *Forward,* which then became the unofficial voice of Jewish labor.[66]

The clash between the DeLeonites and moderate socialists, though eventually decided in favor of the latter, did not obscure the reality that the Russian and Polish Jewish immigrant workers were radical compared to their American counterparts. Their radicalism, in addition to the many differences between themselves and the American born, made for inevitable friction. Rather than regard a union as a means to bargain collectively, the immigrants saw it as an heroic institution to throw off oppression. They looked upon their struggle as not unlike the fight against the czar.[67]

Thus, in April 1891, when the United Garment Workers of America was born, the potential for discord was already present.[68] The founders of this organization of men's clothing workers were cutters, most of whom were native born and of German or Irish descent, and Jewish immigrant shop tailors. The cutters were also skilled craftsmen, more so than the others who were largely basters, operators, and pressers. In deference to the cutters' greater familiarity with the American language and customs, the thirty-six founding delegates of the United Garment Workers elected their leaders to guide the new organization. But the radical tailors had to be mollified with the result that the founders adopted socialist resolutions. Led by the conservative cutters, the membership of under 3,000 immediately joined the American Federation of Labor.[69]

Though the United Garment Workers was also affiliated with the United Hebrew Trades, that connection was soon severed. Unsympathetic to the socialist U.H.T. (United Hebrew Trades), the Garment Workers' national leaders had little concern for the tailors in New York; they preferred to organize ready-made tailors in other parts of the country, which left the city's coat tailors with "an organization on paper only." The coat tailors soon withdrew their delegates from the U.H.T., but the pants, vest, and children's jacket makers' unions remained affiliated.

In the summer of 1893, the United Garment Workers insisted that it would not recognize the three unions still within the Hebrew Trades unless they withdrew from that body. The three unions refused, whereupon the Garment Workers decided to form rival unions. Furthermore, they claimed that the Hebrew Trades disliked national unions and was acting to separate Jewish from American workers. Thereupon, they condemned the U.H.T. as antagonistic to organized labor.

In response, the United Hebrew Trades rejected the indictment, contending that it had always urged workers to join the United Garment Workers and that there were no grounds for conflict between the two labor organizations. Then, at a mass meeting of Jewish trade unions that was called by the U.H.T. to rally support, the U.H.T. secured the passage of a resolution striking back at the Garment Workers. Preambles to that resolution denied that the U.H.T. caused "the present unclean struggle in the Jewish labor movement," or aimed "to separate Jews from other nationalities." On the contrary, they claimed, "the United Hebrew Trades have always been united with all bona fide labor organizations of all nationalities" and "have never kept out any workingman because of his political beliefs, as long as he was prepared to be a faithful union man." The resolution dismissed the Garment Workers' charges as "nothing less than criminal libels committed by intriguers." The U.H.T. would not permit itself "to be split by criminal intriguers ... who serve the interests of capital."[70]

Undeterred by the feud with the United Hebrew Trades, the United Garment Workers gained strength through the nineties, largely as a consequence of militant action. In 1893, New York cutters overcame a lockout and succeeded in having manufacturers hire cutters and tailors who belonged to the Garment Workers rather than the Knights of Labor. A year later, 16,000 coatmakers struck successfully in New York, Brooklyn, and Newark to wipe out the task system of daily team workload assignments.

In 1896 defeat replaced victory. The United Garment Workers lost strikes and turned away from the strike as the favored means of achieving objectives. Instead they chose to promote the union label and cooperate with management. By organizing those employed in making work clothes, the United Garment Workers could control the sale of overalls and work shirts; union men would buy only clothes with the union label. Some employers, appreciating this potential market, even initiated steps to have their plants organized. Yet as the Garment Workers moved increasingly in the direction of favoring native workers and nonmilitancy, its radical and immigrant members became irrevocably estranged.[71]

The Garment Workers may have neglected immigrants, but not women, who amounted to 8,000 of a total of 25,000 members by 1902. In General, the U.G.W. policy was to organize women in separate unions apart from men; however, "mixed" unions frequently arose in factories where men as well as women were employed.[72]

Where women predominated there were few foreigners. In 1901, the eight oldest Garment Workers unions with women were made up almost entirely of native-born girls, "frequently of Irish or German parentage, but in perhaps the majority of cases" of American parentage. There was "a slight sprinkling of Jewish and Polish women, constituting probably not more than one percent of the total number."[73]

New to the country, burdened with dreadful working conditions, and divided along ethnic and ideological lines, the garment workers of the late nineteenth century made significant but limited progress toward establishing viable labor organizations. As the twentieth century began, the United Hebrew Trades was just recovering from the tumultuous takeover by the DeLeonites. However, an infusion of support from well-organized women's garment workers was already visible. The United Garment Workers, having deflected United Hebrew Trades challenges and passed through its militant phase, for the moment seemed secure in its organization of the men's clothing workers. That security, though, was contingent upon the allegiance of Jewish socialist immigrants to conservative American leaders. Within fifteen years the socialists would have their own organization, and would inject dynamism into each major branch of the needle trades.

CHAPTER 7

The Garment Workers: The Making of Responsible Immigrant Unions

IF immigrant workers ever demonstrated loyalty to unionism, they did so in New York City in the years between 1900 and 1920. In a reversal of earlier habits, they not only formed but did everything in their power to maintain their labor organizations. Different in membership and ideology from most unions, those in the garment industry clung to views that organized labor often did not favor. This unorthodoxy was not very welome within the American Federation of Labor, but there was no denying the commitment of the immigrant wage earners to the promotion of working-class ideals.

The rise of the women's clothing industry coincided with the onset of the heavy Jewish immigration from Eastern Europe. Centered in the immigrants' main port of entry, New York, the expansion of the industry, which rose from 11,696 employees in 1870 to 25,192 by 1880, 39,149 by 1890, and 83,739 by 1900, was coterminous with the rise in immigration. In 1880, the capital invested in the industry totaled $8.2 million, which rose to $21.2 million by 1890 and $48.4 million by 1900. The value of the goods produced in 1900 exceeded $159 million, which represented an increase of almost 134 percent above the figure for 1890.[1]

Despite the growth of the industry, through the eighties and nineties its workers were not effectively organized. Though the American Federation of Labor was then rising to prominence on the national level, and the United Garment Workers seemed to be successfully organizing the men's clothing workers, a union for women's garment workers was still in its building stage. Not even the assistance of the Knights of Labor could bring and keep garment workers together in the eighties. The sweatshop thrived as unions came and went, often under the Knights' auspices. Though the Knights' leadership was opposed to strikes, they were unavoidable in many industries. Annually, from 1885 to 1889, cloakmakers in New York and other cities went on strike, but unions formed to direct the walkouts usually died shortly thereafter. As the decade ended, only two garment labor organizations, founded in 1883 and 1884, survived. They were unions of New York City cutters, most of whom were German and Irish.[2]

The lack of a comprehensive organization continued into the nineties, but by then the need for such a central body became even more urgent. As described previously, not only Italians but, in several large cities, Russians, Poles, Bohemians, and Syrians also entered the industry. Furthermore, women were moving in faster than men, especially in the shirtwaist and underwear trades.

Beginning in 1890, the cloakmakers led a movement for an international garment workers' union. The International Cloakmakers' Union of America, founded in 1892, lasted only two years, but was succeeded in 1896 by the United Brotherhood of Cloak Makers' Union no. 1 of New York and vicinity.

Within the next two years the nation's economy revived as did unionism. Acting on a suggestion from the United Cloakmakers' Union of Philadelphia, the United Brotherhood sought to organize a cloakmakers' convention for New York to be held in January 1898. Philadelphia vied with New York to become the convention site, but other doctrinal and political differences could not be resolved, and that meeting did not materialize. In March 1900, the New Yorkers tried again, this time inviting all American and Canadian women's garment workers to a convention in their city in June. At last, on June 3, 1900, delegates representing about two thousand members of seven unions in four cities met and founded the International Ladies' Garment Workers' Union. They elected Herman Grossman president. Herman Robinson, an American Federation of Labor organizer, was on hand to represent his organization, which twenty days later issued a charter to the new union. On July 2, at Philadelphia, the I.L.G.W.U. General Executive Board held its first session, at which time Robinson presented the charter and installed the elected officers.[3]

As historian Joseph Brandes writes, the International Ladies' Garment Workers' Union was founded with meager tangible assets including the charter, "capital of $30, and a desk in the modest office of the New York cloakmakers."[4] By 1903, its membership was close to ten thousand, "about a third of whom were women," but a business decline beginning at the end of that year abruptly halted its upward movement. Only after enduring a "critical period" did the I.L.G.W.U. revive in 1909–1910.[5]

Until that upturn, the union overcame much weakness. One problem was seasonal unionism. Garment workers frequently changed jobs between seasons, which made them "an unstable group, difficult to organize and control." When the slow season and unemployment came, they dropped out of the union. Secondly, there was the tradition of neglecting the union in the aftermath of victory. As in the past, when the union won a battle, it lost members.

Faced with such an unstable membership, in addition to other problems, the union leadership pursued conservative policies. Though I.L.G.W.U. convention resolutions called for socialism and independent politics, actual policy was very cautious, even to the point of discouraging strikes. Rather than risk strike losses, the International turned to the union label, the weapon of the United Garment Workers. In five years only one employer adopted it. Other firms, taking advantage of the depressed economy in 1904 and 1905, were more interested in establishing the open, or nonunion, shop by forming employer associations. This employer offensive resulted in strikes and lockouts which further weakened the union.[6]

Across the country, I.L.G.W.U. locals lost members and income. Pressers' Local 35 of New York, for example, was left with only "ninety members and $23 in its treasury." The result was revolt. In 1904, at the International's Boston convention, conservatives wrested control from the socialists. James McCauley, a cutter from New York, was elected president in place of Benjamin Schlesinger. To prevent further division, the Russian-born John Dyche, a traditional unionist, was elected secretary-treas-

urer. That compromise choice was made possible by the intervention of Samuel Gompers.[7]

In this period of weakness, the I.W.W. made its bid for
supremacy in the garment industry. Supported by immigrants
who arrived after Ruusia's revolution of 1905, the I.W.W. attempted to draw already organized workers and intellectuals
into its own unions. The appeal of industrial unionism was attractive, but the I.W.W.'s tactics were too similar to those of
Daniel DeLeon's Socialist Trade and Labor Alliance. Most
Jewish unionists preferred the moderate socialism of the United
Hebrew Trades. In 1907, the I.W.W. threat abated with the
dissolution of its Jewish Industrial Sub-Council and its "largely
paper" affiliated unions.[8]

Remaining within the fledgling Jewish labor movement, the
great majority of post-1905 immigrants added a sense of activism
and idealism that had been previously missing. Intellectually
alert and culturally aware, they put cultural self-help along with
social uplift among their priorities. To achieve those objectives
they used their simplest and most natural medium of communication, the Yiddish language. Yet, as Will Herberg notes, Yiddish
was more than just a communications medium. It "was also and
above all an instrument of group solidarity and a vehicle of
cultural expression. From this point on, the Jewish labor movement became Yiddishist in a very conscious way."[9]

New York's highly skilled cutters, on the other hand, were
most conscious of their cultural orientation. Organized as Local
6, the cutters were an able, closely knit group consisting of
"either native born or Americanized Irish and German workers."
They aimed, very clearly, to maintain their somewhat elevated
status among women's garment workers by excluding new immigrant workers from their local. Thus, their own kind would also
monopolize the labor supply. Moreover, "they demanded complete jurisdiction over all the cutters in the industry." This position was unacceptable, not only to the immigrant cutters, but
also to other union locals and the leadership of the International.[10]

The controversy surrounding the cutters, which actually began
as early as 1902, was not resolved until 1910. Before it was
finally settled, the International underwent a period of strife.
The question of jurisdiction among cutters' locals lasted until

1906, when Samuel Gompers and Herman Robinson arranged a compromise. All cutters were then put into a new Amalgamated Ladies' Cutters Union of Greater New York, now called Local 10. Local 10 and the cloakmakers' locals together formed a District Council, but in August 1906, when unionized tailors refused to support a strike of cutters, the latter became infuriated. They withdrew from the District Council and complained to the American Federation of Labor that the International had not enforced its constitution and backed their strike.

In 1907, this conflict was settled in favor of the well-organized, English-speaking cutters, who also managed to have Mortimer Julian elected president of the International. Soon afterward, Julian agreed with complainants from Skirtmakers' Local 23 that Local 10 had erred in not supporting a strike of theirs in July. Aggravating matters even more, the District Council's cloakmakers began to call strikes without even consulting the cutters, and then agreed to below standard wage settlements. At the November 1907, convention of the American Federation of Labor, President Julian asked that the International be examined and reorganized. Later that same month, the International retaliated against Local 10 by revoking its charter on the pretext that its members had remained on the job during two strikes in October. On May 28, 1908, the eve of the next I.L.G.W.U. convention, President Julian resigned. Abraham Rosenberg, a cloakmaker, was elected to succeed him.[11]

Backing the cutters in their struggle, a delegate from New York's Central Federated Union asked the A.F. of L. at its November 1908 convention to revoke the International's charter and reorganize the union by calling a convention for that purpose. Regarded as too severe, the resolution failed. By the beginning of 1910, though, the cutters' controversy was at last settled and Local 10 returned to the I.L.G.W.U.[12]

1909 saw prosperity return to the nation's economy and an upturn in the fortunes of the International. The women's shirtwaist business, a relative newcomer to the garment industry, was among the trades benefiting from the good times. In New York, the shirtwaist makers numbered about thirty thousand, almost two thirds of whom were Jewish and a quarter Italian.[13]

About four fifths of them were women, the great majority ranging in age from sixteen to twenty-five.[14]

These workers were discontented with many aspects of their
employment. They were not as unhappy about hours and wages,
which were tolerable, as with the petty indignities and injustices
they were made to suffer. Favoritism, excessive fines, and a
frequent requirement that they pay for their own needles and
thread were particularly galling. In addition, they wanted the
self-respect that comes from belonging to a recognized union
that has a say in determining the conditions of employment.

Long before November 23, 1909, when the shirtwaist makers
finally erupted and went on strike, they had been counseled by
the Women's Trade Union League as to the need for unity and
organization. The W.T.U.L. was a reform group of socially active
feminists such as Jane Addams and Lillian Wald. In September,
these middle-class friends of the garment workers had prodded
Local 25 into two strikes against two firms. However, on November 22, it was teenager Clara Lemlich whose pleas touched off
a general strike. Addressing a mass meeting at Cooper Union
which had heard speaker after speaker urge moderation, Miss
Lemlich passionately demanded a general strike. The audience
immediately gave her what she wanted, which became "the first
great strike by women in American labor history."[15]

The "Uprising of the Twenty Thousand," as this strike was
called, stunned the garment industry. Though the I.L.G.W.U. at
this time had only about two thousand members, more than fifteen
thousand waist and dressmakers walked out of over five hundred
factories.[16] Moreover, the heroism of young immigrant women
on picket lines in defiance of club-wielding policemen was so
extraordinary that it profoundly impressed observers.[17]

Some Italians joined the strike, but most Italians served as
strikebreakers. Italians had evidently not been involved with
Local 25 on the eve of the walkout, which was essentially a
Jewish operation. A thousand Italians did join the Jewish strikers,
but most stayed at work. The Jews made four attempts to win
over the mass of Italians, but the language barrier kept the two
sides apart.

Even the strenuous efforts of two Italian socialist unionists,

Salvatore Ninfo and Arturo Caroti, could not sway the Italian girls. Ninfo, a cloakmaker who had arrived in New York in 1899, directed a specially established office to enlist the Italians. Aided by other socialist cloakmakers, Ninfo sought to persuade the girls, but soon found himself opposed by Italian members of the Industrial Workers of the World, who were making their own appeals. The I.W.W. people urged the girls to prepare for class warfare and denounced the American Federation of Labor. This divisiveness probably confused the Italian workers and gained the "Wobblies," as the I.W.W.ers were called, few recruits.[18]

Caroti was brought onto the scene by the Women's Trade Union League, which induced him to leave his position as manager of a union cooperative store in New Jersey. Immediately assessing the Italian girls, Caroti said, "We must *buy* them off." He would pay the girls to leave the shirtwaist shops. Accordingly, he raised a fund and actually did succeed in removing some of the strikebreakers, but replacement "scabs" were in plentiful supply. Then the money began to run out, and the male relatives of the bought-off girls demanded payment of their wages, which Caroti refused to give them. For the next three months, he visited the girls' homes nightly, pleading with them to help the Jewish and American strikers and not to disgrace Italy by their actions.[19]

The efforts of Ninfo and Caroti failed for several reasons. First, there was the counter appeal by the I.W.W. Second, the I.L.G.W.U. was not only unprepared for the Wobblies, but also for the entire Italian problem which it had not anticipated. The International had not developed an Italian leadership to preclude such an eventuality. Finally, the Italian community as a whole was indifferent if not hostile to the strike. Parents urged their daughters to work, mutual aid societies lent no support, and the Italian press gave only lukewarm backing.[20]

The strike continued until February 15, 1910, when it was officially ended. The workers could not gain recognition of their union by their primary adversary, the manufacturers' association, but they did reach agreements with 339 of that group's 353 member firms. Perhaps even more important, the strikers demonstrated an aroused social consciousness on the part of immigrant working women. For those women there was now a strong Local 25 with more than ten thousand members. For the I.L.G.W.U. the strike marked "the first stage of a revolution" by showing what organized workers were capable of achieving, especially through an industry-wide general strike.[21]

The second stage of that revolution had been in preparation since 1908. Called the "Great Revolt," it was the strike of New York cloakmakers in July 1910. Unlike the spontaneous uprising of the shirtwaist workers, most of whom struck for the first time in 1909, this movement involved men who were also experienced strikers, whose goals were union recognition, higher wages, and a reduction in working hours.[22]

Determined that their strike not suffer from the same Jewish-Italian communications problem that the shirtwaist makers had faced, the leaders of the cloakmakers and the International made several precautionary moves. As early as December 1909, they created a strike fund, and from that point on met regularly to discuss the impending walkout. In April 1910, two publications appeared to report on further developments. The New York Cloak Joint Board began an irregularly issued Yiddish newspaper, the *New Post*, and the International inaugurated a monthly magazine, the *Ladies' Garment Worker* which initially appeared in English, Yiddish, and Italian.[23] In 1918, the union eventually established a weekly journal—called *Justice*—in the same three languages.[24]

At the International's convention in June 1910, the Jewish leadership of the cloakmakers made certain to organize the Italians before the strike. Salvatore Ninfo, who represented all cooperating Italian locals, participated as a delegate from Local 9. His election was made possible by the local's Jewish majority. Local 23 urged the formation of "an Italian local of Cloak and Skirt Makers." Local 38, claiming that it was "impossible for the Jewish working people to organize the Italian working people of our trade," resolved that the International "create an Italian bureau in New York" to organize them. The convention concurred in that resolution. Italian cloak and suit pressers, Local 9 reported, were already organized.[25]

On Thursday, July 7, the strike finally began. The order for workers to leave their shops at 2.00 P.M. appeared in a special

red edition of the *New Post*, printed in English, Yiddish, and
Italian. "Thousands of copies" of the newspaper were distributed
to the cloakmakers immediately after the 9:00 A.M. strike call.
By 2:30 P.M., Manhattan's streets from Thirty-eighth Street
down were filled with workers. Within a few days, an estimated
fifty to seventy thousand were striking, and the cloak and suit
trade was at a standstill.[26]

As the Jews went out, they were joined by most of the Italian
cloakmakers. Some Italians did remain in their shops, but far
fewer than during the shirtwaist strike. The educational and
organizational efforts among the Italians were paying off. In
addition, the Italian workers were able to withstand a new
round of I.W.W. competition for control of the strikers, and
their action received much greater support than the shirtwaist
girls had gotten from the Italian-American community. The
Italian language newspapers stood unanimously behind the
strikers.[27]

With such a united outpouring of workers, and, as in 1909,
public opinion on their side, the cloakmakers triumphed. They
won, though, only with the intervention of Jewish notables
from outside the garment industry, individuals who persuaded
the manufacturers to negotiate and even provided the basis
for settlement of the dispute. From Boston came merchant A.
Lincoln Filene and Louis D. Brandeis, his attorney, and they
were followed by wealthy New Yorkers Louis Marshall and
Jacob H. Schiff. The latter secured the workers' primary demand,
the union shop, by calling it something else, the preferential
shop; employers would now give union members first call to
fill vacant positions.

To resolve future disputes, Brandeis brought what economic
historian Selig Perlman called the "new unionism" to the garment
industry. Brandeis introduced the Protocol of Peace, a system of
Conciliation based on a Board of Grievances on which both
parties were to be represented, and a Board of Arbitration with
representatives of the public who would impartially decide issues
deadlocked on the lower levels. The principle of impartial arbitration, more than conciliation, would emerge from this settlement as fundamental to American unionism both within and
beyond the needle trades.

Regarding conciliation, however, one final achievement of 1910 should be noted, the formation of a Joint Board of Sanitary Control. Labor and management established the mechanism for eradication of the sweatshop and for making the work place hygienic and safe. From this board, the garment industry would later develop an extensive system of health and medical care.[28]

Despite its name, the Protocol of Peace did not usher in an era of harmony. In actuality it produced "an armed truce in which unions and employers' associations jockeyed for advantage and ultimate power." Workers chafed at the theoretical restrictions on strikes, and manufacturers resented what they considered lost control over discipline and productivity. In May 1915, the manufacturers told the International they were abrogating the Protocol and severing union relations. Urged by the press and Mayor John Purroy Mitchel to maintain the Protocol, the I.L.G.W.U. and the Manufacturers' Protective Association agreed to conciliation. The two sides talked, but their essential conflict, between workers' human rights and industrial efficiency, went unresolved. In 1916, the International struck after the Association locked out twenty-five thousand workers. Mayor Mitchel brought pressure on management which produced a settlement, but by then the International no longer wanted any limitation on its right to strike. The unionists would rely on themselves to protect their interests. In other words, the Protocol was dead.[29]

In the aftermath of the shirtwaist and cloak and suit strikes and the creation of the Protocol, the International finally discarded its feeble image of earlier years. A vibrant, respected union, it gained strength through tragedy as well as achievement. On March 25, 1911, a fire broke out at the Triangle Shirtwaist Company at Washington Square, which had been condemned by the Joint Board of Sanitary Control. When it was over, 146 girls were dead; many were killed when they leaped from eighth, ninth, and tenth floor windows, while others were trapped behind locked company doors. Never before had the horrors of the sweatshop been so clearly revealed, or, for that matter, had the need for effective unionism been so vividly demonstrated.[30]

Yet as the International came of age it continued to grapple with problems of ethnic diversity. Between 1910 and 1916, the question of Italian membership took an ironic turn. The Italians, who had, earlier, been difficult to organize, now increased in the labor force in the same proportion as the Jews declined.[31] In 1911, organizers in Cleveland discovered that young Italian girls felt the spirit of unionism. "Steek togetha! Yes, Steek togetha!" they said, despite the loss of a twenty-one-week strike.[32] Arturo Caroti persuaded the International "to provide a separate office for the Italian Waist Makers" so that their individual problems could be dealt with by people speaking their language.[33] In June 1912, President Abraham Rosenberg reported to the International that its "membership includes nine different nationalities," and that "the Italian element alone may be counted in thousands." He advised, therefore, "that the Italian membership should have a representative in the incoming General Executive Board."[34]

Though Rosenberg recommended that the door be opened to Italians, the International's Toronto convention voted to keep it shut. Opponents argued that representation granted to Italians would lead to requests by all other nationalities for the same consideration. Moreover, they contended that the General Executive Board should represent trades rather than nationalities.[35]

Rosenberg's move was an obvious concession to the leaders of the Italians within the International. Since the conclusion of the cloakmakers' strike the Italian leadership had been claiming that the Jewish directors of the union did not understand or sympathize with Italian ways. In 1912, according to Salvatore Ninfo's estimate, twenty thousand Italians and thirty-five thousand Jews were under the jurisdiction of the Joint Board, but the Jews completely controlled the Board and the presidencies of all of the locals in New York.[36]

The Italians thus argued for self-government in the form of Italian-speaking locals and a fair, proportional share of offices in the International. The "tenacious opposition" to their requests, as the Italians saw it, came from "those who did not understand the character and the possibilities of our people," and "caused distrust and in a short time . . . desertions from the union."[37]

So that they would have more of a say in union affairs, the Italians, led by Ninfo, Aldo Cursi, Luigi Cassata, and others, took their case to the 1912 convention. There they introduced five resolutions, but all were rejected. To become influential in the International, the Italians would clearly have to boost themselves. Thus, they began to train their own future leaders and to introduce greater numbers of their own people than ever before to the idea of unionism.[38] The waist and dress trade reported by 1913 that "the shops where the Italian workers are in the majority, and those employing mostly American girls, are now under Union control."[39]

It was gratifying, too, to see that many Americans were organized. The American girls had previously "laughed at the agitation for a Union, avoided the foreign element and refused to come in contact with the other girls." To explain their apparent reversal, as well as that of the Italians, I.L.G.W.U. official Abraham Baroff credited the Protocol of Peace's sanctioning of the union shop.[40]

As American girls changed their attitudes, the drive to win them intensified. In 1913, Local 25 set up an American branch to recruit the more than ninety-three percent of the native-born women in the dress and waist trade who were as yet unorganized.[41] *Ladies' Garment Worker* columnist Pauline Newman explained why those women had to be enrolled: employers were "advertising for American girls only ... because *they* work for lower wages, and take things as they come, while the Jewish girls usually stand up and demand a higher price for their labor."[42] "Many Americans," she also noted, were "still under the impression that a union is either for men or for foreigners." They had to "understand that to belong to the Union is American; that to fight for better conditions is harmony with the American spirit."[43]

By September 1913, Newman reported progress. American girls as well as foreigners were joining the Wrapper and Kimono Workers' Union, Local 41. In one Long Island community, the union controlled the town's only shop. "Most of the workers there are American girls and all of them belong to the Union." Moreover, they were active, interested members.[44] For the benefit of Local 25's membership, which reached "20,000 almost over night," that union's publications began to appear in English and Italian as well as Yiddish.[45]

Through the forces of immigration and organization, the ethnic composition of the garment industry and garment unionism underwent significant change. In October 1914, an I.L.G.W.U.

organizer in Philadelphia discovered that in order to organize the ladies' tailors in that city he "had to reach the Italian element first" as it numbered "about 1,000" while there were "only 200 Jews" in the trade.[46] Another organizer, who recruited among embroidery workers in New Jersey in 1915, discovered that northern Italians in that trade were "slow in their action, but once they organize, they remain organized."[47] Also in 1915, the financial secretary of Cloak Pressers' Local 35 noted that new members usually accounted for one seventh of his union's total membership, which made it necessary "to guard against the new comers [sic] placing in jeopardy the structure we have built up with much powerful effort." He wanted applicants for union membership to be "experienced workers" who would not normally work below the established wage scale and displace unionists.[48]

The truth was that the Jewish union leadership could not hold back the tide they had helped set in motion. The ranks of the garment workers swelled and spread from New York to Chicago and further south and west, and came increasingly to include native-born children of "most ethnic groups." Poles, Bohemians, Lithuanians, Czechs, and others jumped on board—but not the sons and daughters of Jewish immigrant workers, whose parents expected greater accomplishment for their children in business or in the professions. By the 1920s, Italians displaced Jews, whose numbers had fallen to "under twenty percent of the total," as "the largest single unit" in the needle trades.[49] However, as the leadership of the unions remained in Jewish hands, the potential for antagonism was as evident as the need for careful direction.[50]

In the International Ladies' Garment Workers' Union the immigrant had an able and idealistic instrument for improving his standard of living. He belonged to the union, elected officials whom he regarded as advancing his interests, and felt that on the whole his leaders respected him. The United Garment Workers of America was a very different kind of organization. Controlled by Americans or Americanized unionists, the U.G.W. stood for elitism and nativism under the aegis of the American Federation of Labor.

Rather than terminate its feud with the United Hebrew Trades, the Garment Workers renewed and intensified it with the apparent support of the A.F. of L., which regarded immigration and socialism as twin evils. With the assistance of the New York Central Federated Union, the U.G.W. made war on the U.H.T. Renewing the attack begun in the 1890s, the U.G.W. and its allies accused the Hebrew Trades of attempting to divide the American labor movement along racial lines. Simultaneously, the Garment Workers joined a chorus of A.F. of L.–affiliated unions demanding immigration restriction.[51] As early as 1900, the U.G.W. had asked a Federation convention to authorize the Executive Council to draw up and have Congress pass restrictive legislation.[52]

The leaders of the U.G.W. boldly denounced immigrants, but were decidedly timid about moving against management. In dealing with employers they were remarkably cautious, reluctant to strike, and quick to end strikes once they were called. This behavior perhaps may be explained as the result of their experience with partially or unsuccessful strikes. Late in 1901 and into 1902, sixteen thousand workers went out in New York, but little was gained. In 1904, a poorly timed strike took thirty-five thousand workers out for six weeks, only to end in failure. Afterward, it seemed that the United Garment Workers would strike only under optimum conditions and when success was virtually assured.[53]

Yet after 1907 there was considerable unrest in the men's clothing industry. Workers were upset over their union's failure to match gains made in the women's trades. To many of its members, the U.G.W. seemed behind the times.[54]

In September 1910, dissatisfaction with working conditions touched off a strike in Chicago. Only three weeks after the New York cloakmakers' walkout, a wage cut in Hart, Schaffner and Marx's pants shops sparked a general strike. Some thirty-eight thousand men's clothing workers eventually went out, but "without leadership or demands." The public sympathized with the strikers, but the U.G.W. questioned the wisdom of their action. Finally, Garment Workers' president Thomas Rickert announced an agreement with Hart, Schaffner and Marx; the strikers would return to work, but without union recognition and under the old open shop arrangement. Angered, the workers asked the Chicago Federation of Labor to direct them. In addition, they solicited the help of the Women's Trade Union League. At last, in January 1911, the Federation achieved a settlement; the strikers could go back, union members would not be discriminated against, and an arbitration committee would settle outstanding grievances. The arbitration system before long became an "impartial chairman" system similar to that achieved by the women's garment workers.[55]

Chicago was settled, but not New York. In December 1912, sixty thousand workers in that city responded to a strike call issued by an affiliate of the United Garment Workers, the Brotherhood of Tailors. The walkout continued into February, with large manufacturers in particular holding firm and workers beginning to return to their shops. With ten thousand already back, the pressure on the remaining strikers was intensifying. President Rickert, afraid that he would lose control over his members, and convinced that the strike would soon collapse, then worked out a settlement through a mediation board.

Rickert secured a wage increase and a fifty-four-hour week. To explain the settlement to the strikers, the U.G.W. persuaded Abraham Cahan that nothing better was obtainable. Thus, the *Forward* lent its editorial support. However, though the newspaper said, "Bravo," the workers felt betrayed. The *Forward* wound up with the front windows of its building smashed, Cahan was hospitalized with a duodenal ulcer, and Rickert was condemned for having taken matters into his own hands.

As the Brotherhood of Tailors rejected Rickert's settlement, the strike continued. It lasted another three weeks, and achieved improved terms. The work week was set at fifty-three hours, to become fifty-two after a year, and the union received implicit recognition. The workers now felt that they had won a victory, but continued to resent the U.G.W. leadership.[56]

In anticipation of a challenge to their control of the Garment Workers, the incumbent officials made Nashville the site of their 1914 convention. Distant from such radical centers as New York and Chicago, Nashville was a comfortable spot for the conservatives to make their stand against the big city insurgents.

As the convention neared, the verbal warfare between the

two sides continued. The radicals accused the officials of mis-using the union label, acting out of self-interest, deceiving the membership, and collaborating with management. In response, the leadership charged that the insurgents were directed by nonmembers and intellectuals and were aiming to put the Gar-ment Workers under Jewish control. Moreover, Rickert's people contended that the radicals had really wanted from the outset to form their own rival union.[57]

On October 12 the convention convened and the confrontation took place. The credentials committee denied seats to most of the large city delegates, which precipitated a departure of their colleagues who had been seated. With the excluded delegates, the departed insurgents then held their own convention in another hall in Nashville and claimed that only their gathering was legiti-mate. Transacting whatever business they could, they chose Chicago's Sidney Hillman and New York's Joseph Schlossberg president and secretary, respectively. In December, in New York they reorganized as the Amalgamated Clothing Workers of America.[58]

Sidney Hillman, who would ultimately rank among the giants of the American labor movement, was precisely the kind of person abhorred by Rickert. Born in 1887, in Zagare, Lithuania, into a family with a strong rabbinical tradition, he had attended a seminary. However, by the age of seventeen he was already active in the Jewish labor movement. Two years later, after having been confined to a czarist prison for his activities, he left his home for Germany and then England, where an uncle and brother received him. In August 1907, following months of minimal sub-sistence with his relatives, he boarded the liner *Cedric* which took him to New York.[59]

Hillman immediately moved on to Chicago where he stayed with friends of a former teacher who had preceded him in that city. Though highly intellectual, he found work, first as a Sears, Roebuck and Company stock clerk and order packer, and then as a pants cutter for Hart, Schaffner and Marx. As a cutter, Hillman was mediocre, but as a leader of workers he was superb. Consequently, during the Chicago strike of 1910 he was the workers' most articulate spokesman.

Able leadership was essential during that strike. President

Rickert, who negotiated for the U.G.W., was uncomfortably close to management, and William D. Haywood of the Industrial Workers of the World, also present, combined a revolutionary and idealistic stance to win the strikers to his organization. Hillman, the "greenhorn," or newcomer, kept the strikers in line to permit the Chicago Federation of Labor to negotiate an advantageous settlement.[60]

Though the founders of the Amalgamated represented forty thousand workers, they were not in accord with Samuel Gompers and the leadership of the American Federation of Labor. Gompers regarded the Nashville walkout as a treasonous act against an A.F. of L. affiliate, and the formation of the Amalgamated (A.C.W.A.) as an example of the classic crime of "dual unionism." Thus, the Federation refused to recognize the Amalgamated. As early as May 1915, Gompers went before a meeting of the United Hebrew Trades to plead in person that it, too, reject the "secessionists." He argued that the Federation depended on discipline and unity for strength, and that racial or religious division within the labor movement would result in endless and destructive conflicts.[61]

The U.H.T. was only slightly swayed by Gompers's speech. It suggested in response that either the Executive Committee of the Federation or "a committee of prominent persons of the labor movement" study and reconcile the differences between the two factions.[62] Following the lead of New York's Central Federated Union, which had already suspended the Hebrew Trades from membership, Gompers demanded that A.F. of L. affiliates withdraw from the U.H.T. unless the Amalgamated was immediately expelled. Affiliates who failed to terminate their connection with the rebels would be suspended by the A.F. of L.[63]

As the United Hebrew Trades refused to yield to Gompers, the Central Federated Union and the American Federation of Labor took additional action. In August 1915, the Central Federated Union voted overwhelmingly to suspend all members who were still within the U.H.T., and, in November, the A.F. of L. Executive Council directed Gompers to see that all affiliates withdraw from the Hebrew Trades.

To prevent the U.H.T.'s destruction, the Amalgamated then withdrew its membership. Officially, the Hebrew Trades declared, it would now occupy a neutral position between the competing garment unions. Unofficially, the U.H.T.'s relationship with the beleaguered Amalgamated remained close.[64]

Besides Jewish labor, Italians sided with the Amalgamated. During the 1913 strike, Italian socialist members of the United Garment Workers, organized as Local 63, had united themselves with the Jews. The Italians as well as the Jews protested President Rickert's intervention in that walkout and his settlement. Afterward, the Italian leadership worked to organize as many Italians as they could in the men's clothing industry. Their efforts resulted in new Italian locals and Italian branches in locals where Italian membership was small. The Italian Tailors of Greater New York was organized to provide cohesion among the various Italian units. In 1913, Local 63 began to publish a weekly newspaper, *Il Lavoro,* which aided union recruitment.

In 1914, the Italians joined their Jewish brethren in condemning the Garment Workers' choice of Nashville as a convention site and in giving rise to the Amalgamated. Such leaders as August Bellanca and Fiorello LaGuardia served on an agitation committee to arouse Italians against the distant Nashville location. At the convention, all twelve Italian delegates, from locals in New York, Brooklyn, Boston, and Chicago, withdrew with the Jewish dissidents. In founding the Amalgamated, two of those Italians became officers. Ideologically linked by socialism, Italians and Jews together withstood competition from the Garment Workers as they organized workers in additional cities. The early alliance of the two sides against the Garment Workers' leadership thus held firm in succeeding struggles.[65]

After 1915 the clash between the Garment Workers and the Amalgamated continued unabated. The former insisted that its interest was in labor unity and that charges that it was bigoted and anti-Jewish were incorrect.[66] Furthermore, between 1916 and 1918, the A.F. of L. and the Central Federated Union demonstrated their hostility to the Amalgamated by rejecting conciliation efforts and attacking those who sympathized with it.[67]

To calm the situation, the International Ladies' Garment Workers' Union tried, but in vain, to have the A.F. of L. accept the Amalgamated on the basis of its size. The outcast union represented more clothing workers than the Garment Workers.

In 1918, the International revived a proposal it had made as early as 1914. It attempted to have the A.F. of L. set up a Needle Trades Department on the model of the mining and metal trades. This would be a device for coordination of the various unions. But the Federation's· officials opposed the idea, and it was defeated at the A.F. of L. convention.[68] Before the convention met, there had been the suggestion that both sides had behaved rashly, and an article in the I.L.G.W.U.'s journal proposed that "bygones be bygones.... The labor movement is too sacred a cause to permit such methods."[69]

Unfortunately, peace was not restored in 1918, and the Amalgamated Clothing Workers of America would not be recognized by the American Federation of Labor until 1933,[70] despite its membership of almost two hundred thousand by 1920. The Garment Workers, the affiliate in good standing, at that time numbered not more than forty-six thousand, most of whom were in the work clothing industry.[71]

It is evident that for the Ladies' Garment Workers' and the Amalgamated Clothing Workers' Unions the roads to respectability and stability were not easy to follow. Yet by 1920 each established a firm foundation for future growth. Directed by new immigrants, they had succeeded in creating organizations in which new immigrants would prosper.

CHAPTER 8

The Italians in the Labor Market

BETWEEN 1880 and 1914 more immigrants came to the United States from Italy than from any other land. In the eighties and nineties, about 850,000 Italians arrived followed by over three million in the next fourteen years. The annual arrival rate exceeded 100,000 beginning in 1900 and reached a peak of nearly 286,000 in 1906. The flow remained heavy until World War I, which reduced it to less than 2,000 by 1919.[1] As early as 1910, the Italian-born population of the United States reached 1.3 million.[2]

By living frugally and saving to make the return to the Old Country possible, the Italians were frequently compared to the Chinese, the most reviled of immigrants. Like the Asians, these Europeans were regarded as sojourners whose stay in America was to be only temporary.[3] Indeed, nativists—of whom Woodrow Wilson was one—regarded the Italians as "the Chinese of Europe."[4]

As these newcomers became familiar with American ways, many of them also began to protest unbearable industrial working conditions. In several industries they ceased being docile, obedient servants. Instead they joined unions and supported strikes.

Despite the fact that Christoforo Columbus discovered America and that it was named after Amerigo Vespucci, few Italians came to America before 1860. Italian glassmakers appeared at Jamestown in 1621, and settlers later founded colonies in Delaware and New York, but in general British America had little interest in the people of Italy and little contact with them.

Those who came during the colonial period were mainly individuals rather than members of groups. Some were outstanding,

125

such as the musician Giovanni Gualdo, the physician Filippo Mazzei, the language professor Carlo Bellini, and the explorer Giuseppe Maria Francesco Vigo. Similarly, the American Revolution and its aftermath witnessed the arrival of Italian settlers and visitors of education and distinction. Count Luigi Castiglioni, the botanist, and Count Pavlo Andreani, the physicist and naturalist, were among the visitors who appreciated the freedom Americans had won for themselves.[5]

As the Civil War approached, Italian immigration increased somewhat. Though fewer than 4,500 Italians came between 1820 and 1850, almost twice that number arrived during the fifties. Still, by 1860, there were only 10,518 Italian immigrants in the United States.

Mainly northern Italians, the antebellum immigrants were noticeable as traders, plaster statue vendors, and monkey-assisted street musicians. Some like Guiseppe Garibaldi, who made candles in Manhattan while he resided on Staten Island, were political refugees. Others were interested in gold, and rushed to California to find it.[6]

Fearful of a hostile reception in rural areas, the Italians tended to congregate in the nation's eastern cities. There they could depend on the companionship of one another. Thus they populated slum sections, such as New York's notorious Five Points in Lower Manhattan. The living conditions in that center of violence and immorality alarmed the city's Children's Aid Society, which opened an elementary school to give the neighborhood's youth industrial training. Such instruction was designed to keep the young out of the hands of *padroni,* wandering men who virtually enslaved boys as street acrobats and musicians. The *"padrone* system," which the society fought, contributed to a stereotype of Italians as a menace to the young.[7] In time the abuses among children declined, and padronism was identified with the exploitation of adult Italian immigrant workers.[8]

Another unflattering impression Americans had of Italians was that they were Papists, obedient disciples of a foreign potentate, the pope. Protestant Americans had viewed Italians in that way since colonial times,[9] but bigotry flared with particular ugliness during the nativist 1840s and fifties. Fortunately for the Italians, their small numbers spared them the brunt of the era's anti-Catholic and antiforeign attitudes.[10]

After 1860 the immigrant flow from the southern provinces of Italy was greater than before and included a variety of classes and types. Significantly, after 1870 occurred the beginning of a return migration. Of those present as the seventies began, most were still northern Italians, and they were distributed rather evenly across the country. Representing a diversity of educational levels and religions as well as occupations, they contributed to America's cultural and economic development. Only a few Italians were in the West, many having left California following disappointment in the quest for gold. Similarly, there were few working on railroads or bringing music to city streets. By 1880, there were still only 20,000 Italians in New York City, and the mass migration had not yet begun.[11]

Even prior to that time, it became evident that the primary source of emigration was the south of Italy. As early as 1866, emigration from southern sections exceeded that from all other regions of Italy combined. In 1868, 6,875 came from the south as opposed to 4,410 from elsewhere.[12] Between 1876 and 1913, eighty percent of the Italians who arrived in the United States were southerners.[13]

In contrast with the northern Italians, the inhabitants of southern Italy were very much the victims of man and nature. Mainly peasants, they suffered from heavy taxation, low wages, and frequent unemployment. The soil of southern Italy had become eroded and parched—the result of meager rainfall—which sometimes became torrential and caused flooding. Consequently, the average Italian was underfed. In 1880, he consumed a scant twenty-eight pounds of meat, as opposed to 120 pounds for Americans. He relied on pasta, but the wheat from which that was made was in short supply. The 1880s witnessed bread riots by starving city dwellers as well as peasants in Sicily and Calabria in the south and even Lombardy in the north.[14]

As wage earners the Italians faced other handicaps. American wages were two to five times higher. For the same work, even San Francisco's Chinese were paid better than Neopolitan laborers. By coming to the United States, unskilled Italian laborers could expect to earn $1.50 per day. In 1903, a dozen hours of work in Sicily usually earned common laborers, or *braccianti*, about a sixth as much.[15]

As mentioned before, these peasants often emigrated with repatriation in mind. "Persons who come to the United States reduce the rate of wages by ruinous competition, and then take their savings out of the country are not desirable," Congressman Henry Cabot Lodge wrote in 1891. He called them "mere birds of passage," who regard "as home a foreign country, instead of that in which they live and earn money." Accordingly, Lodge continued, they had neither an "interest or stake in the country, and they never became American citizens."[16]

For the next three decades, Lodge's criticism was echoed widely. To the extent that repatriation was a common goal of the Italians, it did have a basis in fact. In 1906, John Foster Carr, a sympathetic observer, described them as "the most mobile supply of labor that this country has ever known." He noted that migratory Italian laborers came and worked "eight or nine months of the year" and then returned "between October and December." In excess of 98,000 returned in 1903 and 134,000 in 1904.[67]

These Italian immigrants were generally unwelcome. Poor, illiterate, and unskilled, they were repudiated even by the northern Italians in the country.[18] To observers of the American labor scene, the newcomers were usually strikebreakers or virtually helpless slaves of other southern Italians who ruled them as labor bosses. "They cannot shift for themselves nor make an intelligent appeal to the natives," explained one observer.[19]

Though they were used to break strikes, much of their strikebreaking was done unwittingly, and was contrary to their actual feelings. For example, in 1882, the Freighthandlers' Central Union struck five railroads in New York and New Jersey. Management then brought immigrant Italians and Jews to break the strike. However, upon learning what purpose they were serving, both Jewish and Italian immigrants stopped working and joined the union.[20]

Beginning in February 1883 and continuing for sixteen months, Italian scabs joined with Germans during a lockout at Troy, New York. The Malleable Iron Company had locked out members of the Troy Iron Molders' International Union no. 2 to compel them to accept a wage cut and break the union. The predominantly Irish ironworkers, to defend their interests, used violence against the scabs. They assauted and shot at them, and even set fire to the church in which their families were housed. The lockout was not broken, but neither was the union. The result was a "stalemate."[21]

The list of incidents in which Italians served as strikebreakers is extensive. It also includes the anthracite coal strike of 1877–1888 and strikes by New York longshoremen in 1887 and Chicago meat packers in 1904. As previously discussed, Italian scabs were prominent in the New York shirtwaist walkout of 1909.[22]

Nonetheless, without denying or excusing their participation, Italians were far from alone in breaking strikes. In 1880, Belgians, Swedes, and Americans, as well as Italians, combined to defeat a coal mine stoppage. Swedes, in fact, were brought into St. Louis to scab in a wire mill in 1881 and into Maryland to mine coal in 1884.[23]

Sometimes Italians fought their own *paesani*, or countrymen, during strikes. In March 1906, Italian miners walked out at Cornwall, Pennsylvania, demanding higher wages and a ten-hour day. The reaction of the mine operator, Pennsylvania Steel, was to send sixty other Italians to replace the strikers. When the scabs arrived, the strikers yelled and jeered at them. However, the newcomers were rescued by armed policemen who assaulted and drove off their tormentors. Under the protection of state police, the scabs worked the mines while strikers paraded through Cornwall singing the Italian national anthem as they waved red handkerchiefs. That display of spirit achieved little. The next day Pennsylvania Steel added a load of Hungarian scabs to the Italians already present, and broke the strike. Police used clubs on those Italian strikers who refused to concede defeat.[24]

To many Americans, southern Italians were worse than scabs; they were slaves of the "*padrone* system." In 1886, an unscrupulous notoriety-seeker told a congressional committee that eighty thousand Italians, five thousand in Chicago alone, were in the United States as virtual slaves of *padroni*. Though that charge could not be substantiated, the view that many Italians were being brought in ignorance and under contract into the country was widely held. A California fruit grower even contended that *padroni* had greater control over Italians than San Francisco's Six Companies had over the Chinese.[25] Edward F. McSweeney, assistant United States commissioner of immigration, told readers of the A.F. of L.'s *American Federationist* that the system was "soulless and absolutely degrading, and made immigrants as practically enslaved as ever were the black men of the south."[26]

The *padroni* of the late nineteenth century were generally not child recruiters. The latter day figures were primarily labor bosses who provided immigrants with numerous services, but often at a very steep price. Padronism never existed as a formal system; it involved personal and irregular arrangements between immigrants and *padroni*. Moreover, as a form of bossism it was not peculiar to Italians. After 1880 it flourished among several other groups as well, including Poles, Hungarians, Armenians, Greeks, Turks, Bulgarians, Austrians, Mexicans, and Macedonians.[27]

By the beginning of the eighties, the early form of padronism was virtually dead. The practice of importing minors, plus some adults, and holding them as indentured servants for as many as three years fell victim to action by both the Italian and American governments and private philanthropic organizations. Though it disappeared, a second system replaced it.

This system provided laborers for American industry. Imported under contract, immigrants paid *padroni* specified amounts for finding them jobs and boarding them. The *padroni* also paid their wages.[28] Though the importation of contract labor had been approved by law in 1864, there is no evidence that more than a few such immigrants were brought in before the Foran Act outlawed the practice in 1885. Both before and after that date, most *padroni* were probably more labor agents rather than importers.[29]

It has been said that the *padrone* was "the first political leader that the Italian immigrant had."[30] Considering the fact that the newcomer who entrusted his fate to this labor agent did so usually in the absence of any alternative to starvation makes it difficult to regard the relationship as "political" rather than economic. As historian Rudolph Vecoli says, the *padroni* "made a business out of ignorance and necessities of his countrymen."[31]

These middlemen of labor exploited not only the opportunities offered by an individualistic economy, but also the peculiarities of the Italian *contadini's* background. The agents, who understood the closeness of southern Italian family ties, served as surrogate fathers, big brothers, or bosses for the young, single men who constituted the bulk of the migration. They shrewdly kept the largely illiterate, Italian-speaking immigrants dependent on their knowledge of the labor market for employment and also directed settlement. "Little Italies" were formed by the activities of the *padroni,* who assisted in organizing "chain migrations" of peasants from villages in Italy to American localities. In other words, the *paesani* were kept together.[32]

The distribution of the Italian immigrant laborers involved a large effort. The bosses directed them to places in Canada as well as throughout the United States. Mainly the newcomers worked at occupations called *sciabola,* or pick and shovel labor, which usually meant railroad or other construction. Such jobs were usually seasonal. Owing to its many railroad lines and geographic centrality, Chicago became "a clearing house for seasonal workers of the entire country as well as the Middle West."[33]

By distributing temporary Italian laborers throughout America, the *padrone* contributed significantly to the nation's industrial development. In addition, it was largely through his influence that Italian settlers found their way to and made new lives in Lincoln, Nebraska, Paterson, New Jersey, Syracuse, New York, and many other cities.[34]

It is also clear that the *padrone's* ability to find jobs was important and should not be minimized. First, he was useful to employers who would have been otherwise unable to hire appreciable numbers of Italians. Many employers simply did not know of another method.[35] Second, he often helped Italians get jobs that might have gone to others. For example, he gave the unskilled Italian a competitive edge over Polish, Irish, and black workers in railroad and public works employment. Poles, even in Cleveland, Chicago, Milwaukee, and Buffalo, where they were either in the majority or close to it, could not find work in subway and street railway construction, street paving and street cleaning. Italians had a monopoly. Lacking the *padrone,* the Poles "had a decided disadvantage in securing public works projects and were frozen out of this very large sector of Philadelphia's unskilled labor market."[36]

In addition to securing a job for the immigrant, the *padrone* usually supplied him with several other forms of assistance. He was often interpreter, banker, moneylender, notary, and counsel. He took care of sending savings back to family in Italy. Therefore, it should come as no surprise that for these social and economic services *padroni* became respected, honored members of their communities. Among the notables were Thomas Marnell of Syracuse, New York, and Lorenzo Columbo of Carneta, Pennsylvania.[37]

Thomas Marnell (born Marinelli) came to the United States in 1877 and worked as a laborer on the Pennsylvania Railroad. By 1883 he was in Syracuse, probably as part of a group of Italian laborers recruited for railroad construction. Within a decade his influence had risen rapidly. He became a foreman, saloon proprietor, court interpreter, special policeman, banker, grocer, steamship agent, notary public, and general contractor. Well known and respected, he became the most influential member of Syracuse's Italian colony. For Italians in need, Marnell was the person they could rely on for help in finding employment, writing letters, bringing families from Europe, lending money, and handling legal problems.[38]

In the early nineties, Lorenzo Columbo, Nicolo Carnato, and Giovanni Dolcetti bought parcels of land in New Italy Town, later called Carneta. Soon afterward they built their own homes on the lots and then gave or sold sections of land to *paesani*, relatives, and their children. By 1895 the colony had forty homeowners. Columbo, a quarry laborer by trade, also speculated in real estate and tried several other business ventures, including the operation of a teamster service. Yet he never became wealthy, probably because of his backing of an indebted relative who could not repay a loan.[39]

The sad truth about the *padrone* is that he was "an indispensable evil."[40] He "rendered useful services," but "too often abused his trust."[41] He betrayed the trusting immigrants either by overcharging or swindling them, or by subjecting them to wretched working conditions.

It was easy to cheat the immigrants. Sometimes they were

asked to pay for first-class rail transportation or rent when an employer had already provided it free of charge. Occasionally laborers paid fees for services which they did not receive. Some laborers worked a few days on a job only to learn that they were being sent home without explanation. These unfortunates were then replaced by new men who paid new commissions.[42] Then there were those laborers who paid their fees and were led to isolated places and there abandoned. Wages went first to the middleman, who deducted arbitrary amounts above legitimate expenses, and then passed on the remainder to the laborer. Often the worker received nothing. Nontheless, he had to buy almost all his provisions from the *padroni* at vastly inflated prices. The low quality goods brought profits "from twenty-five to one hundred per cent above the cost . . . to the seller."[43]

To live and work in the labor camps run by the *padroni* required the utmost stamina. As one college student who worked on a railroad track gang in Indiana recalled, men worked "ten hours every day under the blistering sun, or pouring rain" in an atmosphere marked by "a cringing, all-pervading terror of the boss." The human "dogs" lived in windowless cars, slept on straw bags under vermin-covered blankets, and in general, endured filth and stench.[44] Elsewhere conditions were similar, characterized mainly by "frequent and inexcusable brutality" or "actual slavery."[45]

After 1890 the *padrone* system declined, in part a victim of its own success in introducing Italians to the American world. The many Italian immigrants of the nineties had less need of the middlemen than had their predecessors. By now the earlier arrivals were more familiar with the English language and the ways of American labor, and had risen somewhat in economic status. At the end of the decade, increasing numbers of women and children arrived from Italy, and, as the new century began, also men of more varied occupational backgrounds. Now there were tailors, printers, barbers, artists, and lawyers in addition to peasants.[46] Enough relatives and *paesani* were already at least partly assimilated to be able to help find jobs.[47]

When the Southern Italians came to the United States, they entered a labor market that could readily absorb them. With the other peoples of the "new" immigration, they performed tasks that native-born Americans and "old' immigrants could or would not do. The latter were moving economically upward and away from unskilled and semi-skilled occupations. Therefore, such areas of employment as railroad, canal, and water supply system construction, timber cutting, and fruit, vegetable, and grain harvesting were open to newcomers.[48] In 1893 it led a visitor from Italy to comment: "He tills the soil, builds railroads, bores mountains, drains swamps; opens here and there to the industry of American workmen new fields which would not perhaps be opened but for his cheap labor."[49]

Though the typical Italian laborer moved into pick and shovel occupations, he did so more out of necessity than choice. In southern Italy he had tilled the soil, but had not come to revere the land. On the contrary, he despised it and associated manual labor with degradation. If he could not escape it entirely in America then his hope was that his children would be entering the business or professional world. When he had a choice of where to work, he preferred the city to the countryside.[50]

Loneliness and isolation also contributed to the desire to settle in towns. "The Italian is no lover of the country; he dreads of all things an isolated dwelling," an Italian government authority noted.[51]

One thing he did not dread was hard work. He did not arrive in the United States with a "work ethic" as intense as the native American's, but he did come with a similar feeling that labor was both healthy and useful. He came from a culture that condemned sloth in men and women. For instance, their folk songs warned that lazy girls were apt to remain unmarried.[52]

Family members often worked together. Fearful that American workers would be a liberal influence on women and children, Italians passed up industrial opportunities where such contact and possibility existed.[53] To preclude such problems and maintain parental control over their offspring, children often worked side by side with fathers or relatives.

The industriousness of the Italians was particularly noticeable in the vegetable canneries of New York State. At Buffalo, under the direction and prodding of their parents, Italian children worked longer hours and tended to more tasks than the

American-born youngsters who labored in the same plant, thus contributing to family prosperity.[54] For example, Sicilian laborers at nearby Fredonia were able to save enough money from wages earned by the whole family to enable them to purchase land and create impressive vineyards.[55]

The Italians' "lust for employment" led them to work overtime when possible, sometimes at very low wages. In Boston, at least, by maintaining "an inconceivably low standard of living" they were able to save money and acquire a large amount of real estate. However, as settlement house director Robert Woods observed in 1904, the low wages and living standard did "real injury to the community" and gave "grounds for the enmity which their industrial competitors among the older immigrant elements" felt toward them.[56]

While incurring ill-will, they remained remarkably self-sufficient. In 1904, when the average wage for labor in the North Atlantic States was $1.39 a day, unskilled Italian laborers in New York City proved "most able to care" for themselves and "keep away from charity." In 1906, an observer noted that there were no Italian beggars in American cities.[57]

In public works, industry, and agriculture, the Italian immigrant's impact on the labor market was nationwide. Italians monopolized the street sweeping of San Francisco and the street work of Chicago. They laid a lengthy natural gas pipeline in Indiana and constructed a dam across the Colorado River in Texas and a reservoir at Northampton, Massachusetts. They were prominent in the restoration of Galveston following a hurricane in 1900 and the rebuilding of San Francisco after the earthquake of 1906. Often, they supplanted English or Irish men who had previously done this kind of work.[58]

In railroad construction, they likewise displaced the Irish as the primary source of unskilled labor. Beginning in the nineties, Italian laborers came to be scattered across the country in great numbers, with Chicago as the major distribution center. The Pennsylvania Railroad alone soon employed 13,500 Italians. In 1911, a vice-president of that line noted, "On nearly all the important work we have done in recent years there has been a large percentage of Italian labor, and this applies to work done directly by the railroad or by contractors."[59] From May 1904 through

July 1906, almost seventy-six percent of the railroad contstruction laborers placed by New York employment agencies in jobs in northern states were Italian.[60]

The displacement of other laboring groups by Italians contributed to hard feelings. After a strike by Irish longshoremen on the New York waterfront in 1887, steamship companies brought in Italians. The object was to lessen the likelihood of another stoppage, which it did. The Italians differed radically and linguistically from the Irish, who feared their competition. It also deflected their resentment of abuses by management.

The practice of using Italians as substitutes was not extensively followed until the early nineties, but once they appeared on the scene they proved manageable and reliable, unlike the Irish who were inclined to be bellicose. So antagonistic were the Irish that they initially refused to work in the same gangs with the Italians. The more irritated they became, the easier it was to force them out and replace them with additional Italians. Shrewd foremen regularly exacerbated friction between the Irish and the "Guineas" or "Dagoes," as the Italian competitors were called. Consequently, not only the Irish, but Germans and Scandinavians, too sought employment elsewhere.[61]

The reception Italians received in the West and South was often violent. In 1895, in the coal fields of southern Colorado, American miners murdered six Italians, and then in 1900, four more.[62] Between 1891 and 1910, mobs in five southern states took thirty-two Italian lives.[63] Clearly the most egregious of the killings were those committed in New Orleans on March 14, 1891. Despite their acquittal by a jury of the murder of Superintendent of Police David C. Hennessy, eleven Italian defendants were attacked in prison and lynched.[64]

Rather than condemn this slaughter, Henry Cabot Lodge rationalized it. He said the eleven prisoners were killed because "they were supposed to be members of the Mafia," the secret Sicilian society. In addition, Lodge called "for an intelligent and effective restriction of immigration" which would exclude "dangerous and undesirable elements."[65]

Southern white industrial workers shared Lodge's restrictionist sentiments. Though Italian immigrants were wary of southern prejudice and working conditions resembling peonage, some states actively sought them for industrial purposes. In 1906 Georgia and South Carolina said they would solve their demands for labor by the mass importation of foreigners. Upon investigating the lot of emigrants already in the South, the Italian government said it would not recommend that others go there.

Furthermore, white workers in the two recruiting states also strongly objected. The Georgia Federation of Labor did not want "the scum of Europe" to come and upset southern racial institutions and create northern-style "tenements crowded with unassimilative [*sic*] pauper labor." Fearing competition, whites in South Carolina undermined that state's immigration drive which had begun in 1904. They successfully discouraged the foreigners even though so many cotton mill jobs were then available that immigration would not have posed a serious threat to native employment.[66]

Whether they labored in the North or South, the unskilled *contadini* were generally despised by native American labor. In Chicago, for example, critics compared them unfavorably even with the other recent immigrants. Vehemently disliked, they indeed were the European equivalent of the Chinese.[67]

American workers had genuine cause for concern about those Italians who were exploited by *padroni* industrialists to the detriment of others in the labor force. Italians were not always the first to organize. However, as a class they were not indifferent to labor unity. Furthermore, as they became Americanized and padronism declined, their confidence and the desire to become associated with the unions increased.

When they emigrated, the Italians left a land already familiar with workers' organizations. Trade union activity in Italy had begun among printers in the 1840s, and spread to typographers, hatters, bakers, and construction and woolen textile workers during the sixties and seventies. The organizations that arose were often spontaneous but temporary. They were usually formed during strikes and died afterward, or were mutual-aid bodies that assumed the leadership of strikes in the absence of any other organizations.[68]

Workers' mutual benefit societies became significant in Sicily by the 1860s. The society idea began in the city of Trapani in 1863 and then immediately spread throughout the provinces of southern Italy. By 1870, Sicily had forty-three societies; by January 1, 1895, she had 350, which was second to the 500 in Campania on the mainland.

The appeal of these societies lay in the numerous services they sought to provide in various fields. These included unemployment, health and life insurance and institutions for the economic, and social, cultural, and educational advancement of workers.[69]

Because they were useful, societies were transplanted overseas. In 1908, there were 1,403 societies outside Italy, 394 of which were in the United States. Those in America had 33,462 members, which was clear evidence that Italian immigrants aspired to improve themselves through voluntary associations.[70]

The services offered by these societies often resembled those of American labor organizations, but the reality of bargaining with employers and occasionally taking drastic action against them made union membership a much more consequential experience. At stake were jobs, savings, and the possibility of a return to the homeland. The ability to return usually depended on how much money was set aside for that purpose. As immigrants were aware, a lengthy strike could wipe out the entire amount. Thus, they were reluctant to organize and risk the possibility of loss. On the other hand, the existence of those savings made immigrants more able than natives to endure the loss of wages when they did strike.[71]

Between 1870 and 1900 only a small number of Italians were unionized.[72] Of those who would organize in the succeeding decades, many more would be from the industrial parts of northern Italy than from the agricultural south.[73] Yet, as Edwin Fenton has demonstrated, the key factor in whether Italians, southern *or* northern organized, was bargaining power rather than anything else. Italians could be successfully organized in industries where the nature of the industry was such that they had bargaining power. Where their power was slight, they failed, and "they became devils to unionized workers who soon believed that immigrants could not be organized."[74]

By studying industrial conditions instead of ethnic characteristics the early Italian experience with American unionization begins to make sense. Though almost half of the Italian stone-cutters in America had come from the North, only one of three unions which attempted to organize them, was successful. The International Association of Marble Workers and the Journeymen Stonecutters' Association (Softstones) could not survive in the building materials industry. Unable to prevent the introduction of new machines and substitutes for the materials their skilled members worked on, the organizations folded. On the other hand, the Granite Cutters' International Association, which included craftsmen who inscribed monuments and tombstones and could not be replaced, successfully recruited Italians.[75]

Another example might be found among barbers. In this highly competitive field it was difficult to organize. Between 1886 and 1891 Italians in New York made two attempts in cooperation with members of other nationalities, notably Germans and Jews, to organize the city's barbers. Those efforts failed. Many boss barbers successfully resisted demands for shorter hours, other unionists continued to patronize nonunion barbers, and barbers were apt to ignore union working conditions.[76]

Organized carpenters initially refused to admit Italians to their ranks. Excluded by the Germans and Irish who ran the carpenters' union in New York City in 1880, the Italians established a mutual aid society. However, in 1881, Italians in Brooklyn served as strikebreakers and began developing a reputation in the carpentry industry as cheap laborers who worked long hours. The New York locals of the United Brotherhood of Carpenters and Joiners were thus convinced that the immigration of Italians and others like them should be restricted. Moreover, between 1897 and 1904 the Brotherhood did not attempt to organize Italians, nor did it add a significant number of Italians to its ranks. Of the 255 Italian carpenters in New Jersey in 1900, only a dozen were Brotherhood members.[77]

Italians in other building trades, such as bricklaying and masonry, encountered similar resistance by oldtimers who regarded them as a threat to their standards. However, as Italians were extremely willing to join the unions in the trades, they eventually were admitted despite the hostility of Irish and American workers.[78]

In Buffalo as elsewhere there was considerable interest in

unions among working-class Italians, but native reluctance to admit them kept them out. Unions of skilled craftsmen excluded unskilled immigrants, who in turn avoided such an organization as the Knights of Labor for its advocacy of immigration restrictions. Both Italians and Poles in Buffalo stayed away from the Knights.

Yet tight economic conditions between 1899 and 1912 compelled them to take some kind of positive action. In Buffalo Italian workers went on strike when necessary and moved into or founded unions of their own. During this period, Italian building laborers, longshoremen, shoemakers, tailors, and tile and garment workers acted through such organizations for basically bread-and-butter purposes.[79]

Sometimes when they went on strike, Italian laborers did not even have a union behind them. Especially before 1900, when few were organized, they chose to walk off the job spontaneously to protest uncommonly bad working conditions. These strikes usually occurred on the edges of urban areas, on railroads, and in construction camps. Moreover, most of the walkouts were probably directed against the *padroni* and their system. In October 1880, three hundred Italian laborers demonstrated in Sandwich, Massachusetts, to protest against nonpayment of wages for work in constructing the Cape Cod Canal. Ironically, actions such as this left padronism unaffected and only antagonized Americans residents who did not appreciate having the streets of their town filled with angry immigrants.[80]

In the canneries of New York, Italian women who wished to strike for higher wages found several groups opposed to them. First, they came in conflict with Syrian and Polish workers who did not object to low wages. Second, there were the American workers, who sided with management rather than with the "Eyetalians."[81]

Even in the Colorado mining country, Italians were sometimes the first to strike. In March 1899, members of the Western Federation of Miners went on strike near Lake City, Colorado. Their complaint was a company rule that single male employees had to board at company boardinghouses. The Italians, who made up about forty percent of the miners, rejected the requirement and struck. The American miners, whom the Italians asked to join the strike, stayed on the job. Consequently, the strikers showed up at the mines with rifles and forcibly kept the Americans from working. Six days after the strike began, following the intervention of six companies of soldiers to prevent violence, the mine operators and workers reached an agreement. Company employees could board where they pleased, but Italians had to leave Lake City, and none would be hired in the future.[82]

It seemed to be the fate of Italian immigrant laborers to be unable to overcome their reputation for docility despite their often exceptional strike activity. In coal mining, they followed Irish and American leadership in participating in the anthracite strikes of 1900 and 1902 and a sixteen-month bituminous strike in 1910.[83] On the New York waterfront, six thousand nonunion Italian longshoremen began a six-week strike that probably pulled as many as thirty thousand off the job in 1907.[84]

As mentioned previously, Italians contributed much to the development of unions in the garment industry. There, too, they demonstrated that they were not docile. For example, though Italians constituted less than a quarter of the forty thousand who struck Chicago's Hart, Schaffner and Marx garment factory in 1910 and 1911, their role was crucial in bringing it about. An Italian local of the United Garment Workers, formed just prior to the walkout, was instrumental in starting the action and then in keeping its members on the picket lines. "Sciopero-Sciopero" ("Strike–Strike") Italian women shouted on September 22, 1910, as they quit their worktables and began the strike which ended twenty weeks later.[85]

Only 6,693 of the 85,892 people who lived in the textile city of Lawrence, Massachusetts, in 1910 had been born in Italy.[86] Yet when a general strike including as many as twenty-three thousand workers crippled the woolen and cotton mills in 1912, Italians were prominent. Protesting a pay cut that accompanied a reduction in the work week for women and children from fifty-six to fifty-four hours, the already low-paid and largely unskilled strikers stayed out for fifty-seven working days.[87]

They struck against an industry that was notorious for low wages. In December 1911, the most a worker could earn per week was $8.76, which amounted to an average annual income of only four hundred dollars for family heads. Women and children, who constituted the majority of the work force, received considerably less than that average, as did unskilled mill hands, who earned about six dollars a week. When times were bad in this seasonal industry, the wage level dropped even lower.

The adult male worker's only source of economic or social security came from the labor of his wife and children. Though some parents sneaked children into the mills before their fourteenth birthday, at that age youngsters usually left school for a 6:45 A.M. to 5:30 P.M. workday regardless of their ability to do well at school.

Packed into cheaply constructed wooden tenements, the undernourished and underclad immigrant families suffered the consequences of great population density. Fire, filth, and vermin were common, and the infant mortality rate was extremely high, as much as 172 per thousand in 1909. Respiratory ailments, such as tuberculosis and pneumonia, shortened the lives of the adults, who had difficulty reaching the age of forty.[88]

Though Poles, along with Italians, were ardent strikers,[89] the latter "were the backbone of the strike and provided part of its local leadership." When the walkout began, they rampaged through the factories, destroying machinery. "We are going to fight them for more bread; we are going to get a pair of shoes for our barefoot children; we are going to get another set of underwear for them," said one striker. Later, when the strike was two weeks old, Italians pelted passing trolley cars with pieces of ice.[90]

Italians were in the front ranks of those who provided relief for fellow strikers. They ran four relief distribution stations and two soup kitchens. One station alone gave food to more than a thousand families. Besides the Italians, the Syrian, Polish, Armenian, and Franco-Belgian strikers each maintained a soup kitchen. The Franco-Belgians served those nationalities not fed by the others, about 1,300 persons twice a day. The Italians helped over 600 on the same basis.[91]

Before the strike, the Industrial Workers of the World had about a thousand members in Lawrence, including three hundred who belonged to an Italian branch.[92] That local, prodded by the nineteen-year-old Angelo Rocco, invited the experienced "Wobbly," Joseph Ettor, to Lawrence to help organize the workers and protest their low wages. Ettor arrived during the evening of Saturday, January 13, a day after the work stoppage began.[93]

The twenty-six-year-old Ettor was a veteran of several labor conflicts. A son of Italian immigrants, he was born in Brooklyn and raised in Chicago. Influenced in his radical point of view by his father, he left his trade as iron worker to organize for the Wobblies. From 1905 to 1908 he was an effective and popular agitator on the West Coast. In 1909 he was back in the East for the McKees Rocks, Pennsylvania steel strike, where he addressed the workers in five different languages. Shifting afterward to Brooklyn, Ettor then led striking Italian shoemakers. Finally, he moved on to Lawrence.

On his arrival at the textile city, Ettor formed a strike committee. The strikers did not call for a closed shop or even union recognition, but they did demand a fifteen percent wage increase on the basis of the new, fifty-four hour week, and double the regular rate for overtime.[94]

In stirring the strikers, Ettor had the assistance of several able agitators, including I.W.W. founder William D. "Big Bill" Haywood and editor Arturo Giovannitti. Haywood arrived in Lawrence on January 24, and received a tumultuous welcome at the railroad station. Giovannitti had come to town with his friend, Joseph Ettor.

Born in Italy, Giovannitti had emigrated to the United States in 1900 when he was sixteen years of age. He rejected an affluent family in the Old World for America, where he discovered Marxism, from which it was a short step to syndicalism and then to revolutionary action. He advocated the latter in the Italian paper, *Il Proletario*. Giovannitti was in New York when the Lawrence strike began. On receiving a wire for assistance from the Wobblies of Lawrence, he joined them.[95]

Thus, both Ettor and Giovannitti were at the strike scene. However, within a few weeks of their arrival they and Angelo Rocco were in jail. Rocco was held for a short while on a riot charge, but Ettor and Giovannitti had to stand trial for the murder of a woman by a person unknown. Annie LoPezzi, a bystander at a strikers' parade broken up by police and militia, had been killed by a stray bullet possibly fired by a policeman, Oscar Benoit.

Despite eyewitness evidence against the officer, the two Italians, who had not been present when the shooting occurred, were indicted for incitement to murder by their violent rhetoric. It did not break the strike, nor did it result in convictions.[96]

By March 1912, the strike was finally won, despite intervention by the American Federation of Labor against the leadership of its hated rival, the I.W.W. The workers won wage increases ranging from five to twent-two percent. Moreover, the victory served as a signal for similar demands elsewhere in the industry. "By April 1, about 275,000 textile workers of New England had received wage increases as an indirect result of the Lawrence strike."[97]

By their willingness to strike and organize, the Italian immigrant laborers demonstrated that they were as interested as anyone else in achieving a decent standard of living. They did not win all their battles. Their defeats included, most notably, a disastrous I.W.W.-led strike of the Paterson, New Jersey, silk mills in 1913.[98] But they did disprove the contention that they were mere "*padrone* slaves" whose primary function in the labor market was to break strikes and depress wages.

CHAPTER 9

New Barriers

T HE first steps Congress took to reduce immigration stemmed the flow of Chinese, but these efforts were ineffective against Europeans and other Asians. As the latter continued to arrive, in increasing numbers, organized labor sounded new alarms. To overcome what they regarded as defects in the initial legislation, the unionists urged the exclusion of illiterates and non-Chinese Asians, the Japanese in particular.

Before the 1890s, labor's policy on immigration carefully distinguished between those Europeans who came "voluntarily" and those who were allegedly "induced" to come by unscrupulous employers or steamship companies. The concept of America as a land of opportunity for diverse peoples thus remained valid. With it in mind, unionists who remembered their own transatlantic origins were not yet prepared to bar the great mass of daily arriving Eastern and Southern Europeans.

However, as this influx intensified and the weakness of the restrictions in effect became obvious, American workers began to change their minds. Old World memories and connections and international working-class ideals gave way to economic self-interest tinged with racism. Immigration came to be viewed as a major problem; the time had come to halt the flow.[1]

Samuel Gompers had little in common with Henry Cabot Lodge. On most issues he usually disagreed with the patrician intellectual congressman from Massachusetts. Immigration restriction was the one exception.[2]

In January 1891, Lodge offered the view that the American labor market was "overstocked in many places," which meant "a tendency toward a decline in wages." In America, where everyone voted and people ran the government, Lodge suggested, such a direction was "perilous both socially and politically.[3]

145

Sounding much like Lodge, President Gompers called the immigration question to the attention of the 1891 convention of the American Federation of Labor. "Today," he said, "there is not an industry which is not over-crowded with working people who vainly plead for an opportunity to work." Immigrants were being "dumped" on American shores, he continued, by "societies formed for that purpose," wily shipping companies, and "great corporations" that violated the Alien Contract Labor Law. Finally, Gompers asked the convention delegates to "declare that we will have relief from this pressing evil."[4]

Gompers's concern in 1891, he later wrote, was that the steel industry was then importing cheap labor to create "a surplus of workers to replace those who became Americanized."[5] Closer to home, his own industry, cigarmaking, was experiencing an influx of Russian Jews whose coming upset other Jews already in the trade. In any event, Gompers was ahead of the convention, which did not agree that additional immigration restriction was necessary.[6]

The endorsements by Lodge and Gompers clearly advanced the course of restriction. So, too, did the lynching of the eleven Italians in New Orleans in 1891. The Italian government protested those murders so vehemently that many Americans thought that war with Italy was imminent. As an incident involving the foreign born, only the Haymarket affair of 1886 stimulated greater restrictionist feeling.[7]

Nonetheless, through 1892 and into the following year the A.F. of L. took no action on immigration. Some business-minded observers applauded that inaction. Industrialist and economist Edward Atkinson, for example, contended that those who wanted restriction sought "to create a trade-union *class*" by monopolizing the labor market. Writer George Parker also saw restriction as attempted monopoly, in addition to being an outgrowth of the anti-Chinese movement on the Pacific Coast.

On the other hand, some thoughtful people supported the case for restriction. Lawyer Sydney Fisher agreed with Parker that restriction was labor's equivalent to industry's protective tariff, but he saw nothing wrong with it. "If we protect ourselves against refined sugar, wool, shot-guns, and works of art, why not against human products which degrade the morals of the country and drive its native owners from profitable callings by under-bidding them in wages?"[8]

In 1892, Henry Cabot Lodge introduced a literary test bill in the House of Representatives. His purpose was to keep America's gates open to those immigrants only whom he considered an advantage to the country. He would exclude those he regarded as potentially harmful or only minimally beneficial.[9]

Though Gompers agreed with Lodge, he had some suggestions of his own. In January 1893, he thought an outbreak of cholera in Europe might be a good pretext to demand a year's "suspension of immigration."[10] An alternate proposition of his was to empower the president of the United States "to suspend immigration at any time when the needs of the country demanded it."[11]

Neither Lodge nor Gompers made much headway with their proposals until the middle of 1893, when the United States once again plunged into a major economic depression. Following the lead of the Massachusetts Republican, Gompers asked that illiterates be kept from the country. With unemployment now a serious problem, and labor seemingly at the mercy of capital, union sentiment shifted in the direction of restriction.[12]

In turning against the foreign born at this time, American workers reflected a more widespread change in public opinion. Elements of the working class were not the only ones who had become hostile. From May through October 1893, a series in *The Century* magazine was strongly anti-immigrant. Among other things, the articles accused the foreign born of causing serious social dislocation. "All the trade-unions of the country are controlled by foreigners, who comprise the great majority of their members." These unions allegedly refused to admit Americans.[13] Furthermore, they refused to support the apprentice system.[14] The foreigners in control were determined "to exclude American youths from American trades."[15] When they became angry, they turned to violence, as the Haymarket and Homestead affairs demonstrated.[16] Finally, the unemployed Americans were becoming criminals as a result of the "enforced idleness."[17]

The fear of violence and disorder explains why businessmen advocated a literacy test. With the deepening of the depression, business groups increasingly believed that the desperation of hungry and idle foreigners would result in crime and social conflict. Thus the National Board of Trade, the American Iron and Steel Association, and numerous other business groups felt the need to restrict the number of foreigners.[18] To provide able leadership for those Americans who wished to save their civilization through restriction, several old family Bostonians took action. In early 1894, three members of Harvard's class of 1889, Prescott Farnsworth Hall, Robert De Courcy Ward, and Charles Warren, with some of their classmates, founded the Immigration Restriction League of Boston.[19]

With unemployment continuing, and immigration regarded as a menace to the jobs of Americans,[20] some states legislated against the newcomers. New York and Pennsylvania outlawed the employment of aliens on local and state public works. Idaho said that the only aliens mining corporations could hire were those who had declared that they intended to become naturalized.[21]

Yet Gompers, aware of the continuing resistance to restriction among many in the A.F. of L., proceeded cautiously. Through 1893 he was intent on achieving improved enforcement of the Alien Contract Labor Law. Toward that end he alerted immigration commissioners at Ellis Island, New York, of possible violations, and appealed to David B. Hill of New York, chairman of the United States Senate Committee on Immigration, for amendments to make "violations . . . more difficult and convictions more easy."[22] In his presidential reports of December 1893 and 1894, Gompers stressed his struggle against contract labor.[23]

Under Gompers's editorship, the A.F. of L.'s new monthly, the *American Federationist*, made the case for restriction. "The supreme call of the present hour is an immediate closing of our ports against any and all immigration," said one writer, until all presently unemployed American workers were taken care of.[24] Yet as that request was made, another article in the same number of the magazine revealed relatively little restrictionist sentiment among unionists. Sixty-five labor organizations responded to a circular which asked them to state the issues that concerned their members. Only six responses cited immigration.[25]

The lack of rank and file pressure for restriction continued through the 1896 annual convention. As the Federation's presi-

dent in 1895, John McBride, told that year's convention, his
organization could recommend further restriction as well as
assist federal officials in enforcing the contract labor ban.[26]
In the *American Federationist,* immigration commissioner Edward
McSweeney echoed that theme. Again president in 1896, Gompers
resumed his quest for restrictive measures. In October, he advised the secretary of the Italian labor organization, *Camera Del
Lavoro,* that immigrants from his country were used by capital
to "menace" American workers, and that the A.F. of L. would
shortly move in a restrictionist direction.[27]

Despite Gompers's intentions and warning to the Italians, the
1896 convention refused to recommend further restriction. The
Federation's Special Committee on Immigration endorsed the
Lodge-Corliss literacy test bill then before Congress, but the
convention would not follow suit. Among the many opponents
of the bill was John McBride of the Mine Workers, who would
not blame the nation's industrial depression and unemployment
on immigration. However, rather than drop the immigration
question altogether, the convention referred it to the A.F. of L.'s
1897 meeting in Nashville.[28]

As Grover Cleveland's second presidential administration came
to an end, the Lodge-Corliss bill passed Congress. Though not
endorsed by the A. F. of L., the literacy test did win the backing
of the Knights of Labor and many newspapers, Protestant organizations, and social workers. The North German Lloyd Steamship
Company, which maintained a lucrative immigrant transport
business, strongly opposed it. In late February 1897, Cleveland
vetoed the bill, contending that literacy was not a good test of
citizenship.[29]

In their efforts of 1894 and 1896, the restrictionist leaders of
the A.F. of L. could not convince their membership that labor's
problems came from immigration. Internationalist and foreign-
born workers preferred instead to blame capitalists and not
attack immigrant members of the working-class. Boston's Central
Labor Union even regarded restriction as similar in principle to
the Fugitive Slave Laws.[30]

On the other hand, by 1897 attitudes did change sufficiently
for the Federation to recommend adoption of the literary test.
The *American Federationist* began the year with a forecast that

passage would reduce immigration from Austria-Hungary, Italy, Poland, and Russia "over 40 per cent."[31] In preparation for the Nashville convention, the Executive Council of the A.F. of L. issued a circular to determine the sentiment of its affiliated unions on the issue.[32] Then the New York State Federation of Labor, which represented some 98,000 unionists, recommended an immediate five-year suspension of immigration.[33] Finally, the Knights of Labor repeated their endorsement of the Lodge-Corliss Bill.[34]

In December, Gompers had his way. Backed by the heads of several large unions, including John Mitchell of the Mineworkers, P. J. McGuire of the Carpenters, James Duncan of the Granite Cutters, George Perkins of the Cigarmakers, and M. M. Garland of the Iron and Steel Workers, a literacy test resolution passed by a five-to-one majority. From the very outset of the convention, Gompers had his forces mobilized, and demanded an unequivocal stand for restriction. The opposition, represented by delegates from the Brewery Workers, Boot and Shoe Workers, and Woodworkers and Mineworkers (John McBride), was easily outmaneuvered. Thus, the A. F. of L. officially took its stand on the side or restriction.[35]

With the Federation officially committed to the literacy test, restrictionists received encouragement in their bid to have it become law. Gompers and others in the labor movement could devote even more energy than before to persuading Congress and public opinion. However, while pursuing the "educational test," which many proponents called it, they remained alert to any other alien threats to American workers.

Within a month of the Nashville convention, Gompers was already discussing strategy with the Immigration Restriction League. The Boston organization, which appointed itself leader of the literacy test movement, actually prodded the Federation into taking action. Accordingly, the unionists sent a circular letter to the members of Congress on the subject of restriction.[36] In addition, individual unions sent their petitions. Congress received more than five thousand petitions in 1901–1902, a good proportion coming from labor groups. Among those demanding restriction were the Glass Blowers', Iron Ship Builders', Boiler

Makers', Wood Carvers', Carpenters and Joiners', Granite Cutters', and Electrical Workers' unions.[37]

Those petitions, too, did not arise spontaneously. Charles E. Edgerton, an assistant secretary of the Immigration Restriction League, based in Washington, had communicated "with all local labor unions of the United States" for the purpose of stirring them up.[38]

Yet they did not succeed in pushing an educational test bill through Congress. Following Cleveland's veto, it was indeed difficult for much legislation to be passed. In February 1897, the House of Representatives, but not the Senate, voted to override the rejection. The bill was then reintroduced in the next session of Congress, but this time it passed the Senate and was not even voted on in the House. Two years later neither house took a vote on a new bill. By 1903, when an educational test appeared about to pass, it was withdrawn from the bill in which it was incorporated in order to save the general measure.[39] In November, Gompers explained to his convention and assured his membership that another attempt to enact the test would now be made.[40] The convention then went "on record as opposed to the wholesale immigration of foreign labor" and in favor of a test "to protect American labor."[41]

Though it lacked the ban on illiterate entrants, the immigration law enacted in March 1903, was nonetheless significant. Its primary targets were radicals, especially anarchists, one of whom had assassinated President William McKinley in 1901. Passed in an antiradical climate and signed by McKinley's nativist successor, Theodore Roosevelt, it denied entry to anarchists. Moreover, it permitted the deportation of aliens three years after their arrival if they were found to be anarchists. The existing head tax on all immigrants was doubled. This law "was the first serious effort to restrict immigrants because of their beliefs and associations."[42]

Nonetheless, the supposedly simple, single-shot solution to the problem of immigrant labor was not yet at hand. Unlike the nineties, American society after 1900 was more buoyant than hesitant. The Spanish-American War had helped to restore national self-confidence and had left the nation with an empire.

In addition, prosperity had returned. With this revival, Americans did not suddenly become sympathetic to foreigners; neither did they feel an urgent need to restrict them en masse.

Yet what kept the literacy test from becoming law was less the subsiding of nativism than the emerging opposition to it. The National Association of Manufacturers, expressing the business viewpoint, maintained a continuous lobbying effort in Washington. Even more effective than business in blocking restriction were the immigrants themselves, especially the Russian Jews. All immigrant groups opposed the literacy test, including older ones which were represented by such organizations as the Ancient Order of Hibernians and the German-American Alliance.

Finally, as the immigrants became naturalized they turned to the ballot for protection. Previously the newcomers had tended to associate themselves with the Democratic party, which had permitted the Republican party to be used for nativist purposes. However, around 1900, political patterns began to change. Jews, Slavs, and Italians discovered the Republicans and voted for them. With this new constituency, the Grand Old party muted its nativism. Though endorsed by the Republican national platform in 1896, the literacy test was omitted in 1904. In 1906, Republican Joe Cannon, speaker of the House of Representatives, would fight successfully to keep it from passing Congress.[43]

As it became hotter, the debate on immigration restrictions extended to the halls of the National Civic Federation. Designed to promote cooperation between business and labor in the public interest, this organization provided a forum for the divergent opinions on immigration among its members. On December 6, 1905, banker August Belmont, its president, convened the National Conference on Immigration at New York's Madison Square Garden before 517 assembled delegates.

Belmont asked the delegates to decide whether the federal restrictions thus far imposed on the "human refuse" from Europe went "far enough." First Vice-President Samuel Gompers spoke next, representing labor. "No man in this country," Gompers said, "can attempt to assume an indifference toward this question of immigration." Then he proceeded to condemn "cheap" Chinese labor and demand a general reduction in immigration.[44]

Gompers was not alone. "To get the right kind [of immigrants]," U.S. Commissioner General of Immigration Frank P. Sargent said, "you must make laws that will prevent the other kind [from] coming." In support of his superior, Immigration Commissioner Robert Watchorn demanded the exclusion of "people with weak minds," who were imbecile and whose physical frames were "so depleted and deteriorated" that there was "no hope of recovery."[45]

"I don't own any skyscrapers or big factories, . . . and I'm not the President of a college," said Jesse Taylor, a bank employee from Jamestown, Ohio. "But," he continued, "as one of the plain people of Ohio, I tell you that we don't want the worms and riff-raff from Southern Europe you people have been sending out to us."

Taylor's remarks drew immediate hisses, which were then over-whelmed by cheers. Then, addressing himself to the businessmen present, he warned that unless the American workmen were protected "from alien competition" they would cause trouble.

Several speakers defended the immigrant and attacked his critics. Professor Morris Loeb of New York University likened the Immigration Restriction League to those who drove the Quakers from New England and Anne Hutchinson and Roger Williams from Massachusetts Bay. Archbishop John Ireland of St. Paul insisted that immigrants had made America the world's greatest nation. Scottish-born industrialist Andrew Carnegie asked, "who is there among us who is not either an immigrant himself or has immigrant blood in his veins?" He observed that immigration was not a problem for America, but was one "for the poor, unfortunate countries from which we are draining the best blood."[46]

The American Federation of Labor rejected those views, and included restriction in the political program it formulated the next spring. Coauthored by Gompers and Andrew Furuseth of the Sailors' Union, "Labor's Bill of Grievances" demanded, among other things, protection against labor injunctions and an eight-hour work day.[47] An immigration bill acceptable to Gompers did soon afterward get through the Senate, but, as mentioned above, was killed by Joe Cannon in the House.[48]

In February 1907, the restrictionists again settled for a partial victory. Congress approved a bill without a literacy test, but with the head tax doubled to four dollars, additional classes of persons excluded for mental, physical or economic reasons, a new Division of Information, and a Joint Immigration Commission to investigate the immigration question. Another provision, which would soon be applied to Japanese immigration, empowered the president to negotiate international agreements on regulation, subject to senatorial approval.[49]

The Immigration Commission created by the act was chaired by Senator William Dillingham of Vermont. Terence V. Powderly became chief of the Division of Information of the Bureau of Immigration and Naturalization. With the formation of this division, Congress at last established an agency to improve the regulation and distribution of immigration. Gompers was hopeful that Powderly would bring the "right spirit" to his division, but he was dismayed over the composition of the study commission. Of the nine members, six came from Congress and three were presidential appointees. What bothered Gompers was that none of the latter were drawn from the ranks of organized labor.[50] Three years later, when the commission would issue its forty-one-volume report, he would have little cause for complaint.

On the other hand, he did have reason for being upset over the literacy test, which had become a perennial loser in Congress. The A. F. of L. kept up its pressure, but with no apparent success.[51] Frustrated at the lack of progress, Gompers lashed out at the friends of the immigrant. In July 1911, he publicly identified them, including the National Liberal Immigration League, the National American Federation for the Promotion of Sane and Liberal Immigration Laws, the Young Women's Christian Association, and the Jewish Agricultural and Industrial Society. The various philanthropic societies, Gompers said, aimed to put "the immigrant next against the American workingman with whom he is to compete." The groups worked with the Division of Information and the Bureau of Labor of the Agriculture Department to distribute the newcomers geographically. However, they allegedly conducted those efforts and promoted immigration "regardless of the effect on American labor." Their activities, if unchecked, would reduce American working conditions "to the European level" or substitute the poverty-stricken, dependent immigrant for the independent American in the workplace.[52]

Ever mindful of its enemies, organized labor kept one individual from an appointment to the United States Supreme Court. In 1912, President William Howard Taft considered filling a vacancy on the court with Secretary of Commerce Charles Nagel, an opponent of the literacy test. However, when unions protested that Nagel was a liberal enforcer of the immigration laws, Taft dropped the idea.[53]

Supported by the Immigration Commission's strongly restrictionist report of 1910, which endorsed the literacy test as eminently feasible,[54] Congress passed the Dillingham-Burnett Bill in early 1913. Though it went through with ease, President Taft decided to hold hearings before he would sign. A.F. of L. Secretary Frank Morrison and the Federation's Legislative Committee thereupon met with Taft and argued for restriction and regulation. Soon afterward, Gompers participated in another conference. This one included the president, William Williams, the restrictionist commissioner of immigration at Ellis Island, and William Bennett, a former congressman from New York and Immigration Commission member opposed to restriction. The conferees made their respective appeals to Taft, with Gompers and Bennett lapsing into a heated exchange between one another. As the gathering ended, Gompers felt he had won the day.

He was wrong. On February 14 Taft vetoed the bill. Though he admitted that the measure had some good points, he denied that the literacy test would exclude undesirables. Instead, Taft said, it would bar the "bone and sinew" of the migrating peoples. The Senate then overrode the veto, but the House did not, and the bill died.[55]

Less than two years after Taft's veto President Woodrow Wilson faced a similar situation. In January 1915, a revised Burnett Bill was before him for his approval. Like his predecessor, Wilson called a White House conference on the matter, and, like Taft, afterward rejected the bill because of its literacy test provision. In the view of the United Garment Workers of America, whose Jewish immigrant members had only a month before broken away and formed the rival Amalgamated Clothing Workers of America, this veto was "a grave mistake."[56]

In demanding restriction, the Garment Workers accomplished two things. First, they made war on the immigrant elements that

threatened their own existence, and, secondly, they demonstrated loyalty to the A.F. of L. leadership. As discussed earlier,
Gompers gave them his support.[57]

As the friend of the Amalgamated Clothing Workers, which
the Federation regarded as a traitorous organization, the International Ladies' Garment Workers' Union was in a delicate position. Since the International's founding in 1900, Samuel Gompers
had helped it in many ways. In 1903, for example, he assisted
in organizing corset makers in the Midwest, and, as late as 1914,
he addressed strike rallies in Philadelphia. Appreciative of such
assistance and respectful of the Federation's power, the International's leadership refused to allow ideological differences
to spoil good relations. However, relations with the Federation
also involved complete exclusion from its governing bodies, a
product of racial and religious prejudice as well as fears of radicalism, which would last until 1935.[58]

With such considerations in mind, President Benjamin Schlesinger of the I.L.G.W.U. attempted to harmonize the differences
between the Garment Workers and the immigrant "secessionists." Yet as the International worked to restore peace to the
men's garment industry, it also spoke out on the immigration
question. As a matter of conscience, it could not be silent on
that issue.

In November 1915, at the A.F. of L's San Francisco convention, I.L.G.W.U. delegates tackled both questions. They failed
to end the garment warfare, or to prevent another endorsement
of the literacy test, but they did secure regulations urging European nations and workers "to cease the discriminations now
practiced against the Jewish people.[59]

In an appearance before the House Immigration Committee
in January 1916, socialist congressman Meyer London eloquent-
ly represented the Jewish garment workers on the literacy test.
London, a revered leader of the Jewish labor movement, declared
that organized labor was now "on the wrong track." Instead of
pointing to the immigrant, he suggested, unions should advocate unemployment insurance, abolish child labor in factories,
and make "impossible the competition of millions of women with
men." "Every human being," he further declared, "has a right

to go to any part of the civilized world." God never decreed that any place was reserved for any particular person.[60]

Representative John L. Burnett of Alabama thought otherwise, and once again sent a literacy test bill through Congress. James Lord, president of the A.F. of L's mining department, sent a circular to all senators and representatives urging their votes for it. Lord accused employers of being "utterly selfish and un-American" in opposing restrictions, and asked for congressional approval "in the name of Americanism, justice, and common decency and honesty."[61] Any employer who exploited immigrant labor, the *Garment Worker* advised, should "be considered an enemy of his country and a traitor to its best interests."[62]

In 1916, with the European war threatening to compel the participation of the United States, many Americans found themselves thinking about military preparedness and patriotism. Moreover, a National Americanization Committee was seeking organized labor's support for its movement to Americanize the immigrant through education, parades, and other methods.[63] Thus, it became more fashionable at this time to introduce patriotic arguments in addition to economics, social, and racial pleas for restriction. In supporting the anti-immigrant effort, the *Garment Worker* declared, the trade unionist showed "a patriotic devotion to his country in upholding American ideals."[64]

On March 24, 1916, Congressman Meyer London, in a House speech, identified the three main sources of opposition to immigration. First he cited "the chauvinist element, which fears contamination from foreign stock." Then he called attention to "the representatives of those states," mainly in the South, "where children are exploited, where industry is undeveloped, where agriculture is in a primitive state, and where there is a particularly submissive class of labor." Finally, there was organized labor, which was permitting "itself to play into the hands of the unreasoning chauvinists and of the most reactionary labor-hating element, in the vain hope that labor will improve its condition by limiting the working population of the United States through restrictive immigration."[65]

Six days later the Burnett Bill won overwhelming House approval. In the summer, President Wilson applied political pressure to block Senate passage.[66]

Meeting in Philadelphia in October, the I.L.G.W.U. came out against the bill. In particular, the International objected to a Senate amendment barring political refugees if their offenses were classified as felonious. In other words, America's traditional role as a place of political asylum would end.[67] In November, at the A.F. of L's Baltimore convention, the International's five delegates restated their union's position and voted against restriction. However, of the 394 delegates present, only twenty-two others joined them in championing the cause of the immigrant.[68]

A revised Burnett Bill cleared the Senate on December 14, then went to a conference committee, and, on January 16, 1917, was on its way to President Wilson. Feeling honor-bound to respect pledges he had made to representatives of foreign nationality groups in 1912, Wilson responded with a second veto. The literacy test, he explained was "not a test of character, of quality, or of personal fitness." It would mainly serve to penalize aliens who came from lands of little opportunity. "Tests of quality and of purpose cannot be objected to on principle, but tests of opportunity surely may be." In addition, Wilson objected to a clause allowing the entry of illiterate victims of religious persecution. Inserted in consequence of remarks Wilson had made in rejecting the first Burnett Bill, this provision appeared to him to be a source of potential diplomatic embarrassment.

Unimpressive and unconvincing, Wilson's objections could not sustain his veto. In February, a nonpartisan House overrode it by 287 to 106, and the Senate by sixty-two to nineteen.[69]

The act of February 5, 1917, repealed the immigration laws of 1903 and 1907, raised the head tax to eight dollars, and excluded a total of thirty-three classes of immigrants. Among those barred were idiots, psychopaths, paupers, vagrants, polygamists, anarchists, prostitutes, contract laborers, and, of course, illiterates. The law defined the latter as including "all aliens over sixteen years of age, physically capable of reading, who can not read the English language, or some other language or dialect, including Hebrew or Yiddish." However, a legally admitted alien or United States citizen could "bring in or send for his father or grandfather over fifty-five years of age, his wife, his mother, his grandmother, or his unmarried or widowed daughter, if otherwise inadmissible," whether or not that person was able to read.

The test consisted of "not less than thirty nor more than forty words in ordinary use" in a language or dialect of the immigrant's choice.

Besides the illiterate relatives, the law specifically exempted certain other immigrants from the literacy requirement. Refugees from religious persecution and purely political offenders, whether convicted or not, were in that category.

Comprehensive in scope, this act created a "barred zone" in the Pacific which excluded almost all Asians not already kept out by existing statutes or international agreements. However, it did not bar the Japanese, whose immigration had been limited by "Gentlemen's Agreement" between the United States and their government.[70]

Despite its omission of the Japanese and its exemptions and loopholes, this law's passage pleased Samuel Gompers. In November 1917, the A.F. of L's executive council happily announced that the Federation's "long and persistent struggle . . . to secure the enactment of an immigration law containing the literacy test" had come to an end. The convention then adopted a report which declared that the new law would "check, if not totally stop, the flow of undesirable immigration."[71]

CHAPTER 10

Immigration from Asia

THE Chinese Exclusion Act of 1902, followed two years later by the termination of the Chinese treaty of 1894, marked the successful conclusion of one phase of organized labor's campaign against Asian immigration. This drive introduced racial concepts and fears into the essentially economic argument against foreign competition, laying a foundation for movements against Europeans as well as other Asians. In the case of Europeans, labor critics compared their styles of living and working with the Chinese and judged their threat to be *similar* to that of the Asians. Regarding immigrants from Japan and Korea, who were in many ways different from the Chinese, opponents often ignored distinctions and considered them part of the same threat to America's economy and civilization. On that basis the American Federation of Labor then demanded Japanese and Korean exclusion.

Ever vigilant and mindful of the intense feelings and unusual unity on the Chinese issue, Gompers and others were reluctant to let it die. They insisted on the strict enforcement of the exclusion law, condemned any move to repeal it, and, when new situations arose, urged that its principle be extended.

The belligerent stance had to be maintained. Asked in June 1904, whether to organize the workers in a Chinese restaurant, Gompers replied negatively, saying that such a step "would be unwise and impracticable." It would be the height of inconsistency for a movement to unionize the Chinese against whom we have declared. . . . You cannot organize the Chinese in one place and deny them membership in another place."[1]

In December 1905, as on many other occasions, Gompers explained his objection to Chinese immigration. "I am opposed to the Chinaman . . . because his ideals, his civilization are absolutely in antagonism to the ideals and civilization of America." Historically, "the Chinaman has dominated, or he has been driven out by force. The Chinaman is a cheap man."[2] Following Gompers's lead, James O'Connell, president of the International Association of Machinists, told the National Civic Federation's Immigration Department meeting the following September that the countries to which Chinese "emigrate very rapidly do not assimilate them, but they become Chinaized."[3]

The A.F. of L. certainly did not want that situation to occur in Panama. On November 3, 1903, a revolution assisted by President Theodore Roosevelt made the province of Panama independent of Colombia. Three days later the United States recognized the Republic of Panama, with whom it immediately negotiated the Hay-Bunau-Varilla Treaty. By that document, Americans secured what they had urgently sought, the right to construct a canal across the Isthmus of Panama connecting the Atlantic and Pacific oceans.

Before the treaty was signed, the A.F. of L.'s annual convention wondered what kind of labor would construct the waterway. Rather than have the work done by Italian immigrants, whom the unionists believed especially suited for it, the convention resolved that it be reserved for American citizens.[4]

John Stevens, the project's chief engineer, and his associates never gave serious consideration to the idea of building the canal with American labor. The truth was that they were uninterested in Italian immigrant labor, and that unskilled whites were themselves unwilling to work in Panama. Moreover, even American labor leaders were opposed; they did not want their people sent to a "deathtrap." When inspectors from Japan came to see whether Japanese labor should be sent, they reported that the Isthmus was too dangerous for their men.[5]

On the other hand, Stevens wanted Chinese labor. From his own background in railroad building with James J. Hill in the American West, Stevens had gained a favorable impression of the Chinese. Consequently, he sought to employ as many as fifteen thousand as quickly as possible, and invited bids for contracts to supply them. To permit their employment, David J. Foster of Vermont introduced a bill in the House of Representatives.

Alerted to this attempt to circumvent the principle of Chinese exclusion, Gompers vigorously opposed it, and the bill remained in committee. Panamanians, who were themselves distressed over successful Chinese merchants descended from earlier laborers, did enact a law to exclude additional Chinese. Finally, the Chinese government shared the Japanese view that Panama was an unsafe place for laborers. Thus, Stevens's plan failed. Though the Chinese were kept out, in 1914, when the Panama Canal opened for traffic, it reflected the labor of workers from ninety-seven countries. Almost all the unskilled workers were black, mainly from Barbados.[6]

The Chinese question remained an A.F. of L. obsession throughout World War I. In 1918 and again in 1922, Federation conventions approved the leadership's efforts to bar Chinese coolie labor.[7] By then, however, the Asians who were most bothersome to American workers were those from Japan rather than China. They, too, would have to be excluded.

As the anti-Chinese movement peaked and declined, along with Chinese immigration to the United States, agitation arose against the Japanese. Aimed now at checking the flow from Japan, the new movement much resembled the old. Once again organized labor played a prominent role.

Before 1853, when Commodore Matthew C. Perry's black ships sailed into Edo Bay, Japan had been virtually sealed against contact with the West. Perry's Japan Expedition not only broke that seal, but also led to a commerce treaty in 1858 between the United States and the Asian nation.[8] Though relations were thus established, few Japanese came to America until after 1885, when the government legalized emigration.[9]

In 1880, only 148 Japanese were in the country, but in the nineties the annual flow exceeded a thousand, reaching twelve thousand by 1898. Even with the increase, in 1900 the total Japanese population was only 24,326, 41.7 percent of whom resided in California. As late as 1930, when there were nearly 139,000 of Japanese birth or ancestry in America, they amounted to only .021 and .001 percent of the populations of California and the continental United States, respectively. Numerically, at least, these people did not constitute much of a menace to American civilization.[10]

The Japanese came for three reasons. First, many left poverty-stricken provinces and wages of fourteen cents a day for a land where stories told of wages as high as two dollars a day. Second, Japanese and other low-price laborers were wanted by California farmers to end the labor scarcity caused by the Chinese exclusion legislation. Finally, the Japanese government required subjects who emigrated to return after three years, with that return guaranteed by a responsible individual or agency at home. To provide the guarantees and necessary financing, which only the rare laborer could afford, emigration societies arose. These companies, with agents in Canada and the United States, greatly stimulated emigration. Between 1899 and 1903, nearly 85,000 emigrants left Japan for foreign places besides Korea and China; eight of every ten went to the United States.[11]

Yet as early as 1887 there was evidence in America that the anti-Chinese feeling also included the Japanese. Though "no more than 400 Japanese" were in California at the time, a politically ambitious San Francisco physician named O'Donnell sought unsuccessfully to exploit their presence by crying, "The Japs must go."[12] A year later the *Coast Seamen's Journal*, which spoke for the San-Francisco Trades Council, complained that American ships had Japanese crewmen.[13] In 1890, San Francisco unionists physically attacked fifteen Japanese cobblers who were secretly working in a shop apart from their employer's white employees.[14]

These incidents and others were of little consequence, even when involving the demagogue of former times, Dennis Kearney. In May 1892, he awoke to the Japanese "menace," which he attributed to their importation by "absentee money-lenders." Kearney insisted that the Japanese, like the Chinese before them, had to go, but neither he nor the alarmist *San Francisco Call* could rally much support for such a crusade.[15]

In March 1900, a case of bubonic plague helped change the public's mood. Following the discovery that a resident of San Francisco's Chinatown had contracted the plague, the city's officials imposed a quarantine on the Asiatic sections of the city. Mayor James Duval Phelan, who had been campaigning against the Japanese since 1896, then further exacerbated the situation by making derogatory statements about the Chinese and Japanese. Pressure from local business leaders, who feared the widely publicized plague scare would hurt the economy, compelled Phelan to back down somewhat. Nonetheless, the anti-Japanese movement gained considerable momentum.

In May, Phelan's leadership was again noticeable as he organized a huge anti-Japanese rally in San Francisco. This meeting was chaired by Walter MacArthur of the Sailors' Union. Phelan delivered the major address in which he attacked the Japanese as unassimilable. At Phelan's invitation, Stanford University sociologist Edward Alsworth Ross was on hand to speak and add a touch of academic respectability. The session concluded with requests for Congress to exclude the Japanese as well as the Chinese.[16]

Congress was not swayed, but the American Federation of Labor endorsed this appeal at its Louisville convention in December. The Federation adopted a resolution proposed by the San Francisco Labor Council for Congress to "strengthen and re-enact the Chinese Exclusion Law, including, in its provisions, all Mongolian labor."[17]

Sensitive to American opinion, the Japanese government in 1900 voluntarily limited the emigration of laborers to the United States. Consequently, Japanese arrivals in 1901 totaled only 4,909 down from 12,626 in 1900. This concession, though, did not stop the Californians. In January 1901, Governor Henry T. Gage called Japanese labor "a menace to American labor"; and in November the California Chinese Exclusion Convention made the same accusation.[18]

Anti-Japanese sentiment was mounting and not only in California. By December 1905, the legislatures of Montana, Nevada, and Idaho added their voices to those asking Congress to restrict Japanese labor.[19] In another Western state, Utah, Japanese laborers served as strikebreakers in coal mines beginning in 1903 and 1904.[20]

Gompers, of course, refused to admit Japanese workmen into his Federation. He regarded the necessity for excluding them as well as the Chinese as "obvious," and "steadfastly refused to issue charters to organizations composed of Japanese laborers."[21]

Reflecting his views and those of California labor, in 1903 and 1904, the A.F. of L. called for Chinese exclusion to "be made to apply to the Japanese and Koreans and other Asiatic Mongolian labor."[22] "Morally and industrially," said the United Mine Workers of the Japanese immigrant, "he is a curse to the American nation, and should be excluded from our shores."[23]

Americans readily humiliated Chinese in their midst without fear of retribution by the government of China. In 1905, merchants in South China protested this treatment by boycotting American goods. Though this boycott compelled American businessmen and government officials to worry about future trade with China, its immediate commercial impact was slight. Moreover, there was no threat of war.[24]

Regarding the Japanese, 1905 was the year of the "yellow peril." Americans had traditionally feared an invasion by "hordes" of Chinese. Now they were wary of the Japanese, who were demonstrating their military might by defeating Russia in the Russo-Japanese War, which had begun in 1904. Respectful of Japan's power, Theodore Roosevelt was "utterly disgusted" at the Japanese exclusion movement on the Pacific Coast. "How people can act in this way with the Russo-Japanese war going on before their eyes I cannot understand," he wrote in May 1905. Roosevelt's correspondent, Henry Cabot Lodge, said "the ultimate danger [of antagonizing the Japanese to the point of war] will come from the labor unions." To conciliate the unionists, the Massachusetts senator suggested "an arrangement with Japan by which she excludes our labor and we exclude hers." Japan, Roosevelt noted in response, was "a power jealous, sensitive and warlike, and which if irritated, could at once take both the Philippines and Hawaii from us if she obtained the upper hand on the seas."[25]

Roosevelt discussed the Japanese question with Gompers. In the company of Ralph M. Easley of the National Civic Federation, Gompers had it explained to him first by secretary of state Elihu Root and then by the president. On account of Japanese sensitivity to criticism by Americans, Gompers agreed to Roosevelt's request "to use his influence with the labor representatives" to keep Japanese matters out of the A.F. of L.'s 1905 convention and of the N.C.F.'s National Conference on Immigration.[26] If

Gompers actually made such an effort, it failed miserably. Federation members at both meetings denounced Japanese labor, and his convention even commended the work of the recently formed Japanese and Korean Exclusion League in San Francisco and other western cities.[27]

In California, which had been comparatively quiet since 1901, 1905 saw a resurgence of the anti-Japanese agitation. The *San Francisco Chronicle*, edited by the Sinophobic and Japanophobic John P. Young, led the way. Beginning on February 23 and for several months thereafter, the newspaper featured headlines and stories on the evils and dangers of the Japanese. Coming from the highly conservative and influential *Chronicle*, the warnings were heeded.[28]

In response to the newspaper, San Francisco's unionists launched the Japanese and Korean Exclusion League. Founded on May 7, 1905, this organization would eventually become known as the Asiatic Exclusion League, and draw strength from laboring elements throughout California. Its founders included Patrick Henry McCarthy of San Francisco's Building Trades Council and Andrew Furuseth and Walter MacArthur of the Sailors' Union. Olaf Tveitmoe, the secretary of McCarthy's union, became president. These four men, all of them European immigrants, thus created an instrument for no other purpose than to bar the Japanese.[29]

Determined to demonstrate its good-will, the Japanese government countered the renewed agitation by once again limiting emigration to America. In April 1905, Japanese emigration to Hawaii, which had already been limited to five hundred per ship, was temporarily suspended.[30]

Then came the school segregation crisis. On October 11, 1906, the San Francisco school board ordered the city's Japanese school children to attend a school in Chinatown previously limited to Chinese children. As a consequence of the earthquake and fire of April 1906, which destroyed the Chinese quarter, many Chinese families had abandoned their neighborhood in favor of Oakland and Alameda. Thus, the Chinatown school could accommodate the Japanese pupils, who numbered ninety-three out of a total public school population of 28,736.[31]

The timing of the segregation order was extremely suspicious.

It came just as Mayor Eugene E. Schmitz, a musician by trade and staunch unionist, and "boss" Abraham Ruef, an attorney who controlled the Union Labor party of San Francisco, were about to be indicted on charges of municipal corruption. It was feared that the school board, which they controlled, might be diverting public attention from their plight by moving against the Japanese.[32]

Whatever the reason for the order, Mayor Schmitz and organized labor supported it, while the Japanese government and population of San Francisco were outraged. Japan issued a formal protest, contending that the discriminatory treatment violated treaty rights obtained in 1894. To soothe Tokyo, President Roosevelt first sent Victor H. Metcalf, the secretary of commerce and labor, to investigate the controversy, and then condemned the Californians' action in his annual message to Congress.[33]

With both the Japanese and the San Franciscans firm in their positions, and with war talk in the air, Roosevelt moved to end the impasse. In late January 1907, he invited Schmitz and the school board to Washington. Though already indicted and free on bail, the mayor was the guest of honor at several events. Gompers, who later claimed to have been "confidentially advised of all developments of the problem" by Schmitz, hosted a reception for him.[34]

On February 15, the Roosevelt administration reached an agreement with the California delegation. In exchange for promises that the flow of Japanese laborers would be ended, and that a legal test of the California school law would be dropped, the school board agreed to withdraw the segregation order and permit qualified Japanese children to attend the public schools.[35] Informally, the government of Japan then accepted the "Gentlemen's Agreement" under which no passports would be granted to Japanese laborers for entry to the American mainland.

Unhappy over the bargain with Washington, some Californians sought to subvert it with new, discriminatory legislation. However, though Roosevelt's intervention that effort was aborted, and, on March 13, 1907, the school board at last rescinded the segregation order.[36]

The events of 1906 and 1907 climaxed but did not end the

anti-Japanese movement. The accord with Japan of 1907, followed by another in 1908, greatly reduced immigration to the United States and international tensions as well, but it did not satisfy all parties. Organized labor resumed its campaign to exclude the Japanese, while the California legislature invented devices to reduce their economic competition. In 1915, though not yet able to secure exclusion, Andrew Furuseth did win passage of a seamen's act designed to ensure that foreigners made up no more than a quarter of the crew of any ship of American registry.[37]

After 1908, the California exclusionists had a new grievance against the Japanese. While they were wage laborers, their primary critics were nonfarm elements fearful of cheap labor competition. Agricultural employers, on the other hand, welcomed and depended on this labor. Then the ambitious Japanese acquired land of their own, and employed their countrymen to work it, thereby shrinking the Asian labor supply and angering the white growers. As landowners, the Japanese were regarded as too independent, which meant they had to be checked.

In 1913, California's Alien Land Act sought to achieve that purpose. The law set three-year maximum limits on agricultural land leased to Japanese, and prohibited aliens ineligible for citizenship from purchasing additional land. Seven years later, after the Japanese effectively circumvented this law by buying and selling land in the names of their American-born children, that subterfuge was outlawed. Similarly, the Japanese could not buy or sell land through corporations.[38]

With this land legislation, the anti-Japanese movement in California achieved as much as it could short of federal action. The next goal was the long-discussed act of exclusion, which was a congressional matter. In arguing and lobbying for exclusion, organized labor, as usual, would be highly visible and vocal.

Labor's activities would also include going beyond the literacy test to restrict European immigrants. Though sought since 1892, the test would prove deficient following its enactment in 1917. More a symbolic than actual deterrent, it would nonetheless serve as a significant step toward the passage of legislation of far greater severity in 1921 and 1924.

CHAPTER 11

Beyond the Literacy Test

THE purpose achieved by the passage of the literacy test was mainly symbolic. Enacted during a period of reduced immigration resulting from the continuing and spreading European war, the immigration law of 1917 proved ineffective against a revived flow that followed the cessation of hostilities. By the time Europeans were ready and able to resume their migration, their levels of literacy had risen sufficiently to enable a greater number to meet the requirements.[1]

Almost immediately after the literacy test became law, Americans considered adopting far more stringent measures against the foreign born. In April 1917, with the entry of the United States into the war on the side of England and France against Germany and her allies, American opinion began to question the loyalty of certain foreign-born aliens and even naturalized citizens. German born, in particular, were often suspected of disloyalty and subject to harassment and persecution in any of several ways. It was distinctly uncomfortable to be an "enemy alien."

The conclusion of the war in late 1918 merely gave rise to new fears. Many, including organized labor, worried about how the American economy would reconvert to civilian from military priorities without causing depression and high unemployment. Moreover, as they watched the economic barometer, they studied developments in Russia, whose Bolshevism might spread to America.

By 1919–1920, the United States was in the midst of a "Red Scare" which seemed to call for the purging of radicals, many of whom were born abroad. That purge would reach a climax in 1927 with the execution of two Italian immigrant anarchists,

169

Nicola Sacco and Bartolomeo Vanzetti. Widely believed to have been unfairly convicted in 1921 of murder, the pair were electrocuted despite international expressions of outrage.

Anti-Semitism added to the ugliness of the situation. As early as 1915 it surfaced in Georgia, where a second Ku Klux Klan was born. This KKK hated Jews, Catholics, and foreigners as well as blacks. Appropriately, it arose in the immediate aftermath of vigilante violence. In August, Leo Frank, the Jewish manager of a pencil factory in Atlanta, was lynched by people incited by the former Populist notable Tom Watson. Convicted on flimsy evidence of having raped and murdered Mary Phagan, a factory employee, Frank had had his death sentence commuted to life imprisonment before the lynchers seized him.

Besides Watson, other well-known Americans helped make bigotry fashionable. In 1916, socialite and zoologist Madison Grant published his *The Passing of the Great Race in America,* which warned of the menace to Nordic racial supremacy posed by Eastern and Southern European immigrants. Four years later, industrialist Henry Ford offered his contribution. In Ford's newspaper, the *Dearborn Independent,* readers found the text of *The Protocols of the Elders of Zion,* a czarist forgery which purported to reveal the existence of an international Jewish conspiracy to dominate the world.[2]

The flourishing of such attitudes helped immigration restrictionists to conclude their crusade. The last leg of Samuel Gompers's nativist journey was the easiest as well as the most successful. Not all his wishes would be realized, but by his death in December 1924, it was evident that the age of mass immigration had ended, in good part through his efforts.

America's entry into the war found Gompers ready for it. A supporter of Woodrow Wilson's preparedness program in 1916, he was appointed by the president to the National Council of Defense's advisory committee in October of that year. With that appointment, the former pacifist was transformed into a staunch advocate of peace through military might.[3]

During the war, Gompers served as labor's major spokesman, and threw the weight of the A.F. of L. behind Wilson's foreign policies. He loudly denounced all who were pro-German or pacifist.[4] The latter included many of his old socialist enemies, who regarded the war as essentially a struggle among imperialists, and the hated Industrial Workers of the World.[5]

Unlike European labor movements, the American Federation of Labor deferred pressing demands on its government until the war's conclusion. Gompers felt that labor had to help win the war before its own needs could be satisfied.[6] Nonetheless, in exchange for labor's support, which extended to curtailing strikes, the Wilson administration adopted a sympathetic attitude toward such traditional union demands as the eight-hour day and the right to organize and bargain collectively. Those concerns were considered by a National War Labor Board which the president established in April 1918.[7] In the strong wartime economy, with money abundant, demand for goods high, labor scarce, and immigration down, the A.F. of L. prospered. It added nine hundred thousand members between January 1, 1917, and January 1, 1919.[8]

The Wilson administration's assistance to the Federation involved more than sympathy for Gompers's kind of unionism. It also included an assault on the radical critics of the A.F. of L., particularly the socialists and I.W.W., who were bitterly opposed to Wilson's war policies. In an attempt to destroy the enemies of both Gompers and Wilson, the federal government raided their headquarters and arrested and prosecuted their leaders for allegedly violating wartime Selective Service, Espionage, and Sedition acts.

Wilson clearly understood that by attacking these radicals he was aiding the A.F. of L. Moreover, his help even included passing on to Gompers of I.W.W. membership lists that federal agents had seized in their raids. With these lists in its possession, the Federation could purge its ranks of radicals.

Because it was so closely tied to the government, the A.F. of L. suffered from an abdication of leadership. Gompers avoided policies that might embarrass Wilson, particularly at the Peace Conference to be held in Paris. Accordingly, in 1918 the A.F. of L. president did not propose a program of postwar reconstruction of the American economy. Lacking the independent position of the European trade unions, the Federation was dependent on continued governmental good-will for future growth and progress. Unfortunately, when peace came there was less need than before for cooperation between labor and government, and the A.F. of L's influence declined.[9]

By the spring of 1918, only a year after America's entry, the war's end was already being anticipated. Aware of the conflict's impact on immigration, American labor leaders assumed that peace would reverse the downward trend. Delegates to the International Ladies' Garment Workers' May 1918 convention recognized that the postwar immigrants would require assistance. If peace were to come before their next convention, the delegates resolved, the International should "call a conference of all organized workers whose trades may become affected" by the newcomers. That conference would "create a league for the protection and education of these immigrant workers, which would be of mutual aid to all elements concerned and also to the entire country."[10]

As usual the A.F. of L. was hostile to immigration. In May 1918, Congress had authorized the naturalization of aliens who enlisted in the armed forces of the United States. A month later, the Federation's annual convention, meeting in St. Paul, applauded that legislation and requested further gains. It asked for a change in the immigration laws to require "that all persons eligible for citizenship and who locate permanently in our land, become citizens of our country." Such a law would "discourage that class of immigrants, which has for its purpose the securing of advantages and benefits of our institutions and evade [sic] any of its responsibilities."[11]

That fall a Federation delegation went to Italy, a major source of those unwelcome immigrants. Chaired by President James Wilson of the Pattern Makers' League of North America, the five-person A.F. of L. mission toured the country and met with government representatives. The Americans visited industrial plants in at least ten cities. In Genoa, they held discussions with the royal commissioner of emigration. When the Italian official sought to discuss the condition of his countrymen in America, the visitors objected. In addition, when the Italian Bureau of Emigration presented resolutions in opposition to discrimination against immigrants and in favor of improved conditions for them in the "countries of emigration," they again responded negatively.[12]

Imbued with such negativism, and lacking a constructive reconversion plan, the A.F. of L. leadership began the postwar era by returning to the theme of labor competition. Frank Morrison, the Federation's Canadian-born secretary, presented its case to a sympathetic House Committee on Immigration. Morrison urged that virtually all immigration be suspended for four years. Under the direction of John L. Burnett, on January 29, 1919, the committee favorably reported a bill with that provision, but Congress eventually adjourned without acting upon it.[13]

Morrison's position was clear: the war had demonstrated that the United States could not assimilate diverse peoples and races, and the nation had to protect itself against postwar radicalism and unemployment. He argued that the labor market, which had recently absorbed "a vast addition of women," could expect to be strained by resumed immigration and demobilization. The result would be "a multiplicity of labor such as we never before knew."

Then there was the question of disloyalty. During the war, Morrison contended, "combinations of Germans not only remained German in thought, ideas and sympathies[,] but plotted or connived at plotting the destruction of our industries." Now the problem was "Bolshevik Socialists" like the Wisconsin editor and congressman, Victor Berger, who allegedly represented "a large following—anarchists, anarchistic pacifists and Bolshevists." America did not need any more of his kind.[14]

Appalled at this attack, the immigrant leaders of the I.L.G.W.U. broke their long silence on the immigration issue and openly criticized Gompers and Morrison. They voiced their discontent in the pages of *Justice*, their new weekly newspaper, and at the A.F. of L.'s annual convention in June 1919. In *Justice*, writer Gabriel Kretchmer, whose pseudonym was "Liliput," accused the Federation's president and secretary of exaggerating the nation's unemployment situation. "It is true that there is unemployment in America, but there are always people out of work," including during the war, when three million men were in uniform and industry was busy producing ammunition, uniforms, and military equipment. Moreover, even with America's "gates . . . practically closed" for four years, "the workers did not enjoy such great prosperity"; they had little to expect in the future whether the gates were open or not.

Rather than worry about heavy immigration, which he did not think would materialize because workers would be needed to rebuild Europe, "Liliput" asked for "better and more effective methods" than restrictive laws to help America's wage earners. The writer demanded laws to prohibit the labor of children, protect the health of working women, guarantee a minimum wage, and shorten the work week (beginning with a reduction to forty-four hours).[15]

Unemployment was indeed increasing, *Justice* contended, but it was caused by demobilization, not immigration. Each day tens of thousands of soldiers are being demobilized. . . . A crisis is approaching—a great, terrible crisis, bringing unemployment, hunger and suffering." By their refusal even "to hear anything about reconstruction or demobilization," the leaders of the A.F. of L. allegtdly were helping to hasten the crisis.[16]

The leadership of the Amalgamated Clothing Workers of America, the I.L.G.W.U.'s counterpart in the men's clothing industry, was similarly outraged at the A.F. of L. policies. On April 12, 1919, General Secretary-Treasurer Joseph Schlossberg told a union audience that it was a "sickening spectacle" for labor leaders to impugn the loyalty of fellow workers. Such accusers, Schlossberg said, were defeating "the purpose for which labor organizations were formed," and they were doing it merely to persuade public opinion that they themselves were patriotic.[17]

In June, the dispute over immigration reached the floor of the A.F. of L. convention in Atlanta. When the delegates were asked to endorse the Executive Council's position that immigration be prohibited "for a fixed number of years," Ladies' Garment Worker Max Gorenstein stood in opposition. "I feel it my duty as an immigrant and an American citizen to oppose that as vigorously as I can." There were other methods besides immigration restriction, Gorenstein suggested, to reduce unemployment. "Establish the six-hour day and you will not have to restrict immigration." Finally, he asked, "Is it the desire of this convention to close the doors to those people that are oppressed and persecuted?"

Gorenstein had little support. He was backed by James A. Duncan, of the Seattle Central Labor Council, which despised Gompers,[18] but virtually every other speaker on the issue expressed concern that America rather than the oppressed of the world be protected. Frank Morrison said "the great interests . . . want unemployment; they want cheap labor." In addition, he felt that American civilization could not "withstand the coming into this country of millions of Orientals." John L. Lewis of the United Mine Workers also endorsed prohibition, but he wanted it made clear that the Federation included Mexicans as well as Europeans and Asians in its statement. Mining interests, Lewis claimed, wanted "to import Mexican labor to displace American labor in the mines in certain producing territory." Both Morrison and Lewis had their way; the convention voted in favor of prohibiting "all immigration" for a specified period.[19]

Saul Yanofsky, the editor of *Justice,* was disheartened but not surprised by the outcome of the convention. The Federation's leadership, he noted, was aged and tired. Gompers, for example, was a "weak, fatigued old man with his eyes half extinguished." The sixty-nine-year-old A.F. of L. president, Yanofsky felt, was no longer "the symbol of authority and power, . . . but rather of orderliness, matter of factness. . . ." As for the anti-immigration policy, it "was to be expected," but Yanofsky regarded the challenge to it as a lesson that such thinking was "not necessarily axiomatic for organized labor."[20]

The 1920s began with the I.L.G.W.U. continuing to speak out on the immigration question. In early 1920, President Benjamin Schlesinger offered his assessment based on his firsthand view of the French economy. Differing with those in his union who denied that mass immigration would recur unless prevented by safeguards, Schlesinger in effect recognized the potential for another European influx. Labor conditions in Europe were "so deplorable" as to make America extremely attractive "to the half or wholly starved workers" over there. On the other hand, Schlesinger noted, the low wages earned by European workers might prove injurious to America in yet another way. They made possible the production of cheap manufactured goods which could flood the American markets and cause unemployment even without immigration. To prevent such an occurrence, Schlesinger urged the International to "extend its influence to Europe" to help build unions and raise wages.[21]

Committed to a liberal immigration policy, but aware of the negative potential of a postwar influx of workers, the International sought to preserve the principle of free immigration as well as to maintain high employment. Accordingly, its May 1920, convention called upon the A.F. of L. "to establish immigration bureaus in every port of the United States and Canada." If such a step were taken, immigrant workers would "be cordially received with open arms by organized labor, thus preventing them from falling into the hands of the dark forces of the greedy employers of this country."[22]

The A.F. of L. would not yield on restriction, but it did accept the idea of immigrant assistance. On June 9, 1920, while the Federation's convention was already in session in Montreal, Gompers and Vice-President Matthew Woll were in Chicago before the Republican party's Platform Committee. Woll read a list of demands, which included a call for the "Americanization of those coming from foreign lands," and the enactment of legislation to prohibit immigration completely during periods of high unemployment so as to keep the number of entrants at an assimilable level. Though it did not associate immigration with unemployment, the Republican platform for 1920 incorporated the argument about assimilation and urged tightening of admission standards.[23]

In Montreal, the restrictionist momentum of the A.F. of L. continued unchecked. The convention denied the claims, attributed to manufacturers, that unskilled labor was scarce, and praised the A.F. of L. leadership for valorous service in pursuit of restriction.[24]

By August 1920, the predicted upturn in immigration materialized. Even *Justice* became wary, noting that over five thousand immigrants were arriving daily at Ellis Island. Moreover, about 800,000 had streamed in between July 1, 1919, and June 30, 1920. The immigrant labor movement had always favored unrestricted immigration, but had never been "strong enough to work out a definite and concrete policy toward the incoming workers." To do something now, the United Hebrew Trades called for a conference of the immigrant unions.[25]

Something also had to be done about the garment industry, which was in a depressed state. American manufacturers found European markets unreceptive, which left factories idle and warehouses full of merchandise. "The menace of unemployment is still further strengthened by the oncoming of the fresh stream of immigration that has begun to pour into the country quite recently," observed *Justice* writer Juliet Stuart Poyntz. "These new arrivals crowding into the labor market with their standard of living will naturally tend to increase the supply and lower the price of labor unles[s] definite steps are taken to prevent this situation."[26]

Unlike the A.F. of L., Juliet Poyntz did not urge immigration restriction to deal with the problem. Instead, she advocated national adoption of "the principle of social responsibility for the unemployed." Citing English, German, and Belgian models, she said workers had "a right to sustenance" when they were idle. The creation of "a national system of employment bureaus" to organize the labor market would aid both labor and management. Workers would feel "some sense of security" and industry would have an efficiently distributed labor supply. Furthermore, new immigrants would be effectively and intelligently controlled instead of being left "to collect in pools along the eastern seaboard and underbid in the labor market."[27]

Poyntz and other writers for *Justice* developed two basic themes relative to unemployment and immigration. The first was governmental responsibility for finding jobs and making certain the newcomers would receive decent treatment. Calling crowded conditions at Ellis Island "unbearable," Max Danish accused the government of negligence in insufficiently preparing for the new arrivals.[28] The second theme was union responsibility for "providing work and decent remuneration to all workers." Rather than keep workers out of an industry or country, "a true labor union" has the duty to divide work among all workers in a way that would "afford a living to all of them."[29]

"Those who favor unrestricted immigration," Samuel Gompers said of his critics, "care nothing for the people." They wanted only to flood "the country with unskilled as well as skilled labor of other lands for the purpose of breaking down American standards." In Gompers's opinion, China was "the Utopia of the 'open' shop," a place without strikes. Therefore, believers in free immigration wanted America "Chinaized."[30]

As 1921 began, Gompers and the A.F. of L. lobbied for a suspension of immigration for two years or more.[31] American standards, they maintained, simply had to be protected.[32]

Under the chairmanship of an ardent nativist, Albert Johnson of Washington, the House Committee on Immigration was eager to oblige the Federation president. When Congress convened in November 1920, Johnson immediately revived his previous bill providing for a two-year suspension. Slightly softer than when it had been initially introduced—it exempted relatives of aliens residing in the United States—the bill moved quickly through Johnson's committee and the House, which passed it overwhelmingly. The latter, though, reduced the suspension period to one year.

This bill was meant to be only a temporary measure in response to the rather sudden rush of immigrants. Once it passed, Congress could devise a more permanent policy. Yet as rational as its purpose appeared, behind the scenes it received strong anti-Semitic support, which was so intense that many observers regarded it mainly as a device to exclude Jews.[33]

Indeed, spokesmen for leading Jewish organizations testified against the bill before the Senate Committee on Immigration. John L. Bernstein of the Hebrew Shelter and Immigrant Aid Society, Louis Marshall of the American Jewish Committee, and Max Pine of the United Hebrew Trades all appeared in opposition and denied that an imminent immigrant invasion threatened America. Speaking for organized Jewish labor, Pine said that the new immigration would not subvert or depress the nation's standard of living.[34]

Reminded by a Jewish manufacturer from Brooklyn that he, too, was an immigrant, Gompers became defensive. Though terming the reminder "unkind," he noted that labor objected to those immigrants who adversely affected economic progress. Moreover, he added, "the great majority" of the members of the A.F of L. were native born. "I came into this country as an immigrant," he finally conceded, but he also said that foreign birth did not entitle immigrants to ruin the American economy.

I do not believe that you yourself would urge people to immigrate to this country if by doing so they would break down the American standards. Because we were born across the water is no reason that we should help tear down the splendid economic standards built by the workers of this country. It would be ingratitude run mad for us to encourage the breaking down of these standards.[35]

In the Republican-controlled United States Senate, Gompers's arguments proved less persuasive than those advanced by business interests. Sensitive both to businessmen and foreign-born voters, LeBaron Colt of Rhode Island, chairman of the Senate Immigration Committee, conducted hearings in a manner advantageous to the antirestrictionists. Acting without a sense of urgency, Colt permitted he National Federation of Construction Industries, the National Association of Manufacturers, and other groups to present their case for continued immigration.

This opposition killed the Johnson Bill, but restrictionists in the Senate then proposed a more moderate substitution. Presented by William P. Dillingham of Vermont, who had headed the prewar Immigration Commission, the new bill aimed to reduce immigration by means of a percentage system. European immigrants would be limited to five percent of each nationality in the United States as of 1910.

This plan cleared the Senate with ease, but was modified in the House, which dropped the suspension idea. Instead of five percent of the 1910 population, the House lowered the figure to three, and set an annual maximum of 350,000 Europeans. By this scheme, most would come from Northern and Western Europe; in 1910, those areas still represented the dominant geographic origins of the American people.

Consistent with past practice, Woodrow Wilson vetoed immigration restriction. Without explanation, he withheld his signature from the bill as he left office in March 1921.[36]

Gompers had mixed feelings about the vetoed bill. He wanted restriction, but not Dillingham's plan, which was too mild. The unacceptable measure, he claimed, "did not give proper relief to the American people."[37] Estimating that the current unemployment stood at "about 5,000,000," he considered "all immigration . . . undesirable."[38]

For the moment, though, Gompers had to accept compromise. Wilson's successor as president, Warren G. Harding, called Congress into special session. With Albert Johnson's backing, the percentage plan sailed first through the House and then the Senate. On May 19, 1921, it became law.[39] A month later, at its Denver convention, the American· Federation of Labor endorsed the legislation.[40]

"The law is now three months old," *Justice* columnist Max Danish observed in September. "And during these three months, while immigration has been reduced to a minimum, the number of unemployed in America has increased several million. Marvelous, isn't it? Can anyone explain?"[41]

The Immigration Act of 1921 may not have reduced unemployment, but, nevertheless, it was a highly significant step. Though it was only a temporary, stop-gap law, it imposed the first sharp limitation on European immigration. It made nationality quotas that discriminated against Eastern and Southern Europeans the dominant characteristic of American immigration policy. Subsequent legislation would only reinforce this assault, which would greatly reduce the role of the foreign born in American life.[42]

In fact, as soon as the 1921 law was due to expire, the hardening of attitudes toward the immigrant was apparent. In early 1922, Gompers asked Congress for some new restrictions: keep out all but blood relatives of foreign-born United States citizens, with the law in effect until conditions warranted changing it, or extend the law until June 20, 1924. Though the House had voted a one-year extension, the Senate adopted Gompers's suggestions and chose two years. In addition, the Senate supplied two amendments. One imposed a two hundred dollar penalty on steamship companies for each person brought beyond the quota. The second restricted immigrants who went elsewhere before coming to the United States. It required foreigners who entered the United States from Cuba, Mexico, and Canada to reside beforehand for five years in those places.[43] In June 1922, the A.F. of L. officially approved these developments, over objections of Jewish unions.[44]

As the restriction of Europeans gained momentum, so did the feeling that something must be done to block the Japanese. Despite the Gentlemen's Agreements of 1907 and 1908, Japanese immigrants continued to arrive in alarming numbers. Though the figures for Japanese arrivals did not approach those for Eastern and Southern Europeans during the same periods, they were enough to frighten many Americans. In 1907, Japanese immigration had reached a high of 30,226. Afterward, reflecting the diplomatic arrangements, it dropped, to 15,803 in 1908, 3,111 in 1909, and 2,720 in 1910 The following year it began a gradual ascent to a new maximum of 10,213 in 1918. In the postwar years, it again dipped, to 7,878 in 1921.[45]

Obviously, these Japanese did not constitute a "flood" or "horde," and even included far more women than men.[46] Among these women were "picture brides." By law Japanese men resident in America could bring their wives to join thm. Accordingly, single men through the exchange of photographs chose brides residing in Japan, and married them by proxy. American-born children were automatically citizens of the United States, which to the great dismay of white Californians increased the Japanese presence.[47]

Yet what was most bothersome on the Pacific Coast was the belief that the Japanese provided "impossible competition" for American farmers.[48] Japanese farms, complained California's Governor William D. Stephens in June 1920, accounted for "between 80 and 90 per cent" of the state's berry and vegetable products. With "their wives and their very children in the arduous toil of the soil," Stephens said, the Japanese were "proving crushing competitors" to rural whites.[49]

In fact most of California's Japanese were engaged in agricultural pursuits. They "were mainly small farmers and businessmen." In such occupations they did not significantly compete with organized labor in the state. Nevertheless, to Secretary-Treasurer Paul Scharrenberg of the California State Federation of Labor, who spoke for the A.F. of L. on Japanese matters, the exclusion of the Japanese was a necessity.[50] At the end of 1919, the California Federation's Executive Council actively participated in the organization of the California Oriental Exclusion League.[51]

As wary as ever of Asians, the American Federation of Labor supported the anti-Japanese movement. Even a good-will visit by S. Suzuki, a representative of the Japanese labor movement, to the Federation's 1919 convention, only slightly softened attitudes.[52] In June 1920, the A.F. of L. unanimously endorsed Japanese exclusion.[53] Two months later, Gompers told the Reverend Herbert Welch, the resident bishop for Japan and Korea, that the objection to Asians was on "purely economic grounds." He did not want the workers of Japan to feel that he opposed them because they were Japanese. "It is a question of self-preservation and for that we never will cease to fight."[54]

By January 1921, Gompers offered additional reasons for his attitude. "It is a question of self-preservation, the maintenance of American standards and the dangers that come from the immigraion of Japanese because of it being impossible to assimilate them that animates Labor in opposing their admission to this country," he responded to an inquiry from Nebraska.[55] This rationale went beyond economics.

The A.F. of L. president looked forward to the abrogation of the Gentlemen's Agreement, which would make Japanese exclusion possible. Either by treaty or law, he hoped and expected that America would soon bar "all Orientals."[56]

CHAPTER 12

The Triumph of Restrictionism

AFTER 1921, the advocates of permanent legislation to restrict immigration understood that Congress would not completely close the gates. Although the A.F. of L. and its allies, notably the American Legion and several southerners in Congress, continued to seek such a suspension, it was clear that economic and even diplomatic objections made it unattainable. Nonetheless, the racism and nativism of the twenties demanded that some significant advance be made beyond the 1921 limits.

With that aim in mind, Albert Johnson surrounded himself with some of the nation's leading racists. Johnson actively corresponded and met with Madison Grant, whose views on immigration he much admired. Massachusetts nativist Lothrop Stoddard added his counsel, as did novelist Kenneth Roberts, who contributed a series on immigration restriction to the *Saturday Evening Post*. Eugenicist Harry Laughlin was the scientific authority on the ill effects of inferior races. Finally, helping to formulate strategy to enact a permanent law was wealthy patrician attorney John B. Trevor, a man prejudiced against Jews in particular and immigrants in general.[1]

By February 1923, the combined restrictionist effort produced a new bill, which was introduced in the House of Representatives. According to this proposal, future immigration would be based on two percent of the nationality figures for 1890 rather than on three percent of the 1910 totals. That slight percentage reduction, B. Maiman, *Justice's* Washington correspondent claimed, meant "a tremendous difference." The bill provided for easier admission than before of the relatives of immigrants and aliens. They were free to leave America and then to return, but, he noted, it would exclude the cheap labor desired by "Big Business."[2]

A week later, with the bill already reported out of committee,

Maiman turned more sharply critical. He attacked it as indefensible on both economic and humanitarian grounds. Maiman noted that during the 1921–1922 fiscal year the nation's population had increased only slightly. "The fact is that more grownup men have left this country than have arrived here." Second, he decried the nature of the suggested restriction. *"From countries where the populations [sic] suffer most, the least number of immigrants will be permitted to land."* Finally, he objected to a provision that required prospective immigrants to secure "immigration certificates" from American consuls abroad before they could leave. The idea of such documents, complete with portraits and personal information, Maiman feared, would serve as a "foundation for future laws that might become very dangerous for new arrivals to this country." He regarded this certificate as part of an alien registration scheme.[3]

Subsequent developments made Maiman's alarm seem premature. With economic indicators up and business protesting the immigration restriction already passed, Congress took no further action in 1923. Amendments to Johnson's bill distorted it so much in the House that even the A.F. of L. opposed it, and in the Senate the cause was hopeless.

Gompers vehemently disputed the business argument that a labor shortage existed. Employers such as the United States Steel Corporation and the "Steel Trust," he said, only wanted "waiting lines" at factory gates to give them a "hungry influence" which would permit them "more fully to control the wage situation." America could not "afford to relax its immigration restrictions to meet the desires of corporate greed."[4]

On July 30, 1923, the labor leader celebrated the sixty-ninth anniversary of his arrival in America. "The proudest moment of my life," he recalled, "was when I received my citizenship papers." His family and he had come, he added, "in search of American freedom," and he "always felt inspired with [sic] the spirit of American democracy."[5] On September 3, he told a Labor Day audience that America should "assimilate the foreign-speaking population here instead of throwing open our doors to others."[6]

President Calvin Coolidge felt the same way. In office through the sudden death of Warren G. Harding, Coolidge was a restrictionist with a like-minded secretary of labor, James J. Davis. The

Welsh-born Davis had been an iron worker. As a cabinet member, he proposed "selective immigration" involving a system of immigrant inspection. American authorities abroad would subject applicants for admission to the United States to "just tests of physical and mental health." Such tests would spare these people the expense of coming to America only to discover they could not enter. Once admitted, the alien would be registered. If he were later found unfit for American citizenship," he would be deported.[7]

"Selective immigration" drew fire from many quarters. Arturo Giovanitti, the hero of the 1912 Lawrence strike, called it "a new word for involuntary servitude," which had to "be prevented at all cost" unless the Thirteenth Amendment to the United States Constitution be repudiated.[8] Reflecting the A.F. of L. viewpoint, the United Garment Workers' journal said that registration would be "a monstrous evil, a copy of Prussianism at its worst." That journal, too, questioned its constitutionality.[9] Most important, though, the House Immigration Committee made major changes in Davis's proposals after he submitted them to it.[10]

In October 1923, the A.F. of L.'s convention in Portland, Oregon, virtually ignored the registration idea in favor of other demands. The delegates instructed the Executive Council to ask the Sixty-eighth Congress for "a more stringent immigration policy" with reduced quotas and to "deny admission . . . to all aliens who are ineligible to citizenship under the laws of the United States," meaning the Japanese, who were the primary people in that category. On the other hand, the convention referred to one Executive Council resolution that called for a five-year suspension of immigration, and to another that asked for the United States to "maintain the glorious tradition of keeping its doors open to the victims of racial, religious and political persecution in all lands." The latter statement came from the delegates of the I.L.G.W.U.[11]

Of the groups that traditionally opposed immigration restriction, such as the Ladies' Garment Workers' Union, the American Jewish Committee, the American Jewish Congress, and the National Association of Manufacturers, only the organizations of employers did not strictly adhere to that position. Speaking for Jewish labor and philanthropy, respectively, Max Danish and Louis Marshall continued to raise the cry of discrimination.[12]

Business, though, began to bend. Evidently influenced by the racist theories then prevalent, manufacturers tempered their demand for plentiful labor with an acceptance of some restriction. In December 1923, the Hotel Astor in New York City was the site of a National Immigration Conference. Organized by the employer-run National Industrial Conference Board, this gathering consisted of "500 delegates from 150 organizations."

The conference was noteworthy for the variety of views manufacturers expressed. One delegate suggested excluding skilled workers from the quotas; another proposed admitting "ignorant immigrants ... [to] take the place of the negroes who have been leaving the South in large numbers in recent years"; a third said that character rather than education should be the test of admission to the United States. Most significantly, Marcus W. Alexander, the managing director of the National Industrial Conference Board, thought that the nation would soon be unable to absorb additional immigration. Furthermore, he continued, the large supply of cheap workers had even hurt business by retarding "the invention and manufacture of labor-saving devices." Industrialists had to recognize the existence of this menace.

James A. Emery, counsel to the National Association of Manufacturers, perhaps best summarized the mood of the delegates. What the manufacturers sought, he said, was an "elastic" system which would exclude undesirable immigrants but admit others.[13] Soon afterward, the N.A.M. and the United States Chamber of Commerce both advocated retention rather than lowering of the 1921 quotas, but offered no resistance when Congress then ignored their views and embraced permanent, severe restriction.[14]

As the differences between the leaders of business and labor lessened on the immigration question, congressional action appeared inevitable. Israel Zangwill, an English visitor to New York, was troubled by this prospect. A distinguished playwright and novelist, whose play, *The Melting-Pot*, had stirred American audiences and added a new consciousness of the immigrant experience when it opened in Washington, D.C. and New York in 1908 and 1909,[15] Zangwill was bitter. Samuel Gompers, he told a Jewish audience, "was an outstanding figure," but "his work in restricting immigration for selfish labor reasons is not only un-Jewish, but un-American." Gompers and others, he said, accepted a "100 per cent Americanism" that was "only 1 per cent of the great Americanism symbolized by the Statue of Liberty."[16] As if to concede the point, Gompers and the A.F. of L. soon afterward endorsed the discriminatory Johnson Bill before the House of Representatives as a means of maintaining the nation's racial character, which European immigration menaced.[17]

By mid-January, the bill was out of committee and apparently headed for passage. America was going to become "of, by, and for Anglo-Saxons," Max Danish charged. "It is this pernicious, Ku-Klux-Klan feature of the Johnson bill that is most revolting."[18] In Indianapolis, the United Mine Workers, under President John L. Lewis, voted for restriction and applauded James Davis, whose latest suggestion was that aliens be fingerprinted.[19] In the February *American Federationist*, assistant editor Chester W. Wright rejected the idea of partial or flexible restriction; "the more complete the exclusion the better," he insisted.[20] On March 8, representatives of eleven ethnic groups held a mass meeting at New York's Carnegie Hall to protest Johnson's measure.[21]

With events approaching a climax, Gompers called on "organized labor and friends of humanity" to persuade Congress to pass the bill.[22] Though he rejected alien registration, calling it one of the instruments of unfreedom,[23] he nonetheless devoted space in the April *American Federationist* to the nativist views of James J. Davis.[24] Confirming the A.F. of L.'s alliance with the American Legion on immigration, Gompers also printed a piece by John R. Quinn, the national commander of the veterans' organization.[25] The title of the Federation president's own editorial summed up the views of all three restrictionists: "America Must Not Be Overwhelmed."[26]

In replying to the A.F. of L.'s call for labor support, General Secretary Abraham Baroff of the I.L.G.W.U. told Gompers that his union saw immigration "not merely as an economic question but as a problem of general humanity." The International could not condone excluding the oppressed or accepting race or nationality discrimination as a principle of immigration regulations or restriction.[27] "The immigrant is our brother—a worker like ourselves," Max Danish explained.[28] In Boston, the International's annual convention supported those sentiments with a resolution. Aware that Congress was about to defeat the cause he stood for, one speaker noted that the Statue of Liberty had become a lonely figure and would "probably feel more so as the Johnsons in this country have their way."[29]

Samuel Gompers also addressed that convention. He warned the delegates to be wary of Communists in the labor movement. Tactfully, he did not mention immigration.[30]

Nothing would have been gained by discussing that sensitive subject. Congress was at that moment in the final stages of excluding the Japanese and devising a new quota system for Europeans. The only genuine question that remained was whether President Coolidge would sign the bill Congress was certain to pass.

By the middle of April, both houses had resolved most major issues. Over protests that they were infected by racial and religious hate, first the House and then the Senate voted overwhelmingly to restrict the Europeans. "We were afraid of foreigners; we distrusted them; we didn't like them," Congressman Emanuel Celler of Brooklyn recalled.[31]

The restrictions they approved limited the immigration of each European nationality to two percent of those who resided in the United States in 1890. Each quota would have a minimum of 100 persons. This system would continue until July 1, 1927, when another was expected to supersede it. From then on immigration per country would be computed according to the percentage of each nationality in the American population in 1920, with the annual maximum set at 150,000.

Led by Samuel Shortridge of California, the Senate followed the House in abrogating the Gentlemen's Agreement. Japanese exclusion met with almost no resistance in the House, but in the Senate the story was different—until the Japanese ambassador intervened. Hoping to prevent a diplomatic crisis between his country and the United States, Ambassador Masanao Hanikara wrote Secretary of State Charles Evans Hughes that "grave consequences" would follow exclusion. Hughes made the letter public, which gave Senator Henry Cabot Lodge the opportunity to call the diplomat's remarks a "veiled threat" of war. Not wanting to appear intimidated, the Senate voted to exclude as opposition virtually vanished.

Though he and Hughes objected to the bill's Japanese provision, President Coolidge decided to sign it. Actually, he had little choice. Albert Johnson had warned him that a veto would easily be overridden. Furthermore, even if one could be sustained, there would be the problem of the expiration of the 1922 act. Thus, on May 26, Calvin Coolidge signed the bill which became the Johnson-Reed Act, or the Immigration Act of 1924.[32]

As expected, the congressional action pleased Gompers but dismayed the National Association of Manufacturers. On vacation at Atlantic City when the Senate moved against the Japanese, Gompers asserted America's right to exclude them. "We have enough race problems here without making the Mongolian more acute than it is already," he also noted.[33] The N.A.M. observed that "profound and fundamental" racial differences had motivated Congress, and expressed its "regret." Diplomacy and cooperation, the manufacturers contended, could achieve the same goal as the legislation, "without giving unnecessary offense to a friendly people."[34]

In Congress, the victors rejoiced. Hiram W. Johnson, California's senior senator, was pleased that his state had finally prevailed, and could not foresee problems with Japan. "It is a very great measure," Henry Cabot Lodge said of the new law. Lodge, whose restrictionist leadership dated back to 1891, called it "one of the most important if not the most important, that Congress has ever passed."[35]

When he signed the bill, Coolidge said he regretted that the exclusion clause could not be severed from it. On the other hand, he denied that the provision implied "any change" in America's "sentiment of admiration and cordial friendship for the Japanese people."

Meanwhile, in Japan, ten thousand army reservists demonstrated against what they regarded as a national affront. "If history teaches anything," said one speaker to the former service men, "an eventual collision between Japan and America on the Pacific is inevitable." Another speaker, a lieutenant general, said the Japanese had to "be determined to undergo whatever hardships are necessary in avenging the insult which America has done our country."[36]

The American Federation of Labor could not completely ignore that ill-feeling. At El Paso in November, the Federation's annual convention commended the Executive Council "for its signal legislative victory" in having secured the legislative enactment of "many of the immigration principles for which organized labor has consistently fought".[37]

Despite this praise, Gompers felt it necessary to answer the critics of America and organized labor. To safeguard American freedom and progress, he insisted, the nation must not be "overrun by hordes of underpaid and undeveloped workers ... men who would not defend their standards of life and progress would not defend the chastity of their homes. Self-protection is the first law of nature. ..."[38]

This was the seventy-four-year-old Gompers's last convention. Victorious in the immigration struggle, but tired from decades of fighting for his ideas of unionism, he died soon afterward in San Antonio. On December 13, 1924, he whispered a parting message to his long-time aide, James Duncan, of the Granite Cutters' Union: "Say to the workers of America that I have kept the faith."[39]

The Johnson-Reed Act represented a stupendous victory for the forces of American nativism. For more than four decades the principles and procedures of this law would remain, with slight modification, the foundation of American immigration policy. Even in 1965, when Congress eventually abandoned national origins quotas as the basis for admission, there was no return to the era of unrestricted or free immigration.

The dramatic decline actually began in 1929, when, after two delays, the national origins system went into effect and the stock market crashed. Ironically, by then neither the A.F. of L. nor the United States Chamber of Commerce favored the new, permanent quota arrangement. Both the businessmen and the unionists would have been pleased to retain the two percent plan.[40]

Fully implemented, the 1924 law stood with its 1917 predecessor, which still functioned, as dual bulwarks against the unwelcome of Europe and Asia. In addition, restriction received the support of President Herbert Hoover, who invoked a section of the 1917 act which authorized the exclusion of "persons likely to become a public charge."

From an average in excess of 300,000 per year from 1925 to 1929, immigration dropped to 97,139 in 1931, 35,576 in 1932, and 23,068 in 1933. As intended, the curtailment most affected Eastern and Southern Europe. Between 1924 and 1946, newcomers from there constituted only 18.9 percent of the total American immigration; 43.1 percent came from Northern and Western Europe.[41]

. Under Samuel Gompers's successor, William Green of the United Mine Workers' Union, the American Federation of Labor sought to defend and extend the achievement of 1924. Immediately the Federation moved to protect the law from those who would undermine it. "Propagandists," the A.F. of L.'s 1925 convention heard, were working hard "to place Japan within the immigration quota law and to otherwise lessen existing immigration restrictions against that country." Thus, the barriers erected the previous year required continued zealous guarding.[42]

Andrew Furuseth, speaking for Pacific Coast seamen, complained that a loophole in the law permitted Chinese to enter the United States by posing as crewmen. The law allowed alien seamen to leave ship and stay in the country for sixty days, providing much opportunity to smuggle men and narcotics. Furuseth wanted vessels to be compelled to leave the United States with "the same number of men which they carried on arrival." In addition, American officials should be empowered to examine crews and deport immigrants disguised as seamen at the expense of the ship. Finally, only under the flag of his own country should an immigrant seaman be admitted to an American port.

Furuseth was interested mainly in reducing the number of foreign crewmen on American ships. Toward that end he constantly plied Congress with alien deportation bills well into the 1930s. Opposed by the American shipping industry, none ever passed.[43]

The questions of Mexico and the Philippines likewise carried into the next decade. The 1924 act did not check immigration from either place. Mexicans entered in the absence of restrictions on the western hemisphere, and Filipinos, foreign nationals under American control, came under a special exemption in the law.

The movement to restrict the Mexicans actually began before 1924, but the Johnson-Reed Act gave it renewed impetus. By reducing the European influx, the act increased the proportion of immigrants who were Mexican, despite a new ten-dollar visa fee which did deter some from coming. Restrictionist elements, such as A.F. of L. unions, patriotic societies, and eugenicist groups, thereupon waged a fight to put the Mexicans under a quota. Led in Congress by Representative John Box of Texas, they fought the cattle, farm, and railroad interests of the Southwtst that wanted cheap Mexican labor, legal or otherwise.[44]

The idea of placing a quota on Western Hemisphere countries, introduced in 1925, survived four years of congressional hearings. More racist than economic in nature, the Mexican restriction drive failed in Congress in 1930. Though his opposition had contributed to the defeat, President Hoover then soothed restrictionist feelings by waging a campaign against illegal Mexican aliens and by withholding visas from Mexicans on the grounds that they were potential public charges. This "administrative restriction" was so successful that it satisfied the proponents of a quota and was adopted by Hoover's successor in the presidency, Franklin D. Roosevelt.[45]

The Filipino question, like the Japanese, was a direct consequence of the Pacific Coast's fear of Asians. In 1927, California nativists, with victories over the Chinese and Japanese behind them, demanded Filipino exclusion. Aided two years later by the onset of the Great Depression, the matter reached Congress, where it went unresolved until 1934. The American Federation of Labor, once more allied with the American Legion and other patriotic organizations, again waged war against cheap labor without forgetting the value of exploiting ethnic fears. "This mongrel stream is small, but when it is considered how rapidly it multiplies and grows it is clear that the tide must be stemmed before it gets beyond control," said a member of the restrictionist American Coalition that organized in 1929. Though the Hawaiian Sugar Planters Association and the Pacific American Steamship Association defended Filipino immigration, most of the arguments against it were not economic but racial.

In Congress the question became tied to that of Philippine independence, which would provide a natural pretext for exclusion. Senator Hiram Johnson of California proposed such an arrangement whereby Filipinos would be kept out under the Asian exclusion provisions of the 1924 law. However, Johnson had to settle for a little less. In 1934, an independence bill acceptable to President Roosevelt and the Philippine legislature passed Congress. The Philippine Islands now had an annual quota of fifty immigrants. This compromise quota closed the issue.[46]

Under the leadership of William Green, the A.F. of L. remained, except for a few instances, a staunch defender of the practices and principles of 1924. In 1932 and 1933, Representative Samuel Dickstein of New York sought to remove the aged parents of American citizens from the quota system. The organized labor-patriotic society coalition opposed and helped defeat Dickstein's bill; passage would have been an opening wedge against restriction. In 1933, President Roosevelt allayed Green's fears that he would relax federal administration of the law, especially in excluding those who were likely to become public charges. Regardless of Adolph Hitler's rise to power in Germany that year, which precipitated a new mass movement of refugees, the A.F. of L. held firm. "There is not a country in the world where there is not religious or political persecution," the Federation claimed. On the other hand, in 1935 it did back a bill to report alien Communists and Fascists. As late as March 1938, when President Roosevelt spoke of America's traditional role as an asylum for the oppressed, Green responded by restating his opposition to an increase in the quotas.[47]

By 1939, the A.F. of L. finally demonstrated some flexibility. Senator Robert F. Wagner of New York, himself an immigrant, and Representative Edith Nourse Rogers of Massachusetts, introduced a bill to admit twenty thousand German refugee children for a two-year period above the quotas. Representatives of the Federation, along with those of its new rival, the Congress of Industrial Organizations, testified in behalf of the measure. The bill died anyway, largely because of anti-Semitic fears and propaganda that the refugee children were mainly Jewish.[48]

As Hitler's "Final Solution" for Europe's Jews became known, both the A.F. of L. and C.I.O. participated in efforts to have the American government help them. In March 1943, the labor organizations were among the co-sponsors of a massive rally in New York's Madison Square Garden to "Stop Hitler Now."[49]

The Federation's sympathy for the refugees presaged an easing of its traditional attitude toward Europeans. However, as far as Asians were concerned, the sentiment remained unchanged. Even though the presence of Asians on the West Coast had declined noticeably by 1927,[50] and China was allied with the United States in the war against Japan and Germany, the A.F. of L. and organized veterans and patriots continued to support Chinese exclusion. In 1943, despite their objections, Congress ended the ban and gave the Chinese an annual quota of 105.[51]

As the Chinese received a quota, the Jews of Europe suffered devastating consequences of the national origins system. Countless Jews, kept by discriminatory immigration policy from leaving Nazi-controlled lands for the United States, now faced extermination. Insensitive to their plight during the thirties, Congress, unchallenged by the president, did nothing to facilitate their entry into the country. Indeed, by as late as 1943 the United States government had made no special effort to rescue them.

President Roosevelt offered sympathy rather than substantive action to ease the flow of refugees to America or the rest of the world. Though their situation disturbed him, he refused to fight for them. Roosevelt called an international refugee conference in 1938 and supported another conference begun by the British in 1943, but would not clash with Congress or even his own State Department over immigration policy. Congress would not change the quota law, and the State Department scrutinized immigrants so carefully before admitting them that quota spaces went unused. According to Assistant Secretary of State Breckinridge Long, liberal admission of immigrants would provide easy entry for foreign agents and thus constitute a threat to the nation's security.

Besides these sources of opposition, other factors complicated efforts to rescue the refugees. American Jews were divided into Zionist and non-Zionist camps that quarreled over where refugees should be resettled. In addition, very few people outside the

United States wanted a mass of Jewish refugees settled within their midst.

In 1944, transcending these and even other obstacles, Roosevelt at last acted to save some of the Jews. Prodded by a Treasury Department report that accused the United Staes of acquiescing in their murder by its inaction, the president established a War Refugee Board. This agency helped to relocate Jewish refugees to safe places in Europe, North Africa, and the United States. To circumvent the quota system, Roosevelt called the temporary American havens "Emergency Rescue Shelters." Unfortunately, this venture was too limited in scope and undertaken long after many Jews, who might have been saved, had already perished.[52]

As World War II ended, the national origins system still stood as a barrier against the foreign born. This system both restricted immigration and symbolized prejudice and fear. It reflected, among other things, organized labor's view that working class immigrants should be regarded as strangers rather than brothers.

American workers had come to feel this way for several reasons. First, foreigners often differed from the natives along ethnic lines, including race, religion, language, dress, and custom. Second, companies frequently hired foreigners in order to keep wages low and unions out. Finally, labor organizations often exacerbated intergroup animosities by attacking the most recent immigrant additions to the work force. Through such attacks unions became the protectors of the native-born workers against their foreign-born enemies, and nativist union leaders gained in power and prestige.

Led by Samuel Gompers, the American labor movement entered the twentieth century opposed more to immigration than to industrial capitalism, with which it had learned to live. Foes of the nation's economic system, notably the Industrial Workers of the World, were also anathema to the American Federation of Labor. Though they were within the A.F. of L., the immigrant socialists of the International Ladies' Garment Workers' Union had no policymaking influence in the parent body.

During the twenties, the Federation's anti-immigrant crusade triumphed brilliantly. Congress excluded the Japanese and severely restricted Europeans. America was at last safe, nativists believed, from the threat of heavy immigration. During the thirties and forties, refugees from Nazism constituted little competition for the American worker.

Notes and References

Chapter One

1. John Higham, *Strangers in the Land: Patterns of American Nativism, 1860–1925* (New Brunswick, N.J., 1955), pp. 45–46.

2. George Rogers Taylor, *The Transportation Revolution, 1815–1860*, vol. 4, *The Economic History of the United States* (New York, 1951), pp. 207–40; Norman Ware, *The Industrial Worker, 1840–1860* (Gloucester, Mass., 1959), pp. 1–9, 71–100.

3. Gerald N. Grob, *Workers and Utopia: A Study of Ideological Conflict in the American Labor Movement, 1865–1900* (Evanston, Ill., 1961), pp. 3–5.

4. John R. Commons and Associates, *History of Labour in the United States*, 4 vols. (New York, 1918–1935), 1:169–84, 575–623; Edward Pessen, *Most Uncommon Jacksonians: The Radical Leaders of the Early Labor Movement* (Albany, 1967), pp. 3–4, 9, 34–36.

5. Stephen Salsbury, "The Effect of the Civil War on American Industrial Development," in *The Economic Impact of the American Civil War*, ed. Ralph Andreano (Cambridge, 1962), pp. 161–68.

6. David Montgomery, *Beyond Equality: Labor and the Radical Republicans, 1862–1872* (New York, 1967), pp. 90–134.

7. Charlotte Erickson, *American Industry and the European Immigrant, 1860–1885* (Cambridge, 1957), pp. 6–12; Philip Taft, *Organized Labor in American History* (New York, 1964), pp. 300–301.

8. Grob, *Workers and Utopia*, p. 11; Charlotte Todes, *William H. Sylvis and the National Labor Union* (Westport, Conn., 1975), p. 58.

9. Grob, pp. 11–12.

10. William M. Dick, *Labor and Socialism in America: The Gompers Era* (Port Washington, N.Y., 1972), pp. 10–11.

11. Grob, *Workers and Utopia*, p. 18.

12. Erickson, *American Industry and the European Immigrant*, p. 59; Joseph G. Rayback, *A History of American Labor* (New York, 1966), pp. 119–20.

13. Edward C. Kirkland, *Industry Comes of Age: Business, Labor, and Public Policy, 1860–1897* (New York, 1961), p. 326.

197

14. C. K. Yearley, Jr., *Enterprises and Anthracite: Economics and Democracy in Schuylkill County, 1820–1875* (Baltimore, 1961), p. 166.

15. Rowland Tappan Berthoff, *British Immigrants in Industrial America, 1790–1950* (Cambridge, 1953), p. 60.

16. Erickson, *American Industry and the European Immigrant,* pp. 190–91.

17. Ware, *The Industrial Worker,* pp. 22–23.

18. Grob, *Workers and Utopia,* pp. 35–36.

19. Rendig Fels, *American Business Cycles, 1865–1897* (Chapel Hill, 1959), pp. 98–99, 101.

20. H. C. Carey, "Capital and Labor," in *Report of the Committee on Industrial Interests and Labor, Constitutional Convention of Pennsylvania* (Philadelphia, 1873), pp. 8–9.

21. Robert V. Bruce, *1877: Year of Violence* (Chicago, 1970), passim.

22. Erickson, *American Industry and the European Immigrant,* p. 49.

23. Kirkland, *Industry Comes of Age,* p. 359.

24. Grob, *Workers and Utopia,* pp. 34–35.

25. Dick, *Labor and Socialism in America,* pp. 11–13.

26. Moses Rischin, "From Gompers to Hillman: Labor Goes Middle Class," *Antioch Review* 13 (June 1953):196.

27. Samuel Gompers, *Seventy Years of Life and Labor,* 2 vols. (New York, 1925), 1:21–22.

28. Ibid., 1:2–3, 5–7.

29. Ibid., 1:17.

30. Stuart Bruce Kaufman, *Samuel Gompers and the Origins of the American Federation of Labor, 1848–1896* (Westport, Conn., 1973), pp. 38–39.

31. Ibid., pp. 101–2.

32. Ibid., pp. 106–7.

33. Dick, *Labor and Socialism in America,* pp. 21–25.

34. Ibid., p. 25.

35. *Journal of United Labor,* 7 (November 25, 1886):2210; Norman Ware, *The Labor Movement in the United States, 1860–1895* (Gloucester, Mass., 1959), pp. 316–19.

36. Ira M. Leonard and Robert D. Parmet, *American Nativism, 1830–1860* (Huntington, N.Y., 1979), pp. 49–109.

37. Leonard Pitt, "The Beginnings of Nativism in California," *Pacific Historical Review* 30 (February, 1961):23–24.

38. Pitt, "The Beginnings of Nativism in California"; Ira B. Cross,

A History of the Labor Movement in California (New York, 1935), pp. 16–17.

39. The tax law was repealed in 1851, but reenacted in 1852 at three dollars per month. In 1853, 1855 and 1856 the legislature again changed the rate, finally settling at four dollars. Though amended afterward, the law remained basically intact until it was declared unconstitutional in 1870. Cross, p. 17; Pitt, "The Beginnings of Nativism in California," p. 28.

40. Pitt, "The Beginnings of Nativism in California"; Cross, pp. 73–75; Ping Chiu, *Chinese Labor in California, 1850–1880: An Economic Study* (Madison, 1963), p. 13..

41. Gunther Barth, *Bitter Strength: A History of the Chinese in the United States* (Cambridge, 1964), p. 1.

42. Mary Roberts Coolidge, *Chinese Immigration* (New York, 1969), pp. 41, 43, 43, n.

43. Alexander Saxton, *The Indispensable Enemy: Labor and the Anti-Chinese Movement in California* (Berkeley, 1971), pp. 7–8; Elmer Clarence Sandmeyer, *The Anti-Chinese Movement in California* (Urbana, 1939), pp. 28–29; Philip P. Choy, "Golden Mountain of Lead: The Chinese Experience in California," *California Historical Quarterly* 50 (September 1971):270.

44. Chiu, *Chinese Labor in California*, pp. 43–47.

45. Cross, *A History of the Labor Movement in California*, pp. 78–79.

46. George H. Tinkham, *California Men and Events: Time 1769–1890* (Stockton, Calif., 1915), p. 231.

47. Cross, *A History of the Labor Movement in California*, pp. 79–80.

48. Cross, *History of the Labor Movement,* pp. 80–81; Sandmeyer, *The Anti-Chinese Movement in California,* pp. 78–79; Taft, *Organized Labor in American History,* p. 301.

49. Saxton, *The Indispensable Enemy*, pp. 10–11.

Chapter Two

1. Irwin Yellowitz, *Industrialization and the American Labor Movement, 1850–1900* (Port Washington, N.Y., 1977) pp. 131–32.

2. Mary Roberts Coolidge, *Chinese Immigration* (New York, 1969), p. 128.

3. Ping Chiu, *Chinese Labor in California, 1850–1880: An Economic Study* (Madison, 1963), p. 49.

4. Vernon H. Jensen, *Heritage of Conflict: Labor Relations in the Nonferrous Metals Industry up to 1930* (New York, 1968), pp. 14–15.

5. Chicago *Workingman's Advocate*, February 6, 1869.

6. Ibid., May 29, 1869.

7. Ibid., June 12, 1869.

8. Ibid., July 17, 1869.

9. Ibid., August 7, 1869.

10. Jonathan Grossman, *William Sylvis, Pioneer of American Labor* (New York, 1945), p. 263.

11. *Workingman's Advocate*, September 4, 1869.

12. Frederick Rudolph, "Chinamen in Yankeedom: Anti-Unionism in Massachusetts in 1870," *American Historical Review* 53 (October 1947): 14–16; Stuart Creighton Miller, *The Unwelcome Immigrant: The American Image of the Chinese, 1785–1882* Berkeley, 1969), p. 194; Philip S. Foner, *History of the Labor Movement in the United States*, 4 vols. (New York, 1947–1965), 2:488.

13. T. V. Powderly, *Thirty Years of Labor, 1859 to 1889* (Columbus, 1889), p. 413.

14. Yellowitz, *Industrialization and the American Labor Movement*, p. 132.

15. George E. McNeill, ed., *The Labor Movement: The Problem of To-Day* (Boston, 1887), p. 431.

16. Powderly, *Thirty Years of Labor*, pp. 413–14; Rudolph, "Chinamen in Yankeedom," pp. 27–28; John Philip Hall, "The Knights of St. Crispin in Massachusetts, 1869–1878," *Journal of Economic History* 18 (June 1958):168.

17. Powderly, *Thirty Years of Labor*, pp. 414–15.

18. Elmer Clarence Sandmeyer, *The Anti-Chinese Movement in California* (Urbana, 1939), p. 47.

19. Ira B. Cross, *A History of the Labor Movement in California* (New York, 1966), p. 81.

20. Ibid., pp. 82–83.

21. Alexander Saxton, *The Indispensable Enemy: Labor and the Anti-Chinese Movement in California* (Berkeley, 1971), pp. 18–20, 23–24, 26–27, 29–30.

22. Robert Seager II, "Some Denominational Reactions to Chinese Immigration to California, 1856–1892," *Pacific Historical Review* 28 (February 1959):49–51, 53.

23. Philip Taft, *Organized Labor in American History* (New York, 1964), pp. 301–2.

24. Henryk Sienkiewicz, "The Chinese in California," Translated,

with Forward, by Charles Morley, *California Historical Society Quarterly* 34 (December 1955):301–16.

25. Roger R. Olmsted, "The Chinese Must Go!," *California Historical Quarterly* 50 (September 1971):285–86. Sandmeyer, *The Anti-Chinese Movement in California, p.* 17; Saxton, *The Indispensable Enemy,* pp. 10–11.

26. Coolidge, *Chinese Immigration,* p. 131.

27. George H. Tinkham, *California Men and Events: Time 1769–1890* (Stockton, Calif., 1915), p. 237, n.; Henry George, "The Kearney Agitation in California," *Popular Science Monthly* 17 (August 1880):438; Richard Dillon, *Humbugs and Heroes: A Gallery of California Pioneers* (Garden City, N.Y., 1970), p. 188.

28. George, "The Kearney Agitation in California," p. 439.

29. George, "The Kearney Agitation in California," p. 438; Ralph Kauer, "The Workingmen's Party of California," *Pacific Historical Review* 13 (September 1944):279.

30. Saxton, *The Indispensable Enemy,* pp. 113, 118.

31. Frank Roney, *Frank Roney, Irish Rebel and California Labor Leader: An Autobiography,* ed. Ira B. Cross (Berkeley, 1931), p. 270.

32. Tinkham, *California Men and Events,* p. 237, n.

33. Roney, *Frank Roney,* p. 271.

34. Chiu, *Chinese Labor in California,* pp. 137–38.

35. Saxton, *The Indispensable Enemy,* pp. 121–22; Roney, *Frank Roney,* pp. 285–88.

36. Kauer, "The Workingmen's Party of California," pp. 283–85.

37. Saxton, *The Indispensable Enemy,* pp. 119–20.

38. Kirk H. Porter and Donald Bruce Johnson, eds., *National Party Platforms, 1840–1956* (Urbana, 1956), pp. 50, 54.

39. James D. Richardson, comp., *A Compilation of the Messages and Papers of the Presidents, 1789–1898,* 10 vols. (Washington, 1900–1902), 1:514–20.

40. Cross, *A History of the Labor Movement in California,* p. 86.

41. *Journal of United Labor,* 1 (August 15, 1880):39; Gerald N. Grob, *Workers and Utopia: A Study of the Ideological Conflict in the American Labor Movement, 1865–1900* (Evanston, Ill., 1961), p. 57.

42. Sandmeyer, *The Anti-Chinese Movement in California,* p. 91; Roy L. Garis, *Immigration Restriction* (New York, 1927), pp. 292–94.

43. *Journal of United Labor,* 1 (December 15, 1880):79.

44. Federation of Organized Trades and Labor Unions of the United States and Canada, *Report of the First Annual Session* (Cincinnati, 1882), pp. 3–4; Philip Taft, *The A.F. of L. in the Time of Gompers* (New York, 1957), pp. 11–12.

45. FOTLU, *Report of the First Annual Session*, pp. 4, 20.

46. FOTLU, *Report*, p. 20; Taft, *The A.F. of L. in the Time of Gompers*, p. 12.

47. Garis, *Immigration Restrictions*, pp. 294–95.

48. Grob, *Workers and Utopia*, p. 58.

49. Federation of Organized Trades and Labor Unions of the United States and Canada, *Report of the Second Annual Session* (Cincinnati, 1883), p. 9.

50. Samuel Gompers, *Seventy Years of Life and Labor*, 2 vols. (New York, 1925), 1:216–17.

51. Ibid., 2:161.

52. Bernard Mandel, *Samuel Gompers: A Biography* (Yellow Springs, 1963), pp. 141–42. See also Arthur Mann, "Gompers and the Irony of Racism," *Antioch Review* 13 (June 1953):203–14, and Fred Greenbaum, "The Social Ideas of Samuel Gompers," *Labor History* 7 (Winter 1966):43.

53. U.S. Immigration Commission, *Reports of the Immigration Commission*, 41 vols. (New York, 1970), 3:420.

54. *Journal of United Labor* 3 (June 1882):252.

55. Ibid., 3 (September 1882):299.

56. Ibid., 4 (February 1884):636–37.

57. Garis, *Immigration Restriction*, pp. 295–96.

58. Grob, *Workers and Utopia*, p. 58; Knights of Labor, *Record of Proceedings of the Ninth Regular Session of the General Assembly* (n.p., n.d.), pp. 10–11; Powderly, *Thirty Years of Labor*, pp. 420–21.

59. Sandmeyer, *The Anti-Chinese Movement in California*, pp. 97–98.

60. Jules Alexander Karlin, "The Anti-Chinese Outbreak in Tacoma, 1885," *Pacific Historical Review* 23 (August 1954):271–80.

61. Jules Alexander Karlin, "The Anti-Chinese Outbreaks in Seattle, 1885–1886," *Pacific Northwest Quarterly* 39 (April 1948):103–12.

62. H. Brett Melendy, *The Oriental Americans* (New York, 1971), p. 40.

63. Federation of Organized Trades and Labor Unions of the United States and Canada, *Report of the Fifth Annual Session* (n.p., n.d.), p. 17.

64. W. W. Stone, "The Knights of Labor on the Chinese Labor Question," *Overland Monthly*, 2d ser. 7 (March 1886):225.

65. *Journal of United Labor* 7 (September 25, 1886):2176.

66. Knights of Labor, *Record of Proceedings of the Tenth Regular Session of the General Assembly* (n.p., 1888), pp. 190–92.

67. Federation of Organized Trades and Labor Unions of the

United States and Canada, *Report of the Sixth Annual Session* (n.p., n.d.), p. 7; American Federation of Labor, *Proceedings of the First Annual Convention* (n.p., n.d.), p. 17; Taft, *The A.F. of L. in the Time of Gompers*, pp. 37–38, 290.

68. Garis, *Immigration Restriction*, pp. 296–300.

69. Knights of Labor, *Proceedings of the Seventeenth Regular Session of the General Assembly* (Philadelphia, 1893), p. 5.

70. Garis, *Immigration Restriction*, p. 302.

71. John C. Appel, "American Labor and the Annexation of Hawaii: A Study in Logic and Economic Interest," *Pacific Historical Review* 23 (February 1954), 3–4.

72. Ibid., pp. 4–11. Another anti-imperialist argument made by labor people concerned defense and reflected an awareness of a Japanese-American rivalry in the Pacific. As one union publication said, "It is not a question of whether the annexation is desirable or not, but whether Hawaii shall become a station for attack by Japan or a station for defense for the United States" ("The Annexation of Hawaii," *Locomotive Firemen's Magazine* 23 (August 1897):96.

73. Samuel Gompers, "Travail of Imperialism and Expansion," *American Federationist* 5 (October 1898):159.

74. Samuel Gompers, "Imperialism. Its Dangers and Wrongs," *American Federationist* 5 (November 1898):182–83.

75: Richard E. Welch, Jr., *George Frisbie Hoar and the Half-Breed Republicans* (Cambridge, 1971), pp. 221–50.

76. Sandmeyer, *The Anti-Chinese Movement in California*, p. 106.

77. Knights of Labor, *Record of Proceedings of the Twenty-Fourth Regular Session of the General Assembly* (n.p., n.d.), pp. 56–57; American Federation of Labor, *Record of Proceedings of the Twentieth Annual Convention* (Washington, 1900), pp. 17, 179.

78. International Ladies' Garment Workers' Union, *Report of the Proceedings of the Second Annual Convention* (n.p., 1901?), pp. 5, 7, and *Report of the Proceedings of the Third Annual Convention* (New York, 1902), pp. 23–24; Louis Levine (pseud. Louis Lorwin), *The Women's Garment Workers* (New York, 1969), p. 111.

79. Knights of Labor, *Record of Proceedings of the Twenty-Fifth Regular Session of the General Assembly* (n.p., n.d.), pp. 28–29.

80. *Proceedings and List of Delegates, California Chinese Exclusion Convention* (San Francisco, 1901), pp. 14–20.

81. American Federation of Labor, *Report of Proceedings of the Twenty-First Annual Convention* (Washington, 1901), pp. 21–23, 63–69, 154–55.

82. [Samuel Gompers and Herman Gutstadt], *Some Reasons for*

Chinese Exclusion: Meat vs. Rice (Washington, 1902); Mandel, *Samuel Gompers,* p. 186. The Chinese responded with their own pamphlet, *Truth versus Fiction, Justice versus Prejudice: Meat for All, Not for a Few; A Plain and Unvarnished Statement Why Exclusion Laws against the Chinese Should NOT be Re-enacted; Respect Treaties and Make General, Not Special Laws* (n.p., 1902?).

83. Knights of Labor, *Proceedings of the Seventeenth Regular Session of the General Assembly,* p. 65.

84. Terence V. Powderly, *The Path I Trod,* ed. Harry J. Carman et al. (New York, 1940), p. 298; T. V. Powderly to William C. Arnold, April 9, 1897, Terence V. Powderly Papers, Catholic University of America, Washington, D.C., microfilm edition.

85. *Journal of the Knights of Labor* 17 (April 22, 1897):2; *New York Times,* July 19, 27, 1897; Sameuel Gompers, "Is Labor Honored by Such an Appointment?," *American Federationist* 5 (August 1897): 117; Powderly, *The Path I Trod,* p. 299.

86. Delber L. McKee, *Chinese Exclusion versus the Open Door Policy, 1900–1906: Clashes Over China Policy in the Roosevelt Era* (Detroit 1977), pp. 28–36. See also Delber L. McKee, " 'The Chinese Must Go!': Commissioner General Powderly and Chinese Immigration, 1897–1902," *Pennsylvania History* 44 (January 1977):40–41.

87. McKee, *Chinese Exclusion versus the Open Door Policy,* pp. 53–58.

88. Ibid., p. 59.

89. Ibid., pp. 59–60; Samuel Gompers, "Chinese Must Not be Permitted to Come," *American Federationist* 9 (March 1902): 124–25; Executive Council, American Federation of Labor to President of the United States, April 15, 1902, selections from the Samuel Gompers Papers, State Historical Society of Wisconsin, Madison, Wisc., microfilm.

Chapter Three

1. U.S. Bureau of the Census, *The Statistical History of the United States from Colonial Times to the Present* (Stamford, Conn., 1965), pp. 7, 66.

2. U.S. Bureau of Labor, *First Annual Report of the Commissioner of Labor, March, 1886* (Washington, 1886), p. 245; Wisconsin Bureau of Labor and Industrial Statistics, *Second Biennial Report, 1885–1886* (Madison, Wisc., 1886), p. 422.

3. U.S. Immigration Commission, *Reports, 3:* 9–11.

4. Maldwyn Allen Jones, *American Immigration* (Chicago, 1960), pp. 193–96.

5. Ibid., pp. 198–99.

6. Rudolph J. Vecoli, "*Contadini* in Chicago: A Critique of *the Uprooted*," *Journal of American History* 51 (December 1964): 406–7.

7. U.S. Bureau of the Census, *Statistical History of the United States*, pp. 56–57.

8. Jones *American Immigration*, pp. 201–02; Samuel Joseph, *Jewish Immigration to the United States from 1881 to 1910* (1914; Reprint New York: Arno Press and the New York Times, 1969), pp. 58–64, 93; Irving Howe, *World of Our Fathers* (New York, 1976), pp. 5, 26.

9. Philip Taylor, *The Distant Magnet: European Emigration to the U.S.A.* (New York, 1972), pp. 27–44.

10. Joseph Schachter, "Net Immigration of Gainful Workers into the United States, 1870–1930," *Demography* 9 (February 1972): 88–97.

11. John Higham, *Strangers in the Land: Patterns of American Nativism, 1860–1925* (New Brunswick, N.J., 1955), pp. 47–48.

12. Herbert G. Gutman, "The Buena Vista Affair, 1874–1875," *Pennsylvania Magazine of History and Biography* 88 (July 1964): 251–253, 256–287.

13. Jules I. Bogen, *The Anthracite Railroads: A Study in American Railroad Enterprise* (New York, 1927), p. 54.

14. Higham, *Strangers in the Land*, pp. 48–49.

15. Ibid., pp. 43–44.

16. *Journal of United Labor* 3 (May 1882):222.

17. *New York Times*, May 9, 1882.

18. Higham, *Strangers in the Land*, p. 43; *Jones, American Immigration*, pp. 250–51; Marion T. Bennett, *American Immigration Policies: A History* (Washington, 1963), pp. 16–18.

19. *New York Times*, May 3, 1883.

20. Erickson, *American Industry and the European Immigrant*, pp. 153–58.

21. Knights of Labor, *Record of Proceedings of the Eighth Regular Session of the General Assembly* (n.p., n.d.), pp. 575–76, 726.

22. *New York Times*, January 15, 1885; *Journal of United Labor* 5 (January 25, 1885):896–97.

23. Federation of Organized Trades and Labor Unions, *Report of the Fourth Annual Session* (Washington, 1884), p. 20; Gabriel Ed-

monston to Henry W. Blair, December 2, 1884, and Gabriel Edmonston to W. W. McLelland, December 2, 1884, Gompers Letterbooks.

24. Erickson, *American Industry and the European Immigrant,* pp. 158–61.

25. Morrell Heald, "Business Attitudes Toward European Immigration, 1880–1890, "*Journal of Economic History* 13 (Summer 1953):303.

26. Federation of Organized Trades and Labor Unions, *Record of Proceedings of the Fifth Annual Session* (n.p., n.d.), p. 8.

27. Ibid., pp. 103, 164–65.

28. Knights of Labor, *Record of Proceedings of the Ninth Regular Session of the General Assembly* (n.p., n.d.), p. 10.

29. Ibid., pp. 17–18.

30. Ibid., pp. 121, 164–65

31. Wisconsin Bureau of Labor and Industrial Statistics, *Second Biennial Report, 1885-1886* Madison, 1886), pp. 416–27.

32. U.S. Bureau of Labor, *First Annual Report,* pp. 246–47.

33. S. M. Jelley, *The Voice of Labor* (Chicago, 1887), pp. 327, 335, 338.

34. Erickson, *American Industry and the European Immigrant,* pp. 168–69.

35. *Journal of United Labor* 7 (March 12, 1887):2316.

36. Ibid., 7 (April 9, 1887):2345.

37. Ibid., 7 (April 30, 1887):2370.

38. Ibid., 7 (May 14, 1887):2385.

39. Ibid., 7 (June 11, 1887): 2421.

40. Ibid., 7 (June 18, 1887):2427.

41. Ibid., 7 (September 10, 1887):2487.

42. Ibid., 7 (December 24, 1887):2546.

43. Ibid., 7 (February 11, 1888):2574.
view 147 (August 1888):166, 168.

44. T. V. Powderly, "A Menacing Irruption," *North American Review* 147 (August 1888):166, 168.

45. *Journal of United Labor* 9 (September 6, 1888):2693.

46. Ibid., 9 (September 20, 27, October 4, 11, 1888):2701, 2705, 2709, 2713.

47. Report of the General Investigation of Woman's Work and Wages," p. 2, in Knights of Labor, *Record of Proceedings of the Twelfth Regular Session of the General Assembly* (Philadelphia: Journal of United Labor, 1888).

48. Samuel Gompers to Daniel McLaughlin, January 18, 20, 1888;

Gompers to Thomas Magone, January 18, 20, 1888, Gompers letter-books, Library of Congress, Washington, D.C., microfilm edition.

49. American Federation of Labor, *Report of Proceedings of the Third Annual Convention* (Philadelphia, 1899), p. 31.

50. American Federation of Labor, *Report of Proceedings of the Ninth Annual Convention* (Philadelphia, 1890), pp. 16–39.

Chapter Four

1. David Brody, *Steelworkers in America: The Nonunion Era* (New York, 1969), pp. 96–97.

2. Victor R. Greene, *The Slavic Community on Strike: Immigrant Labor in Pennsylvania Anthracite* (Notre Dame, 1968), p. 14.

3. U.S. Bureau of Labor, *Report on Conditions of Employment in the Iron and Steel Industry*, 4 vols. (Washington, 1911–1913), 3:112.

4. Carroll D. Wright, "The Amalgamated Association of Iron and Steel Workers," *Quarterly Journal of Economics* 7 (July 1893): 400–401.

5. U.S. Bureau of Labor, *Report on Conditions in Iron and Steel*, 3:113.

6. Brody, *Steelworkers: Nonunion Era*, p. 119.

7. Henry George, "Labor in Pennsylvania," Pt. 3, *North American Review*, 143 (October 1886):361.

8. Brody, *Steelworkers: Nonunion Era*, pp. 119–21.

9. John E. Bodnar, "The Formation of Ethnic Consciousness: Slavic Immigrants in Steelton," in *The Ethnic Experience in Pennsylvania*, ed. John E. Bodnar (Lewisburg, Pa., 1973), pp. 310–11.

10. John Bodnar, *Immigration and Industrialization: Ethnicity in an American Mill Town, 1870–1940* (Pittsburgh, 1977) p. 76.

11. Ibid., p. 77.

12. Bodnar, "Formation of Ethnic Consciousness," p. 312.

13. Bodnar, *Immigration and Industrialization*, pp. 78–80.

14. Ibid., pp. 54–55.

15. Michael P. Weber, "Residential and Occupational Patterns of Ethnic Minorities in Nineteenth Century Pittsburgh," *Pennsylvania History* 44 (October 1977):328.

16. Gabriel Kolko, *Main Currents in Modern American History* (New York, 1976), p. 70.

17. Ibid., p. 77.

18. Bodnar, *Immigrants and Industrialization*, p. 54.

19. Ibid., pp. 41–43.

20. Edward W. Bemis, "The Homestead Strike," *Journal of Political Economy* 2 (June 1894), 369, n., 372.

21. Foster Rhea Dulles, *Labor in America: A History* (3rd ed.; Northbrook, Ill., 1966), pp. 167–68.

22. Leon Wolff, *Lockout: The Story of the Homestead Strike of 1892* (New York, 1965), p. 241.

23. Andrew A. Marchbin, " Hungarian Activities in Western Pennsylvania," *Western Pennsylvania Historical Magazine* 22 (September 1940):165.

24. Eli Ginzberg and Hyman Berman, eds., *The American Worker in the Twentieth Century* (New York, 1963), pp. 44–47.

25. Margaret F. Byington, *Homestead: The Households of a Mill Town* (New York, 1910), p. 160.

26. Marchbin, "Hungarian Activities," p. 166.

27. James C. Davis, ed., "Growing Up in an Iron Town at the Turn of the Century: A Memoir by John Griffen Pennypacker," *Pennsylvania History* 44 (July 1977):247; Byington, *Homestead*, pp. 12–13.

28. Bodnar, *Immigrants and Industrialization*, pp. 39–40, 43.

29. Byington, *Homestead*, pp. 14–15.

30. John A. Fitch, *The Steel Workers* (New York, 1910), pp. 147–48.

31. Byington, *Homestead*, p. 4.

32. U.S. Immigration Commission, *Reports*, 8:91.

33. Ibid., 8:390.

34. Ibid., 8:388.

35. Robert L. Tyler, "The I. W. W. and the West," *American Quarterly* 12 (Summer 1960):179.

36. Rufus D. Smith, "Some Phases of the McKee's Rocks Strike," *Survey* 20 (October 2, 1909):38.

37. Paul U. Kellogg, "The McKee's Rocks Strike," *Survey* 20 (August 7, 1909):656.

38. Tyler, "The I. W. W. and the West," pp. 179–80.

39. Tyler, "The I. W. W.," p. 180; M. T. C. Wing, "The Flag at McKee's Rocks," *Survey* 23 (October 2, 1909):45.

40. Melvyn Dubofsky, *We Shall Be All: A History of the Industrial Workers of the World* (Chicago, 1969), pp. 206–9.

41. Bodnar, *Immigration and Industrialization*, p. 44.

42. Ibid., pp. 48–49.

43. Dulles, *Labor in America*, p. 233.

44. Ibid., pp. 233–34.

45. Brody, *Steelworkers: Nonunion Era*, pp. 222–25.

46. Ibid., pp. 258–60.

47. David J. Saposs, "The Mind of Immigrant Communities," in The Commission of Inquiry, The Interchurch World Movement, *Public Opinion and the Steel Strike* (New York: Harcourt Brace and Company, 1921), pp. 226, 235–38.

48. Brody, *Steelworkers: Nonunion Era,* pp. 261–62.

49. Irving Bernstein, *The Lean Years: A History of the American Worker, 1920–1933* (Baltimore, 1966), p. 51.

Chapter Five

1. Frank Julian Warne, "The Union Movement Among Coal-Mine Workers," *Bulletin of the U. S. Bureau of Labor,* no. 51 (March 1904), p. 380.

2. Amy Zahl Gottlieb, "The Influence of British Trade Unionists on the Regulation of the Mining Industry in Illinois, 1872," *Labor History* 19 (Summer 1978):397–405.

3. Clifton K. Yearley, Jr., *Britons in American Labor: A History of the Influence of the United Kingdom Immigrants on American Labor* (Baltimore, 1957), p. 135.

4. Gottlieb, "The Influence of British Trade Unionists," pp. 413–14.

5. James Rodechko, "Irish-American Society in the Pennsylvania Anthracite Region: 1870–1880," in *The Ethnic Experience in Pennsylvania*, ed. Bodnar, pp. 20–21.

6. Wayne G. Broehl, Jr., *The Molly Maguires* (Cambridge, 1964).

7. Yearley, *Britons in American Labor,* pp. 84–86.

8. Harold W. Aurand, *From the Molly Maguires to the United Mine Workers: The Social Ecology of an Industrial Union, 1869–1897* (Philadelphia, 1971), pp. 119–20.

9. Ibid., pp. 27–29.

10. McAlister Coleman, *Men and Coal* (New York, 1969), pp. 40–44.

11. Aurand, *From the Molly Maguires,* pp. 89–93.

12. Warne, "The Union Movement Among Coal-Mine Workers," pp. 385–87.

13. Aurand, *From the Molly Maguires,* pp. 118–20, 132.

14. Ibid., pp. 122–30.

15. G. O. Virtue, "The Anthracite Mine Laborers," *Bulletin of the Department of Labor,* no. 13 (November 1897), p. 750.

16. Greene, *The Slavic Community on Strike,* pp. 79–110.

17. Aurand, *From the Molly Maguires,* pp. 131–35; Warne, "The Union Movement Among Coal-Miners," p. 387.

18. John Brophy, *A Miner's Life*, ed. John O. P. Hall (Madison, 1964), p. 22.

19. Warne, "The Union Movement Among Coal-Mine Workers," p. 388.

20. Brophy, *A Miner's Life*, pp. 22–23.

21. Ibid., p. 23.

22. Henry Rood, "The Mine Laborers in Pennsylvania," *Forum* 14 (September 1892):121.

23. Brophy, *A Miner's Life*, pp. 29–30, 32.

24. Virtue, "The Anthracite Mine Laborers," p. 753.

25. U. S. Industrial Commission, *Reports of the Industrial Commission on Immigration* (New York, 1970), p. 32.

26. Ibid., pp. xxxiii–xxxiv.

27. Ginzberg and Berman, eds., *The American Worker in the Twentieth Century*, p. 56.

28. Joseph M. Gowaskie, "From Conflict to Cooperation: John Mitchell and Bituminous Coal Operators," *Historian* 38 (August 1976):674–75.

29. Peter Roberts, *The Anthracite Coal Industry* (New York, 1901), p. 104. See also Peter Roberts, *Anthracite Coal Communities* (New York, 1904), pp. 19–21.

30. These percentages were based on a survey of 92,485 employees of 116 of a total of 140 athracite companies and 55,583 employees of 398 bituminous companies. Frank J. Sheridan, "Italian, Slavic, and Hungarian Unskilled Immigrant Laborers in the United States," *Bulletin of the U. S. Bureau of Labor*, no. 72 (September 1907), p. 413.

31. Greene, *The Slavic Community on Strike*, pp. 129–51; Chris Evans, *History of the United Mine Workers of America, 1860–1900*, 2 vols. (Indianapolis, 1918), 2:610–12; Michael Novak, *The Guns of Lattimer* (New York, 1978), pp. 123–34, 199–237.

32. Greene, pp. 121–25.

33. Greene, *The Slavic Community on Strike*, p. 124.

34. United Mine Workers of America, *Proceedings of the Ninth Annual Convention* (Indianapolis, 1898), p. 28.

35. Patrick Dolan to M. D. Ratchford, August 8, 1898, John Mitchell Papers, Catholic University of America, Washington, D.C., microfilm edition. Dolan's "find," John Hepner, did not last very long. He allegedly appeared "intoxicated when under pay," and spent "more of his time . . . destroying confidence of the miners in National officials than in trying to organize them." John Mitchell to Louis Goaziou, August 31, 1899.

36. Dolan to Ratchford, August 30, 1898.

37. Ibid., August 22, 1898.

38. United Mine Workers of America, *Proceedings of the Twelfth Annual Convention* (Indianapolis, 1901), pp. 51, 90.

39. Frank Julian Warne, *The Coal-Mine Workers: A Study in Labor Organization* (New York, 1905), pp. 33–34.

40. *Constitution of the National United Mine Workers of America, Revision 1901* (n.p., n.d.), p. 16.

41. Carter Goodrich, *The Miner's Freedom: A Study of the Working Life in a Changing Industry* (Boston, 1925), pp. 109–10.

42. William Warner to John Mitchell, August 14, 1899, Mitchell Papers.

43. Greene, The Slavic Community on Strike, pp. 127–44; Victor R. Greene, "A Study in Slavs, Strikes and Unions: The Anthracite Strike of 1897," *Pennsylvania History* 31 (April 1964), 211–12.

44. Warne, "The Union Movement Among Coal-Mine Workers," p. 412.

45. John Mitchell to William D. Ryan, September 24, 1900, Mitchell Papers.

46. United Mine Workers of America, *Proceedings of the Twelfth Annual Convention*, p. 53.

47. United Mine Workers of America, *Minutes of the National Executive Board*, April 11, 1901, Mitchell Papers.

48. John Mitchell to William Hawthorne, May 2, 1899.

49. United Mine Workers of America, *Proceedings of the Thirteenth Annual Convention* (Indianapolis, 1902), pp. 55–56.

50. Warne, *The Coal-Mine Workers*, pp. 29–30.

51. United Mine Workers of America, *Proceedings of the Nineteenth Annual Convention* (Indianapolis, 1908), p. 26.

52. Greene, *The Slavic Community on Strike*, pp. 170–71.

53. Warne, "The Union Movement Among Coal-Mine Workers," p. 412; Dulles, *Labor in America*, p. 189.

54. Elsie Glück, *John Mitchell: Labor's Bargain with the Gilded Age* (New York, 1929), pp. 4–7.

55. Coleman, *Men and Coal*, pp. 59–63.

56. Ibid., p. 68.

57. Coleman, *Men and Coal*, p. 69; Glück, *John Mitchell*, p. 72.

58. United States Anthracite Coal Commission, *Report to the President on the Anthracite Coal Strike of May-October, 1902* (Washington, 1903), pp. 33–35.

59. Coleman, *Men and Coal*, p. 70.

60. William Henry Harbaugh, *Power and Responsibility: The Life and Times of Theodore Roosevelt* (New York, 1961), pp. 166–81.

61. Aurand, *From the Molly Maguires*, pp. 200–203.

62. John Mitchell to T. V. Powderly, January 6, 1902, Mitchell Papers.

63. Louis N. Hammerling to John Mitchell, July 15, 1902, Mitchell Papers.

64. Ibid., August 15, 1903.

65. Hammerling to Mitchell, November 29, December 1, 1902; Mitchell to Boise Penrose, Mitchell to Matthew S. Quay, and Mitchell to Samuel W. Pennypacker, December 3, 1902; Hammerling to Mitchell, November 17, 1904, February 8, 1905; Mitchell to Hammerling, February 1, 5, 1905, Mitchell Papers; James O. Morris, "The Acquisitive Spirit of John Mitchell, UMW President (1899–1908)," *Labor History* 20 (Winter 1979):27–28.

66. Hammerling to Mitchell, December 27, 1902, October 17, 1903, November 5, 1904, Mitchell Papers.

67. Mitchell to Hammerling, January 1, 1903, November 7, 1904, Mitchell Papers.

68. During his presidency of the United Mine Workers, Mitchell received a considerable amount of income beyond his salary from questionable practices. Morris, "The Acquisitive Spirit of John Mitchell," pp. 8–43.

69. John Mitchell, "The Case of the Non-Unionist," *American Federationist* 10 (December 1903):1304.

70. John Mitchell, *Organized Labor* (Philadelphia, 1903), pp. 180–84.

71. United Mine Workers of America, *Proceedings of the Seventeenth Annual Convention* (Indianapolis, 1906), p. 55.

72. Immigration Department, National Civic Federation, *Facts About Immigration: Being the Report of the Proceedings of Conferences on Immigration held in New York City, September 24 and December 12, 1906* (n.p., 1907), pp. 68–69.

73. Glück, *John Mitchell*, pp. 197–219.

74. John Mitchell, "Immigration and the American Laboring Classes," *Annals of the American Academy of Political and Social Science* 34 (July 1909):125–29.

75. United Mine Workers of America, *Proceedings of the Sixteenth Annual Convention* (Indianapolis, 1905), pp. 176–85, 205–6.

76. Graham Àdams, Jr., *Age of Industrial Violence, 1910–15* (New York, 1966), pp. 151–61; George S. McGovern and Leonard F. Guttridge, *The Great Coalfield War* (Boston, 1972), pp. 210–68.

Chapter Six

1. Joel Seidman, *The Needle Trades* (New York, 1942), pp. 30–31; Morris Hillquit, "Rise of the Russian Jew," *American Hebrew* 126 (November 22, 1929):36.

2. Judith Greenfeld, "The Role of the Jews in the Development of the Clothing Industry in the United States," *YIVO Annual of Jewish Social Science* 2–3 (1947–1948):180.

3. Mabel Hurd Willett, *The Employment of Women in the Clothing Trade* (New York, 1902), pp. 33–34.

4. Jesse Eliphalet Pope, *The Clothing Industry in New York* (Columbia, 1905), p. 27.

5. Moses Rischin, *The Promised City: New York's Jews, 1870–1914* (Cambridge, 1962), p. 62; Greenfeld, "The Role of the Jews," p. 182.

6. Robert Ernst, *Immigrant Life in New York City, 1825–1863* (New York, 1949), p. 77.

7. Ibid.

8. Egal Feldman, "Jews in the Early Growth of New York City's Men's Clothing Trade," *American Jewish Archives* 12 (April 1960): 4–6, 13.

9. Seidman, *The Needle Trades*, pp. 32–33; Rischin, *The Promised City*, p. 62.

10. Greenfeld, "The Role of the Jews," p. 183.

11. William Morris Leiserson, "The Jewish Labor Movement in New York" (B.A. thesis, University of Wisconsin, 1908), p. 17.

12. Pope, *The Clothing Industry*, pp. 41–43.

13. Melech Epstein, *Jewish Labor in U.S.A.*, (2 vols. (New York, 1969), 1:87–90.

14. Abraham Menes, "The East Side and the Jewish Labor Movement," *Voices from the Yiddish: Essays, Memoirs, Diaries*, ed. Irving Howe and Eliezer Greenberg (Ann Arbor, 1972), p. 204.

15. Abraham Cahan, *The Education of Abraham Cahan*, trans. by Leon Stein, Abraham P. Conan, and Lynn Davison (Philadelphia: Jewish Publication Society of America, 1969), p. 400.

16. Pope, *The Clothing Industry*, pp. 52–53, 56.

17. Seidman, *The Needle Trades*, pp. 33–34.

18. Will Herberg, "The Jewish Labor Movement in the United States," *American Jewish Year Book* 53 (1952):4.

19. Selig Perlman, "Jewish-American Unionism, Its Birth Pangs and Contribution to the General American Labor Movement," *Pub-*

lications of the American Jewish Historical Society 41 (June 1953): 302–3.

20. Solomon F. Bloom, "The Saga of America's 'Russian' Jews: The Molding of a Generation in the Industrial Crucible," *Commentary* 1 (February 1946):6.

21. Jacob Lestchinsky, "The Socio-Economic Physiognomy of Jewish Immigration to the United States," *YIVO Annual of Jewish Social Science* 9 (1954), 377–78.

22. Roy B. Helfgott, "Trade Unionism Among the Jewish Garment Workers of Britain and the United States," *Labor History* 2 (Spring 1961):205–6.

23. Menes, "The East Side and the Jewish Labor Movement," pp. 204–5.

24. Ibid., pp. 205–6.

25. Herberg, "The Jewish Labor Movement in the United States," p. 5.

26. Elias Tcherikower, ed., *The Early Jewish Labor Movement in the United States*, trans. Aaron Antonovsky (New York, 1961), pp. 153–55; Nathan Goldberg, "Occupational Patterns of American Jews," *Jewish Review* 3 (April 1945):7.

27. Menes, "The East Side and the Jewish Labor Movement," pp. 205–6.

28. Pope, The Clothing Industry, p. 293; Burton J. Hendrick, "The Jewish Invasion of America," *McClure's Magazine* 40 (March 1913):134, 136.

29. C. Bezalel Sherman, "Nationalism, Secularism and Religion in the Jewish Labor Movement," in *Voices from the Yiddish*, ed. Howe and Greenberg, pp. 221–22.

30. Menes, "The East Side and the Jewish Labor Movement," p. 213.

31. C. Bezalel Sherman, "Labor in the Totality of Jewish Life," *YIVO Annual of Jewish Social Science* 9 (1954):381.

32. Melvyn Dubofsky, *When Workers Organize: New York City in the Progressive Era* (Amherst, 1968), p. 17; Perlman, "Jewish-American Unionism," pp. 305–7.

33. Edwin Fenton, *Immigrants and Unions, A Case Study: Italians and American Labor, 1870–1920* (New York, 1975), p. 467.

34. Louise C. Odencrantz, *Italian Women in Industry: A Study of Conditions in New York City* (New York, 1919), p. 38.

35. Fenton, *Immigrants and Unions*, pp. 468–69; Willett, *The Employment of Women in the Clothing Trade*, p. 38.

36. Thomas Kessner, *The Golden Door: Italian and Jewish Im-*

migrant Mobility in New York City, 1880–1915 (New York, 1977), pp. 75–77.

37. Pope, *The Clothing Industry,* pp. 53–54; Hyman Berman, "Era of the Protocol, A Chapter in the History of the International Ladies' Garment Workers' Union, 1910–1916" (Ph.D. dissertation, Columbia University, 1956), pp. 24–25.

38. Fenton, *Immigrants and Unions,* pp. 466–67.

39. Dubofsky, *When Workers Organize,* pp. 17–18.

40. J. M. Budish and George Soule, *The New Unionism in the Clothing Industry* (New York, 1920), pp. 64–65.

41. Odencrantz, *Italian Women in Industry,* p. 206.

42. Ibid., pp. 77–78, 104.

43. Ibid., pp. 105, 293.

44. Greenfeld, "The Role of the Jews," p. 199.

45. United States Industrial Commission, *Reports of the Industrial Commission on Immigration: Including Testimony with Review and Digest* (New York, 1970), pp. xxiv, 316.

46. Abraham M. Rogoff, *Formative Years of the Jewish Labor Movement in the United States (1890–1900)* (New York, 1945), pp. 40–41.

47. Greenfeld, "The Role of the Jews," p. 100.

48. Rogoff, *Formative Years of the Jewish Labor Movement,* p. 41.

49. Willett, *The Employment of Women in the Clothing Trade,* p. 36; Harry Best, *The Men's Garment Industry of New York and the Strike of 1913* (New York, 1914), p. 6; Leiserson, "The Jewish Labor Movement in New York," p. 20.

50. Seidman, *The Needle Trades,* p. 34.

51. Tcherikower, *The Early Jewish Labor Movement,* pp. 361–62. Though the Polish and Russian Jews easily displaced German, Irish, and Swedish garment workers in New York, they did not have the same effect in Chicago. There the other groups held firm and the Jews constituted only a fourth of the work force, which was a third of their strength in New York, by 1900. See Wilfred Carsel, *A History of the Chicago Ladies' Garment Workers' Union* (Chicago, 1940), p. 13.

52. Leiserson, "The Jewish Labor Movement in New York," pp. 13–14.

53. Abraham Cahan, "The Body and Soul of the Labor Movement," *Ladies' Garment Worker* 7 (November 1916):14.

54. United States Industrial Commission, *Reports on Immigration,* pp. xxvi, 327.

55. Rogoff, *Formative Years of the Jewish Labor Movement*, pp. 43–44.

56. Leiserson, "The Jewish Labor Movement in New York," pp. 17–18.

57. Tcherikower, *The Early Jewish Labor Movement*, p. 308.

58. Tcherikower, *Early Jewish Labor Movement*, pp. 308–10; Leiserson, "The Jewish Labor Movement in New York," pp. 58–59.

59. Norma Fain Pratt, *Morris Hillquit: A Political History of an American Jewish Socialist* (Westport, Conn., 1979), pp. 20–21.

60. Morris Hillquit, "Speech at Carnegie Hall Celebration of the Fortieth Anniversary of the United Hebrew Trades, December 22, 1928" (Morris Hillquit Papers, State Historical Society of Wisconsin, Madison, Wisconsin, microfilm edition), p. 2.

61. Herberg, "The Jewish Labor Movement in the United States," p. 8; Mandel, *Samuel Gompers*, p. 141; Moses Rischin, "The Jewish Labor Movement in America," *Labor History* 4 (Fall 1963):231–32.

62. L. Glen Seretan, *Daniel DeLeon: The Odyssey of An American Marxist* (Cambridge, 1979), pp. 143–44.

63. Donald B. Robinson, *Spotlight on a Union: The Story of the United Hatters Cap and Millinery Workers International Union* (New York, 1948), pp. 177–78.

64. Robinson, *Spotlight on a Union*, p. 178; Charles H. Green, *The Headwear Workers: A Century of Trade Unionism* (New York, 1944), p. 95.

65. Herberg, "The Jewish Labor Movement in the United States," p. 13.

66. Seidman, *The Needle Trades*, pp. 86–87.

67. Ibid., p. 87.

68. Ibid.

69. Rogoff, *Formative Years of the Jewish Labor Movement*, p. 46; Budish and Soule, *The New Unionism in the Clothing Industry*, pp. 73–74.

70. Leiserson, "The Jewish Labor Movement in New York," pp. 56–57.

71. Seidman, *The Needle Trades*, pp. 88–89; Budish and Soule, *The New Unionism in the Clothing Industry*, pp. 74–75.

72. Willett, *The Employment of Women in the Clothing Trade*, p. 168.

73. Ibid., pp. 190–91.

Chapter Seven

1. Greenfeld, "The Role of the Jews," pp. 187–88.

2. Louis Levine, *The Women's Garment Workers* (New York, 1969), pp. 32–43.

3. Levine, *Women's Garment Workers*, pp. 77–91, 99–104; Rogoff, *Formative Years of the Jewish Labor Movement*, pp. 79–81.

4. Joseph Brandes, "From Sweatshop to Stability: Jewish Labor Between Two World Wars," *YIVO Annual of Jewish Social Science* 16 (1976):17.

5. Herberg, "The Jewish Labor Movement in the United States," p. 11; Irving Howe, with Kenneth Libo, *World of Our Fathers* (New York, 1976), pp. 296–97.

6. Seidman, *The Needle Trades*, pp. 96–99.

7. Epstein, *Jewish Labor in U. S. A.*, I, 366–67.

8. Rischin, *The Promised City*, pp. 190–91.

9. Herberg, "The Jewish Labor Movement in the United States," pp. 15–16.

10. Hyman Berman, "Era of the Protocol, A Chapter in the History of the International Ladies' Garment Workers' Union, 1910–1916" (Ph.D. dissertation, Columbia University, 1956), p. 52.

11. Levine, *The Women's Garment Workers*, pp. 135–39.

12. Seidman, *The Needle Trades*, p. 101.

13. Herberg, "The Jewish Labor Movement in the United States," p. 17.

14. Levine, *The Women's Garment Workers*, p. 144.

15. Dubofsky, *When Workers Organize*, pp. 50–52.

16. Herberg, "The Jewish Labor Movement in the United States," p. 17; Levine, *The Women's Garment Workers*, pp. 154–55.

17. Howe, *World of Our Fathers*, pp. 299–300.

18. Fenton, *Immigrants and Unions*, pp. 489–90.

19. Adriana Spadoni, "The Italian Working Woman in New York," *Collier's* 44 (March 23, 1912):14.

20. Fenton, *Immigrants and Unions*, pp. 492–93.

21. Levine, *The Women's Garment Workers*, pp. 165–67.

22. Seidman, *The Needle Trades*, p. 104.

23. Levine, *The Women's Garment Workers*, pp. 177–78; International Ladies' Garment Workers' Union, *Report and Proceedings of the Tenth Convention . . . 1910* (n.p., n.d.), p. 77; "The International Union in 1910," *Ladies' Garment Worker* 2 (January 1911):1.

24. "Convention Decides Upon A Weekly Official Organ," *Ladies' Garment Worker* 9 (June 1918):27–31.

25. International Ladies' Garment Workers' Union, *Report and Proceedings* . . . *1910*, pp. 49, 74–75, 83; Fenton, *Immigrants and Unions*, pp. 496–97.

26. Levine, *The Women's Garment Workers*, pp. 181–82ffi *Ladies' Garment Worker* 2 (January 1911):2.

27. Fenton, *Immigrants and Unions*, pp. 498–99.

28. Selig Perlman, *A History of Trade Unionism in the United States* (New York, 1950, p. 220; Perlman, "Jewish-American Unionism," pp. 298, 311–25; Herberg, "The Jewish Labor Movement in the United States," pp. 18–19; Jack Barbash, "Ethnic Factors in the Development of the American Labor Movement," in Industrial Relations Research Association, *Interpreting the Labor Movement* (Champaign, Ill.: Twin City Printing Co., 1952), p. 72; Dubofsky, *When Workers Organize*, pp. 60–66.

29. Dubofsky, *When Workers Organize*, pp. 86–97.

30. Leon Stein, ed., *Out of the Sweatshop: The Struggle for Industrial Democracy* (New York, 1977), pp. 188–201; Ronald Sanders, *The Downtown Jews: Portrait of an Immigrant Generation* (New York, 1969), pp. 393–96.

31. Berman, "Era of the Protocol," p. 24.

32. Emily Krial, "Report of Cleveland Action Committee," *Ladies' Garment Worker* 3 (January 1912):5–6.

33. "What the New York Women's Trade Union League is Doing To Organize Women," *Ladies' Garment Worker* 3 (January 1911):5.

34. International Ladies' Garment Workers' Union, *Report and Proceedings of the Eleventh Convention* . . . *1912* (n.p., n.d.), p. 5.

35. International Ladies' Garment Workers' Union, pp. 100–101; Fenton, *Immigrants and Unions*, p. 506.

36. Fenton, *Immigrants and Unions*, pp. 503–4; International Ladies' Garment Workers' Union, *Report and Proceedings* . . . *1912*, pp. 89–90.

37. M. D. Danish, "Local News and Events," *Ladies' Garment Worker* 8 (July 1917):20–21.

38. Fenton, *Immigrants and Unions*, pp. 507–8.

39. Abraham Baroff, "Splendid Results of a Bloodless Struggle in The Waist and Dress Trade," *Ladies' Garment Worker* 4 (June 1913):1–2.

40. Ibid, p. 2.

41. Berman, "Era of the Protocol," p. 24.

42. Pauline M. Newman, "Our Women Workers," *Ladies' Garment Worker* 4 (July 1913):21.

43. Ibid., pp. 20–21.

44. Pauline M. Newman, "Our Women Workers," *Ladies' Garment Worker* 4 (September 1913):18.

45. Pauline M. Newman, "Our Women Workers," *Ladies' Garment Worker* 5 (January 1914):20–21; "Need of Amalgamating Our Press," *Ladies' Garment Worker* 5 (August 1914):7–8.

46. "Organizers' Reports," *Ladies' Garment Worker* 6 (March 1915):18.

47. H. Dubinsky, "Reports of Organizers," *Ladies' Garment Worker* 6 (June 1915):21.

48. A. A. Kazen, "Annual Report of Cloak Pressers' Union, Local No. 35," *Ladies' Garment Worker* 6 (April 1915):17.

49. J. B. S. Hardman, "The Jewish Labor Movement in the United States: Jewish and Non-Jewish Influences," *American Jewish Historical Quarterly* 52 (December 1962):104.

50. Herman Feldman, *Racial Factors in American Industry* (New York, 1931), p. 221.

51. Melvyn Dubofsky, "Organized Labor and the Immigrant in New York, 1900–1918," *Labor History* 2 (Spring 1961):187–89.

52. American Federation of Labor, *Report of Proceedings of the Twentieth Annual Convention . . . 1900* (Washington, 1900), pp. 148–49.

53. Best, *The Men's Garment Industry of New York and the Strike of 1913*, pp. 13–14.

54. Budish and Soule, *The New Unionism in the Clothing Industry*, p. 85.

55. Herberg, "The Jewish Labor Movement in the United States," pp. 21–22. For more extensive treatment of the role of the Women's Trade Union League, see Cecyle S. Neidle, *America's Immigrant Women* (Boston, 1975), pp. 147–51.

56. Herberg, "Jewish Labor Movement," pp. 22–23; Sanders, *The Downtown Jews*, pp. 404–12.

57. Budish and Soule, *The New Unionism in the Clothing Industry*, pp. 86–87.

58. Budish and Soule, *New Unionism*, pp. 87–88; Herberg, "The Jewish Labor Movement in the United States," p. 23.

59. Matthew Josephson, *Sidney Hillman: Statesman of American Labor* (Garden City, N.Y., 1952), pp. 17–37.

60. Moses Rischin, "From Gompers to Hillman: Labor Goes Middle Class," *Antioch Review* 13 (June 1953):195–96; George Soule, *Sidney Hillman: Labor Statesman* (New York, 1939), pp. 12–30.

61. Epstein, *Jewish Labor in U. S. A.*, 2:44–48.

62. A. I. Shiplacoff to Samuel Gompers, June 23, 1915, Benjamin

Schlesinger Correspondence, International Ladies' Garment Workers' Union Archives, New York, N.Y.

63. International Ladies' Garment Workers' Union, Minutes of the Fifth Quarterly Meeting of the General Executive Board, October 18–21, 1915, microfilm, p. 333, I.L.G.W.U. Archives.

64. Dubofsky, "Organized Labor and the Immigrant in New York, 1900–1918," pp. 195–96.

65. Fenton, *Immigrants and Unions*, pp. 531–34.

66. "The Racial Hatred Serpent," *Garment Worker* 15 (November 12, 1915):4; In August 1917, General Secretary-Treasurer Abraham Baroff complained to the I.L.G.W.U.'s General Executive Board that Gompers had been attacking the Jewish unions whenever he had a chance to discredit them. Moreover, Gompers allegedly permitted an anti-Semitic attack to be printed in the *American Federationist*. International Ladies' Garment Workers' Union, Minutes of the Fourth Quarterly Meeting of the General Executive Board, August 17–23, 1917, microfilm, p. 701, I.L.G.W.U. Archives.

67. Dubofsky, "Organized Labor and the Immigrant in New York, 1900–1918," pp. 196–97; Howe, *World of Our Fathers*, p. 304.

68. Budish and Soule, *The New Unionism in the Clothing Industry*, p. 93; A. Rosebury, "Light and Shade at the St. Paul Convention," *Ladies' Garment Worker* 9 (July 1918):10–11; International Ladies' Garment Workers' Union, Minutes of the Third Quarterly Meeting of the General Executive Board, January 22–26, 1915, microfilm, p. 219, I.L.G.W.U. Archives.

69. A. Rosebury, "The American Federation of Labor and The Jewish Trade Unions," *Ladies' Garment Worker* 9 (March 1918):-12–15.

70. Dubofsky, "Organized Labor and the Immigrant in New York, 1900–1918," p. 197.

71. Budish and Soule, *The New Unionism in the Clothing Industry*, p. 95.

Chapter Eight

1. U.S. Bureau of the Census, *Statistical History of the United States*, pp. 56–57.

2. U.S. Bureau of the Census, *Sixteenth Census of the United States: 1940*, 2:43.

3. Rudolph Vecoli, "The Italian-Americans," *Center Magazine* 7 (July–August 1974):31.

4. Alexander DeConde, *Half Bitter, Half Sweet: An Excursion into Italian-American History* (New York, 1971), p. 101.

5. Ibid., pp. 3–8.

6. Robert F. Foerster, *The Italian Emigration of Our Times* (Cambridge, 1919), p. 323.

7. DeConde, *Half Bitter, Half Sweet,* p. 15.

8. Robert F. Harney, "The Padrone and the Immigrant," *Canadian Review of American Studies* 5 (Fall 1974):101–2.

9. Giovanni Schiavo, *The Italians in America Before the Civil War* (New York, 1934), p. 11.

10. Deconde, *Half Bitter, Half Sweet,* pp. 15–16.

11. Foerster, *The Italian Emigration of Our Times,* pp. 324–5; Luciano John Iorizzo "Italian Immigration and the Impact of the Padrone System" (Ph.D. dissertation, Syracuse University, 1966), pp. 30–31.

12. Betty Boyd Caroli, *Italian Repatriation from the United States, 1900-1914* (New York, 1973), p. 29.

13. Samuel L. Baily, "The Italians and the Development of Organized Labor in Argentine, Brazil, and the United States, 1880-1914," *Journal of Social History* 3 (Winter 1967–1970:127; Alberto Pecorini, "The Italian as an Agricultural Laborer," *Annals of the American Academy of Political and Social Science* 33 (March 1909):158.

14. Andrew F. Rolle,*The Immigrant Upraised: Italian Adventurers and Colonists in an Expanding America* (Norman 1968), pp. 20–22.

15. Ibid., pp. 27–28.

16. Henry Cabot Lodge, "Lynch Law and Unrestricted Immigration," *North American Review* 107 (May 1891):608–09.

17. John Foster Carr, "The Coming of the Italian," *Outlook* 82 (February 24, 1906), 421–22. The demographic nature of the Italian migrants reveals that most expected to return. They were typically young men. Between 1869 and 1910, seventy-eight percent of them were male, and from 1881 to 1930 between sixty-nine and eighty-three percent were in the fourteen to forty-four age group. As the years passed, this group's desire to return seemed to increase. Though only ten percent of the 1887–1890 arrivals went back, the return rate for the three decades beginning in 1891 constantly accelerated to where it reached eighty-two percent for the 1910–1920 arrivals.

Among the Italian immigrants arriving in America each year were many who had been there previously. Roughly fifteen percent of the 1899–1910 arrivals were in this category. "If no duplication occurred because of repeated journeys by the same individual, more than one and one-half million Italians returned to their home country between

1900 and 1914 after a period of temporary residence in the United States." Called *"Americani,"* the returnees constituted "nearly one in 20" of the Italian peninsula's inhabitants. See Silvano M. Tomasi, *Piety and Power: The Role of the Italian Parishes in the New York Metropolitan Area, 1880-1930* (Staten Island, N.Y., 1975), pp.18–21; Caroli, *Italian Repatriation from the United States, 1900–1914*, p. 41.

18. Foerster, *The Italian Emigration of Our Times*, p. 325.

19. John Koren, "The Padrone System and Padrone Banks," *Bulletin of the Department of Labor, no.* 9 (March 1897), 115.

20. Foner, *History of the Labor Movement in the United States*, 2:17–18.

21. Daniel J. Walkowitz, *Worker City, Company Town: Iron and Cotton-Worker Protest in Troy and Cohoes, New York, 1855–84* (Urbana, 1978), pp. 232–33, 240–41, 243.

22. Foerster, *The Italian Emigration of Our Times*, pp. 402–3.

23. Richarl L. Ehrlich, "Immigrant Strikebreaking Activity: A Sampling of Opinions Expressed in the *National Labor Tribune, 1878–1885*," *Labor History* 15 (Fall, 1974):541–42.

24. Bodnar, *Immigration and Industrialization*, pp.43–44.

25. Rudolph J. Vecoli, "Chicago's Italians Prior to World War I: A Study of Their Social and Economic Adjustment" (Ph.D. dissertation, University of Wisconsin, 1962), pp. 406–7.

26. Edward F. McSweeney, *"Immigration," American Feferation* 2 (December, 1895):1974.

27. Humbert S. Nelli, "The Italian Padrone System in the United States," *Labor History* 5 (Spring 1964):153; Koren, "The Padrone System and Padrone Banks," p. 125.

28. Iorizzo, "Italian Immigration and the Impact of the Padrone System," pp. 74–75.

29. Nelli, "The Italian Padrone System in the United States," p. 154; Koren, "The Padrone System and Padrone Banks," pp. 113–14; Erickson, *American Industry and the European Immigrant, 1860–1885*, pp. 83–87.

30. Giovanni Ermenegildo Schiavo, *Italian-American History*, (2 vols. (New York, 1947–1949), 1:537.

31. Vecoli, *"Contadini* in Chicago: A Critique of *The Uprooted*," p. 412.

32. Vecoli, *"Contadini in* Chicago"; John S. MacDonald and Leatrice D. MacDonald, "Urbanization, Ethnic Groups, and Social Segmentation," *Social Research* 29 (Winter 1962):437–45.

33. Humbert S. Nelli, *The Italians in Chicago, 1880–1930: A Study*

in Ethnic Mobility, (New York, 1970), p. 59; Koren, "The Padrone System and Padrone Banks," p. 114.

34. Luciano J. Iorizzo, "The Padrone and Immigrant Distribution," in *The Italian Experience in the United States,* ed. Silvano M. Tomasi and Madeline H. Engel (Staten Island, N.Y.: Center for Migration Studies, 1970), pp. 73–75.

35. Charles B. Phipard, "The Philanthropist-Padrone," *Charities* 12 (May 7, 1904):470.

36. Caroline Golab, *Immigrant Destinations* (Philadelphia, 1977), pp. 25, 108.

37. Iorizzo, "Italian Immigration and the Impact of the Padrone System," pp. 125–33; Luciano J. Iorizzo and Salvatore Mondello, *The Italian-Americans* (New York, 1971), 141, 143–57; Clement Lawrence Valletta, *A Study of Americanization in Carneta: Italian-American Identity Through Three Generations* (New York, 1975), pp. 97–100.

38. Iorizzo and Mondello, *The Italian-Americans,* pp. 143–44.

39. Valletta, *A Study of Americanization in Carneta,* pp. 97–100, 104.

40. Schiavo, *Italian-American History,* 1:538.

41. Nelli, "The Italian Padrone System in the United States," p. 164.

42. Nelli, *The Italians in Chicago, 1880–1930,* pp. 59-60.

43. S. Merlino, "Italian Immigrants and Their Enslavement," *Forum* 15 (April 1893):186.

44. Dominic T. Ciolli, "The 'Wop' in the Track Gang," *Immigrants in America Review* 2 (July 1916):61–62.

45. Gino C. Speranza, "Forced Labor in West Virginia," *Outlook* 74 (June 13, 1903):408; Merlino, "Italian Immigrants and Their Enslavement," pp. 186–87.

46. Nelli, "The Italian Padrone System in the United States," pp. 164–65; Koren, "The Padrone System and Padrone Banks," p. 116.

47. Helen Zeese Papanikolas, "Life and Labor Among the Immigrants of Bingham Canyon," *Utah Historical Quarterly* 33 (Fall 1965):295–96.

48. Iorizzo, "The Padrone and Immigrant Distribution," p. 43.

49. Merlino, "Italian Immigrants and Their Enslavement," p. 184.

50. Vecoli, "*Contadini* in Chicago: A Critique of *The Uprooted,*" pp. 407, 410.

51. Frank J. Sheridan, "Italian, Slavic, and Hungarian Unskilled Immigrant Laborers in the United States; *Bulletin of the Bureau of Labor,* no. 72 (September 1907), p. 406.

52. Daniel T. Rodgers, *The Work Ethic in Industrial America,*

1850–1920 (Chicago, 1978), pp. 171–72. When asked what they wanted to be when they grew up, boys between age nine and fourteen in schools run by the Children's Aid Society of New York indicated that they did not wish to follow their father's trade. Of sixty-six children asked, forty-nine wanted to go beyond their fathers, ten wanted to follow, four were undecided, and one said he was dependent on any job he could get because his father was out of work as a result of illness. See Lilian Brandt, "A Transplanted Birthright," *Charities* 12 (May 7, 1904):495–96.

53. Virginia Yans-McLaughlin, "A Flexible Tradition: South Italian Immigrants Confront a New York Experience," *Journal of Social History* 7 (Summer 1974):435.

54. Ibid.

55. Alice Bennett, "Italian-American Farmers," *Survey* 22 (May 1909):173–74.

56. Robert A. Woods and Albert J. Kennedy, *The Zone of Emergence: Observations of the Lower Middle and Upper Working Class Communities of Boston, 1905–1914*, ed. Sam Bass Warner, Jr., 2d ed. (Cambridge, 1969), p. 202; Robert A. Woods, "Notes on the Italians in Boston," *Charities* 12 (May 7, 1904):451. More recently, it has been demonstrated that rather than being unique, the Italian immigrants' economic adjustment in Boston paralleled that of the Irish of the "old" immigration. See Stephan Thernstrom, *The Other Bostonians: Poverty and Progress in the American Metropolis, 1880–1970* (Cambridge, 1973), p. 135.

57. Carr, "The Coming of the Italian," p. 421; Kate Holladay Claghorn, "The Italian Under Economic Stress," *Charities* 12 (May 7, 1904):502; Herbert N. Casson, "The *Italians* in America," *Munsey's Magazine* (October 1906): 123. "The thrift and endurance" of New York City's 220,000 Italians was reflected in their ten thousand shops and over two hundred banking and industrial concerns which had capital valued at more than $50,000. See Tomasi, *Piety and Power*, p. 27.

58. Foerster, *The Italian Emigration of Our Times*, pp. 354–55.

59. Ibid., p. 359.

60. Sheridan, "Italian, Slavic and Hungarian Unskilled Immigrant Laborers in the United States," p. 421.

61. Charles B. Barnes, *The Longshoremen* (New York, 1915), pp. 5–8.

62. George E. Cunningham, "The Italian, A Hindrance to White Solidarity in Louisiana, 1890–1898," *Journal of Negro History* 50 (January 1965):25.

63. Iorizzo, "The Padrone and Immigrant Distribution," p. 50; Iorizzo, "Italian Iimmigration and the Impact of the Padrone System," p. 212.

64. J. Alexander Karlin, "The Italian-American Incident of 1891 and the Road to Reunion," *Journal of Southern History* 8 (May 1942): 242; Gambino, *Vendetta, passim.*

65. Lodge, "Lynch Law and Unrestricted Immigration," pp. 604, 611.

66. "Southern Peonage and Immigration," *Nation* 85 (December 19, 1907):557; Rowland T. Berthoff, "Southern Attitudes Toward Immigration," *Journal of Southern History* 17 (August 1951): 348–49. Iorizzo and Mondello, *The Italian-Americans,* pp. 133–34. On immigrant peonage, see Pete Daniel, *The Shadow of Slavery: Peonage in the South, 1901–1969* (Urbana, 1972), pp. 82–109.

67. Vecoli, "Chicago's Italians Prior to World War I," pp. 401–2.

68. Daniel L. Horowitz, The Italian Labor Movement (Cambridge, 1963), pp. 37–39.

69. John W. Briggs, *An Italian Passage: Immigrants to Three American Cities, 1890–1930* (New Haven, 1978), pp. 17–20.

70. Ibid., p. 36.

71. Kolko, *Main Currents in Modern American History,* p. 79.

72. Fenton, *Immigrants and Unions,* p. 197,

73. Foerster, *The Italian Emigration of Our Times,* p. 404.

74. Edwin Fenton, "Italians in the Labor Movement," *Pennsylvania History* 26 (April 1959):137–38, 148.

75. Fenton, "Italians in the Labor Movement," p. 137; Edwin Fenton, "Italian Immigrants in the Stoneworkers' Union." *Labor History* 3 (Spring 1962):189.

76. Fenton, *Immigrants and Unions,* pp. 260–63.

77. Ibid., pp. 412–13.

78. Ibid., pp. 383–85, 428.

79. Virginia Yans-McLaughlin, *Family and Community: Italian Immigrants in Buffalo, 1880–1930* (Ithaca, 1977), pp. 129–30.

80. Fenton, *Immigrants and Unions,* pp. 197–201.

81. Yans-McLaughlin, *Family and Community,* pp. 199–200.

82. U.S. Bureau of Labor, *A Report on Labor Disturbances in the State of Colorado from 1880 to 1904, Inclusive* (Washington, 1905), pp. 102–5.

83. Foerster, *The Italian Emigration of Our Times,* p. 403.

84. Foerster, *Italian Emigration;* Barnes, *The Longshoremen,* pp. 115–21.

85. Vecoli, "Chicago's Italians Prior to World War I," pp. 376–78.

86. Chas. P. Neill, *Report on Strike of Textile Workers in Lawrence, Mass. in 1912*, U.S. Senate Document no. 870, 62d Cong. 2d sess., p. 189.

87. Ibid., pp. 19–20, 31.

88. Dubofsky, *We Shall Be All*, pp. 230–32.

89. Neill, *Report on Strike of Textile Workers in Lawrence, Mass. in 1912*, p. 31.

90. Donald B. Cole, *Immigrant City: Lawrence, Massachusetts, 1845–1921* (Chapel Hill, 1963), pp. 186–87.

91. Neill, *Report on Strike of Textile Workers in Lawrence, Mass. in 1912*, pp. 67–68.

92. Ibid., p. 63.

93. Dubofsky, *We Shall Be All*, pp. 228, 241.

94. Ibid., p. 242.

95. Ibid., p. 237.

96. Foner, *History of the Labor Movement in the United States*, 4:335–37, 343–46.

97. Foner, *History of the Labor Movement*, 4:338–43; Dubofsky, *We Shall Be All*, p. 253.

98. Dubofsky, *We Shall Be All*, pp. 263–283.

Chapter Nine

1. Higham, *Strangers in the Land*, pp. 70–71.

2. Gompers, *Seventy Years of Life and Labor*, 2:172.

3. Henry Cabot Lodge, "The Restriction of Immigration," *North American Review*, 152 (January 1891):34.

4. American Federation of Labor, *Report of Proceedings of the Eleventh Annual Convention* (New York, 1892), pp. 14–15.

5. Gompers, *Seventy Years of Life and Labor*, 2:155.

6. Higham, *Strangers in the Land*, p. 71.

7. John Higham, *Send These To Me: Jews and Other Immigrants in Urban America* (New York, 1975), p. 39.

8. Edward Atkinson, "Incalculable Room for Immigrants," *Forum* 13 (May 1892):369–70; George F. Parker, "What Immigrants Contribute to Industry," *Forum* 14 (January 1893):600–601; Sydney G. Fisher, "Alien Degradation of American Character," *Forum* 14 (January 1893):615.

9. John A. Garraty, *Henry Cabot Lodge: A Biography* (New York, 1953), pp. 141–42.

10. Samuel Gompers to P. J. McGuire, January 9, 1893, Gompers letterbooks.

11. Gompers to Executive Council of the American Federation of Labor, January 16, 1893.

12. Higham, *Strangers in the Land*, pp. 71–72; Mandel, *Samuel Gompers*, p. 188.

13. "American Boys and American Labor," *Century* 46 (May 1893):151.

14. "The Disappearance of the Apprentice System," *Century* 45 (June 1893):315.

15. "Hostility of Foreign to American Labor," *Century* 46 (July 1893):475.

16. "Foreign Control of Labor-Unions," *Century* 46 (August 1893: 635–36.

17. "Idleness and Crime," *Century* 46 (September 1893):789–90; "Substitutes for the Extinct Apprentice System," *Century* 46 (October 1893):953.

18. Higham, *Strangers in the Land*, p. 70.

19. Barbara Miller Solomon, *Ancestors and Immigrants: A Changing New England Tradition* (Cambridge, 1956), pp. 82–102.

20. Rena Michaels Atchison, *Un-American Immigration: Its Present Effects and Future Perils* (Chicago, 1894), pp. 105–6.

21. Higham, *Strangers in the Land*, p. 72.

22. Gompers to John B. Weber, January 31, 1893; Gompers to Executive Council of the American Federation of Labor, August 7, 1893, and Gompers to David B. Hill, June 23, 1893, Gompers letter-books.

23. American Federation of Labor, *Report of Proceedings of the Thirteenth Annual Convention* (New York, 1894), p. 13; American Federation of Labor, *Report of Proceedings of the Fourteenth Annual Convention* (New York, 1895), pp. 12–13; "The A. F. of L. Convention," *American Federationist* 1 (January 1895):255.

24. C. Ben Johnson, "Close the Ports," *American Federationist* 1 (December 1894):216; "Pregnant Thoughts Suggested to the Convention," *American Federationist* 1 (December 1894):242–45.

25. American Federation of Labor, *Report of Proceedings of the Fifteenth Annual Convention* (n.p., 1896), pp. 15–16.

26. McSweeney, "Immigration," pp. 173–75.

27. Samuel Gompers, "Immigration and Organization," *American Federationist* 3 (December 1896):219. Mandel, *Samuel Gompers*, p. 188.

28. American Federation of Labor, *Report of Proceedings of the Sixteenth Annual Convention* (Washington, 1897), pp. 99–100; Gom-

pers, *Seventy Years of Life and Labor*, 2:159–60; "Immigration Referred," *American Federationist* 3 (February 1897):257.

29. Garraty, *Henry Cabot Lodge*, pp. 141–42, 145; Gustav H. Schwab, "A Practical Remedy for Evils of Immigration," *Forum* 14 (February 1893):811; Knights of Labor, *Proceedings of the Twentieth Regular Session of the General Assembly* ('Washington, 1896), p. 80; Henry Cabot Lodge, ed., *Selections from the Correspondence of Theodore Roosevelt and Henry Cabot Lodge, 1884–1918*, 2 vols. (New York, 1925), 1:259 n.–260 n.

30. Higham, *Strangers in the Land*, p. 72.

31. Lee Johnson, "The Sword of Damocles Over the Head of the American Laborer," *American Federationist* 3 (January 1897):234.

32. Samuel Gompers, "Shall Immigration Be Restricted?," *American Federationist* 4 (July 1897):97.

33. "Too Much Immigration," *Locomotive Firemen's Magazine* 23 (September 1897):219.

34. Knights of Labor, *Proceedings of the Twenty-First Regular Session of the General Assembly* (Washington, 1897), p. 56.

35. American Federation of Labor, *Report of Proceedings of the Seventeenth Annual Convention* (Washington, 1898), pp. 14, 50–51, 53, 95, 97–98; A. T. Lane, "American Labour and European Immigrants in the Late Nineteenth Century," *Journal of American Studies* 2 (August 1977):241–60.

36. Samuel Gompers to The Immigration Restriction League (Boston), January 10, 1898, Gompers letterbooks.

37. Prescott F. Hall, *Immigration: And Its Effects Upon the United States* (New York, 1907), pp. 125–313.

38. Immigration Restriction League, *Report of the Executive Committee for the period from May 16, 1901, to June 30, 1902* (n.p., n.d.), p. 2.

39. Hall, *Immigration*, pp. 267–71.

40. American Federation of Labor, *Report of Proceedings of the Twenty-Third Annual Convention* (Washington, 1903[?]), p. 25.

41. Ibid., pp. 160–259.

42. Curran, *Xenophobia and Immigration, 1820–1930*, pp. 123–24.

43. Jones, *American Immigration*, pp. 260–62; Gompers, *Seventy Years of Life and Labor*, 2:172.

44. "Minutes of the National Conference on Immigration, December 6–7, 1905," National Civic Federation Papers, New York Public Library, pp. 1–2; *New York Times*, December 7, 8, 1905.

45. "Minutes of the National Conference on Immigration," pp. 30, 48.

46. *New York Times,* December 8, 1905. In September 1906, the Immigration Department of N.C.F. held a meeting which served as a follow up to the 1905 conference. Labor again presented its case. See National Civic Federation, *Facts About Immigration* (n.p., 1907), pp. 69–76.

47. Marc Karson, *American Labor Unions and Politics, 1900–1918* (Carbondale, 1958), pp. 42–43.

48. American Federation of Labor, *Report of the Proceedings of the Twenty-Sixth Annual Convention* (Washington, 1907), p. 28.

49. Jeremiah W. Jenks and W. Jett Lauck, *The Immigration Problem: A Study of American Conditions and Needs,* 6th ed. (New York, 1926), pp. 380–83.

50. Samuel Gompers, "For Better Distribution of Immigrants," *American Federationist* 14 (August 1907), 556–58; American Federation of Labor, *Report of Proceedings of the Twenty-Seventh Annual Convention* (Washington, 1907), p. 39. In February 1909, Gompers charged that the Division of Information "had been used simply as a strikebreaking agency." He "submitted data showing the percentage of unemployed and indicating how immigrants were referred to positions where strikes existed without giving them information of that fact." Powderly and Secretary of Commerce and Labor Oscar Straus denied the charge and defended the bureau. See Gompers, *Seventy Years of Life and Labor,* 2:168.

51. American Federation of Labor, *Report of Proceedings of the Twenty-Eighth Annual Convention* (Washington, 1910), p. 38.

52. Samuel Gompers, "Schemes to 'Distribute' Immigrants," *American Federationist* 18 (July 1911):519–21, 529.

53. Zosa Szajkowski, "*Yahudi* and the Immigrant: A Reappraisal," *American Jewish Historical Quarterly* 63 (September 1973):33.

54. Gompers felt that the Immigration Commission gave "splendid endorsement to the economic position" of the A.F. of L. on the immigration question. See American Federation of Labor, *Report of the Proceedings of the Thirty-First Annual Convention* (Washington, 1911), p. 66.

55. American Federation of Labor, *Report of Proceedings of the Thirty-Third Annual Convention* (Washington, 1913), p. 52; "From Near and Far, *Life and Labor* 3 (March 1913):94.

56. Gompers, *Seventy Years of Life and Labor,* 2:172–73; American Federation of Labor, *Report of the Proceedings of the Thirty-Fifth Annual Convention* (Washington, 1915), pp. 107–8; "The President's Veto," *Garment Worker* 14 (February 5, 1914):4; Arthur S. Link, *Wilson: The New Freedom* (Princeton, 1956), pp. 274–76.

57. "Immigrant Problems of the Future," *Garment Worker* 14 (February 12, 1915):5; "Why Organized Labor Favors Literacy Test," *Garment Worker* 14 (February 19, 1915):5; Samuel Gompers, "Secession is Treason," *Garment Worker* 15 (November 12, 1915):5.

58. Robert Asher, "Jewish Unions and the American Federation of Labor Power Structure 1903–1935," *American Jewish Historical Quarterly* 65 (March 1976):218–24.

59. "Echoes of the San Francisco Convention," *Ladies Garment Worker* 7 (January 1916):5–6; American Federation of Labor, *Report of Proceedings of the Thirty-Fifth Annual Convention*, p. 397; International Ladies' Garment Workers' Union, *Report and Proceedings of the Thirteenth Convention 1916* (n.p., n.d.), pp. 49–50; "Resolution on Civic Rights for Jewish People," *Ladies' Garment Worker* 7 (January 1916):19.

60. Meyer London, Rough Draft of Remarks Before House Immigration Committee, January 21, 1916, Meyer London Papers, Tamiment Library, New York.

61. American Federation of Labor, *Report of Proceedings of the Thirty-Sixth Annual Convention* (Washington, 1916), p. 158.

62. "Protecting American Labor," *Garment Worker* 15 (February 25, 1916):4.

63. Edward George Hartmann, *The Movement to Americanize the Immigrant* (New York, 1948), pp. 140–47.

64. "Against Cheap Labor," *Garment Worker* 15 (March 10, 1916):4.

65. Meyer London, "Immigration: Speech of Hon. Meyer London of New York in the House of Representatives, March 24, 1916" (Washington, 1916), pp. 3–6.

66. Arthur S. Link, *Wilson: Campaigns for Progressivism and Peace, 1916–1917* (Princeton, 1965), p. 327.

67. International Ladies' Garment Workers' Union, *Report and Proceedings of the Thirteenth Convention*, pp. 174–86.

68. "Our International at the Baltimore A.F. of L. Convention," *Ladies' Garment Worker* 7 (December 1916):7; American Federation of Labor, *Report of Proceedings of the Thirty-Sixth Annual Convention*, pp. 278, 293, 335.

69. Link, *Wilson: Campaigns for Progressivism and Peace, 1916–1917*, pp. 327–28.

70. Though they were not immediately excluded, the Japanese could have been under this law had the "Gentlemen's Agreement" ceased to function. The clause that barred the Asians contained the following sentence: "No alien now in any way excluded from, or

prevented from entering the United States shall be admitted to the United States." See Jenks and Lauck, *The Immigration Problem*, pp. 425–26, 468–73; Garis, *Immigration Restriction*, pp. 306–7.

71. American Federation of Labor, *Report of Proceedings of the Thirty-Seventh Annual Convention* (Washington, 1917), pp. 118, 386–87.

Chapter Ten

1. Samuel Gompers to Jere L. Sullivan, June 24, 1904, Gompers letterbooks.

2. "Minutes of the National Conference on Immigration," pp. 159–60.

3. National Civic Federation, *Facts About Immigration*, p. 74.

4. American Federation of Labor, *Report of Proceedings of the Twenty-Third Annual Convention*, p. 205.

5. David McCullough, *The Path Between the Seas: The Creation of the Panama Canal, 1870–1914* (New York, Simon and Schuster, 1977), pp. 473–75.

6. McCullough, *Path Between the Seas*, pp. 471–72, 474–75; Gompers, *Seventy Years of Life and Labor*, 2:166–67; American Federation of Labor, *Report of Proceedings of the Twenty-Sixth Annual Convention*, pp. 25–26; Thomas F. Tracy and Arthur E. Holder, "How Labor Fared in the 59th Congress," *American Federationist* 14 (April 1907):245–52; McKee, *Chinese Exclusion versus the Open Door Policy*, p. 213.

7. American Federation of Labor, *Report of Proceedings of the Thirty-Eighth Annual Convention*, p. 331; American Federation of Labor, *Report of Proceedings of the Forty-Second Annual Convention* (Washington, 1922), p. 323.

8. Samuel Eliot Morison, *"Old Bruin": Commodore Matthew C. Perry, 1794–1858* (Boston, 1967), pp. 261–69, 318–38, 440–42.

9. Raymond Leslie Buell, "The Development of the Anti-Japanese Agitation in the United States, I," *Political Science Quarterly* 37 (December 1922):606–7.

10. Roger Daniels, *The Politics of Prejudice*, 2d ed. (Berkeley, 1977), pp. 1–2; U.S. Immigration Commission, *Reports*, 23:5.

11. Buell, "Anti-Japanese Agitation in the United States, I," pp. 607–8.

12. Yamato Ichihashi, *Japanese in the United States* (New York, 1969), p. 229.

13. Daniels, *The Politics of Prejudice*, p. 19.

232   LABOR AND IMMIGRATION

14. Ichihashi, *Japanese in the United States*, pp. 229–30.

15. Daniels, *The Politics of Prejudice*, pp. 20–21.

16. Daniels, *Politics of Prejudice*, pp. 21–22; Ichihashi, *Japanese in the United States*, pp. 230–31; Fred H. Matthews, "White Community and Yellow Peril," *Mississippi Valley Historical Review* 50 (March 1964):613–14.

17. American Federation of Labor, *Report of Proceedings of the Twentieth Annual Convention*, p. 179.

18. Buell, "Anti-Japanese Agitation in the United States, I," p. 609.

19. Thomas A. Bailey, *Theodore Roosevelt and the Japanese-American Crisis: An Account of the International Complications Arising from the Race Problems on the Pacific* (Gloucester, Mass., 1964), p. 12.

20. U.S. Immigration Commission, *Reports*, 23:53.

21. Samuel Gompers to J. D. McGaguday and J. A. Owens, August 5, 1903, and Gompers to T. J. Ryan, August 29, 1903, Gompers letterbooks.

22. American Federation of Labor, *Reports of Proceedings of the Twenty-Third Annual Convention*, pp. 26, 204; *New York Times*, November 10, 1903; American Federation of Labor, *Reports of Proceedings of the Twenty-Fourth Annual Convention*, pp. 2, 170, 172.

23. United Mine Workers of America, *Minutes of the Fifteenth Annual Convention* (Indianapolis, 1904), p. 151.

24. Jerry Israel, *Progressivism and the Open Door: America and China, 1905–1921* (Pittsburgh, 1971), pp. 24–26; "Organized Labor and the Isthmian Canal," *National Civil Federation Review* 2 (July–August 1905):20.

25. Daniels, *The Politics of Prejudice*, pp. 68–69; Theodore Roosevelt to Henry Cabot Lodge, May 15, June 5, 1905; Lodge to Roosevelt, June 3, 1905, Henry Cabot Lodge, ed., *Selections from the Correspondence of Theodore Roosevelt and Henry Cabot Lodge, 1884–1918*, 2:122, 126–27, 134–35.

26. Ralph M. Easley to Franklin MacVeagh, July 18, 1907, National Civic Federation Papers.

27. American Federation of Labor, *Report of Proceedings of the Twenty-Fifth Annual Convention*, pp. 190–92, 216; Minutes of the National Conference on Immigration, pp. 384–86.

28. Daniels, *The Politics of Prejudice*, pp. 25–26.

29. Ibid., pp. 27–29.

30. Buell, "Anti-Japanese Agitation in the United States, I," p. 617.

31. George Kennan, "The Japanese in the San Francisco Schools," *Outlook* 86 (June 1, 1907):246–49.

32. Buell, "Anti-Japanese Agitation in the United States, I," p. 623; Robert F. Heizer and Alan F. Almquist, *The Other Californians: Prejudice and Discrimination Under Spain, Mexico, and the United States to 1920* (Berkeley, 1970) p. 181.

33. Raymond A. Esthus, *Theodore Roosevelt and Japan* (Seattle, 1966), pp. 128–45.

34. Walton Bean, *Boss Ruef's San Francisco: The Story of the Union Labor Party, Big Business, and the Graft Prosecution* (Berkeley: University of California Press, 1967), pp. 182–83; Gompers, *Seventy Years of Life and Labor,* 2:165.

35. Esthus, *Theodore Roosevelt and Japan,* pp. 160–61.

36. Ibid., pp. 163–66.

37. Ibid., pp. 176–79; A. E. Yoell, "Oriental vs. American Labor, "*Annals of the American Academy of Political and Social Science* 34 (September 1909):247–56; Water MacArthur, "Opposition to Oriental Immigration," *Annals of the American Academy of Political and Social Science* 34 (September 1909):239–46; American Federation of Labor, *Report of Proceedings of the Twenty-Ninth Annual Convention,* p. 329, *Thirtieth Convention,* p. 312, *Thirty-Fifth Convention,* p. 109; Hyman Weintraub, *Andrew Furuseth: Emancipator of the Seaman* (Berkeley, 1959), pp. 132–37; "Analysis of Seamen's Act," *Garment Worker* 15 (November 26, 1915):4.

38. Spencer C. Olin, Jr., *California's Prodigal Sons: Hiram Johnson and the Progressives, 1911–1917* (Berkeley, 1968), pp. 82–90; Robert Higgs, "Landless by Law: Japanese Immigrants in California Agriculture to 1941," *Journal of Economic History* (March 1978):-214–19.

Chapter Eleven

1. Higham, *Strangers in the Land,* p. 308.

2. There are numerous accounts of the intolerance during the war and the "Red Scare" afterward. Among them are H. C. Peterson and Gilbert C. Fite, *Opponents of War, 1917–1918* (Seattle, 1957); Stanley Coben, *A. Mitchell Palmer: Politician* (New York, 1963), pp. 196–245, and "A Study in Nativism' The American Red Scare of 1919–20," *Political Science Quarterly* 79 (March 1964):52–75; and Robert K. Murray, *Red Scare: A Study in National Hysteria* (New York, 1955).

3. Harold C. Livesay, *Samuel Gompers and Organized Labor in America* (Boston, 1978), pp. 175–76.

4. Ronald Radosh, *American Labor and United States Foreign Policy* (New York, 1969), pp. 9–11.

5. Simeon Larson, *Labor and Foreign Policy: Gompers, the A.F.L. and the First World War, 1914–1918* (Rutherford, N.J., 1975), pp. 29–30.

6. Ibid., p. 27.

7. Radosh, *American Labor and United States Foreign Policy*, pp. 14–17; Dulles, *Labor in America*, pp. 225–26.

8. Livesay, *Samuel Gompers and Organized Labor in America*, p. 177.

9. William Preston, Jr., *Aliens and Dissenters: Federal Suppression of Radicals, 1903–1933* (Cambridge, 1963), pp. 118–51; Larson, *Labor and Foreign Policy*, pp. 31–32, 160–61.

10. International Ladies' Garment Workers' Union, *Report and Proceedings of the Fourteenth Annual Convention, p.* 194.

11. American Federation of Labor, *Report of Proceedings of the Thirty-Eighth Annual Convention*, pp. 118, 288.

12. American Federation of Labor, *Report of Proceedings of the Thirty-Ninth Annual Convention* (Washington, 1919), pp. 186–90.

13. Ibid., p. 121; Marion T. Bennett, *American Immigration Policies: A History* (Washington, 1963), pp. 40–41.

14. Frank Morrison, "New Problems of Immigration," typed manuscript, no date, National Civic Federation Papers, pp. 1–5.

15. Liliput [Gabriel Kretchmer], "The Fear of Mass Immigration in America," *Justice* 1 (February 8, 1919):5.

16. M. Koltchin, "Demobilization and the Workers," *Justice* 1 (February 15, 1919):5, and "Demobilization and the Unemployed," *Justice* 1 (February 22, 1919):5.

17. Joseph Schlossberg, "Problems of Labor Organization," Amalgamated Educational Series, Pamphlet no. 2 (New York, 1921), pp. 12–13.

18. Robert L. Friedheim, *The Seattle General Strike* (Seattle, 1964), p. 27.

19. American Federation of Labor, *Report of Proceedings of the Thirty-Ninth Annual Convention*, pp. 364–68; Ruth Krouse, "The Attitude of the American Federation of Labor Towards Immigration" (M.A. thesis, Columbia University, 1931), pp. 20–21.

20. S. Yanofsky, "First Impressions o fthe A. F. of L. Convention," *Justice* 1 (June 28, 1919):4.

21. S. Yanofsky, "Labor in Europe and America," *Justice* 2 (March 12, 1920):4.

22. International Ladies' Garment Workers' Union, *Report and*

Proceedings of the Fifteenth Convention (n.p., n.d.), p. 103; *Justice* 2 (May 14, 1920):3.

23. In 1920 the A.F. of L. issued the same demands to the Democrats, but their platform merely upheld the existing Asian exclusions. See Samuel Gompers, "The Republican Party Platform," *American Federationist* 27 (July 1920):657, 661; Porter and Johnson, *National Party Platforms*, pp. 223, 235–36.

24. American Federation of Labor, *Report of Proceedings of the Fortieth Annual Convention* (Washington, 1920), pp. 104–5, 385; Krouse, "The Attitude of the American Federation of Labor Towards Immigration," p. 21.

25. "Topics of the Week: Flow of Immigration Begins," *Justice* 2 (August 27, 1920):2.

26. Juliet Stuart Poyntz, "The Menace of Unemployment," pt. 1, *Justice* 2 (September 3, 1920):5.

27. Juliet Stuart Poyntz, "The Menace of Unemployment," pt. 2. *Justice* 2 (September 10, 1920):3.

28. M. D. Danish, "Topics of the Week: The Immigration Chaos," *Justice* 2 (October 1, 1920):2.

29. "The Immigration Policy of the A. F. of L.," *Justice* 2 (December 3, 1920):4.

30. Samuel Gompers to Herman S. Hettinger, December 11, 1920, Gompers letterbooks.

31. Gompers to William T. Lakin, January 6, 1921.

32. Gompers to Lionel J. Salamon, January 22, 1921.

33. Higham, *Strangers in the Land*, pp. 309–10.

34. Max D. Danish, "Topics of the Week: Immigration Alarm Subsiding," *Justice* 3 (January 14, 1921):2.

35. Gompers to Salamon, January 27, 1921, Gompers letterbooks.

36. Higham, *Strangers in the Land*, pp. 310–11.

37. Gompers to Ralph H. Long, March 9, 1921, and Gompers to Bert Miller, March 12, 1921, Gompers letterbooks.

38. Gompers to Remo I. Robb, March 29, 1921.

39. Higham, *Strangers in the Land*, p. 311; Bennett, *American Immigration Policies*, p. 42.

40. American Federation of Labor, *Report of Proceedings of the Forty-First Annual Convention* (Washington, 1921), p. 307.

41. Max D. Danish, "Topics of the Week: No Mercy for Surplus Immigrants," *Justice* 3 (September 16, 1921):2.

42. Higham, *Strangers in the Land*, p. 311; William S. Bernard, ed., *American Immigration Policy: A Reappraisal* (New York, 1950), pp. 24–25.

43. American Federation of Labor, *Report of Proceedings of the Forty-Second Annual Convention* (Washington, 1922), p. 103.

44. Ibid., p. 328.

45. U.S. Bureau of the Census, *The Statistical History of the United States from Colonial Times to the Present*, p. 58.

46. Robert Higgs, "Landless by Law: Japanese Immigrants in California Agriculture to 1941," *Journal of Economic History* 38 (March 1978):206.

47. Daniels, *The Politics of Prejudice*, pp. 44–45.

48. State Board of Control of California, *California and the Oriental: Japanese, Chinese, and Hindus: Report . . . to Gov. Wm. D. Stephens, June 19, 1920, Revised to January 1, 1922* (Sacramento, 1922), p. 117.

49. William D. Stephens to Bainbridge Colby, June 19, 1920, *California and the Oriental*, pp. 8–9.

50. Daniels, *The Politics of Prejudice*, p. 87; Paul Scharrenberg, "The Attitude of Organized Labor towards the Japanese, *"Annals of the American Academy of Political and Social Science* 93 (January 1921):34–38.

51. Philip Taft, *Labor Politics American Style: The California State Federation of Labor* (Cambridge, 1968), p. 175.

52. Mollie Ray Carroll, *Labor and Politics* (New York, 1969), pp. 122–23.

53. Lazarus Marcovitz, "At the A. F. of L. Convention," *Advance* 4 (July 2, 1920):2.

54. Samuel Gompers to the Reverend Herbert Welch, August 31, 1920, Gompers letterbooks.

55. Gompers to Ralph E. Sawyer, January 17, 1921.

56. Gompers to W. S. Drysdale, January 25, 1921, and Gompers to John A. O'Connell, January 25, 1921. Gompers continued to regard this attitude towards Asians as economic. For example, in September 1921, he told the General Executive Board of the I.L.G.W.U. of the Cigarmakers' Union's success in ridding its trade of various evils, including "Chinese coolies." A moment later he announced that the Cigarmakers' had begun an organizational drive to enroll "every member of our craft, without regard to race, color or religion, or any other conditions." See President Gompers' Address before N.Y. Cloak Joint Board," *Justice* 3 (September 16, 1921):7.

Chapter Twelve

1. Higham, *Strangers in the Land*, pp. 313–14.

2. B. Maiman, "The New Immigration Bill," *Justice* 5 (February 16, 1923):7.

3. B. Maiman, "The Danger Point in The New Immigration Bill," *Justice* 5 (February 23, 1923):3.

4. Higham, *Strangers in the Land*, pp. 317–18.

5. "Immigration, Utilize First What We Have," *American Federationist* 30 (June 1923):489–93.

6. *New York Times*, July 31, 1923.

7. *New York Times*, September 4, 1923.

8. Higham, *Strangers in the Land*, p. 318; James J. Davis, "America and Her Immigrants," *Congressional Digest* 2 (July–August 1923):292–93.

9. Arturo Giovanitti, "The Menace of Facism," *Justice* 5 (September 28, 1923):11.

10. "No Prussian Scheme Here, Mr. Secretary," *Garment Worker* 23 (December 21, 1923):4

11. Higham, *Strangers in the Land*, p. 319.

12. American Federation of Labor, *Report of Proceedings of the Forty-Third Annual Convention* (Washington, 1923):354–55; Samuel Gompers to Morris Sigman, November 14, 1923, Morris Sigman Correspondence, I.L.G.W.U. Archives.

13. Naomi W. Cohen, *Not Free to Desist: The American Jewish Committee, 1906–1966* (Philadelphia, 1972), pp. 139–42; *New York Times*, November 19, 1923; Max D. Danish, "Topics of the Week: Immigration Again," *Justice* 5 (December 7, 1923):2.

14. *New York Times*, December 14, 15, 1923.

15. Higham, *Strangers in the Land*, pp. 317–18.

16. Philip Gleason, "The Melting Pot: Symbol of Fusion or Confusion?" *American Quarterly* 16 (Spring 1964):24.

17. *New York Times*, December 16, 1923.

18. Higham, *Strangers in the Land*, pp. 321–22.

19. M. D. D. [Max D. Danish], "In the Week's News," *Justice* 6 (January 18, 1924):1.

20. *New York Times*, January 25, February 1, 1924.

21. Chester M. Wright, "Rigid Exclusion and Safety," *American Federationist* 31 (February 1924):144.

22. "To Protest the Johnson Bill," *Justice* 6 (March 7, 1924):3.

23. "The Immigration Restriction Bill," *Garment Worker* 23 (April 4, 1924):8.

24. Samuel Gompers, "No Prussianism for the U. S.," *American Federationist* 31 (March 1924):249.

25. James J. Davis, "An American Immigration Policy," *American Federationist* 31 (April 1924):289–94.

26. John R. Quinn, "America and Immigration: Keep Our Country a True Democracy," *American Federationist* 31 (April 1924):295–99.

27. Samuel Gompers, "America Must Not Be Overwhelmed," *American Federationist* 31 (April 1924):313–17. "Immigration, for the protection of the American people," was the first of the A.F. of L.'s nine legislative aims. See *New York Times,* March 31, 1924.

28. "International Declines to Support Johnson Bill," *Justice* 6 (April 4, 1924):2: "Immigration Theory and Practice." *Justice* 6 (April 11, 1924):6.

29. Max D. Danish, "High Lights of a Liberal Immigration Policy," *Justice* 6 (May 9, 1924):5.

30. International Ladies' Garment Workers' Union. *Report and Proceedings of the Seventeenth Convention* (n.p., n.d.), pp. 145, 243–44.

31. Ibid., p. 45.

32. Emanuel Celler, *You Never Leave Brooklyn* (New York, 1953), p. 4.

33. Peter H. Wang, *Legislating Normalcy: The Immigration Act of 1924* (San Francisco, 1975), pp. 102–12.

34. *New York Times,* May 19, 1924.

35. Ibid., May 22, 1924.

36. Ibid., May 27, 1924.

37. Ibid.

38. American Federation of Labor, *Report of Proceedings of the Forty-Fourth Annual Convention* (Washington, 1924), p. 186.

39. Ibid., p. 247.

40. Livesay, *Samuel Gompers and Organized Labor in America,* p. 181.

41. Robert A. Divine, *American Immigration Policy, 1924–1952* (New Haven, 1957), pp. 41–42; Higham, *Strangers in the Land,* p. 324.

42. Bernstein, *The Lean Years,* pp. 305, 322; William S. Bernard, ed., *American Immigration Policy: A Reappraisal* (New York, 1950), pp. 41, 280.

43. American Federation of Labor, *Report of Proceedings of the Forty-Fifth Annual Convention* (Washington, 1925), pp. 169–70.

44. American Federation of Labor, *Report,* pp. 175–77; Weintraub, *Andrew Furuseth,* pp. 168–69.

45. Divine, *American Immigration Policy,* pp. 52–57; American

Federation of Labor, *Report of Proceedings of the Forty-Fifth Annual Convention*, pp. 51, 68.

46. Mark Reisler, *By the Sweat of Their Brow: Mexican Immigrant Labor in the United States, 1900–1940* (Westport, Conn., 1976), pp. 169–83, 198–218, 230–31; Harvey A. Levenstein, "The A. F. of L. and Mexican Immigration in the 1920's; An Experiment in Labor Diplomacy, "*Hispanic American Historical Review* 48 (May 1968): 206–19.

47. Divine, *American Immigration Policy*, pp. 68–75; J M. Saniel, ed., *The Filipino Exclusion Movement, 1927–1935* (Quezon City, Philippines, 1967), passim.

48. Divine, *American Immigration Policy*, pp. 87, 88, 93, 96, 105–6.

49. Divine, *American Immigration Policy*, pp. 99–102; J. Joseph Huthmacher, *Senator Robert F. Wagner and the Rise of Urban Liberalism* (New York, 1968), p. 269; David S. Wyman, *Paper Walls: America and the Refugee Crisis, 1938–1941* (Amherst, 1968), pp. 75–92.

50. Henry L. Feingold, *The Politics of Rescue: The Roosevelt Administration and the Holocaust, 1938–1945* (New Brunswick, N.J., 1970), pp. 174–75.

51. Eliot Grinnell Mearns, *Resident Orientals on the American Pacific Coast: Their Legal and Economic Status* (New York, 1927), pp. 194–95.

52. Feingold, *The Politics of Rescue*, pp. 22–24, 99–119, 128–31, 190–207, 214–22, 240–94; Robert Dallek, *Franklin D. Roosevelt and American Foreign Policy, 1932–1945* (New York, Oxford University Press, 1979), pp. 444–48.

Selected Bibliography

ABBOTT, EDITH. *Historical Aspects of the Immigration Problem.* Chicago: University of Chicago Press, 1926.

————. *Immigration: Select Documents and Case Records.* Chicago: University of Chicago Press, 1924.

————. *Women in Industry: A Study in American Economic History.* New York: D. Appleton and Company, 1910.

ADAMS, GRAHAM, JR. *Age of Industrial Violence, 1910–1915.* New York: Columbia University Press, 1966.

AMALGAMATED CLOTHING WORKERS OF AMERICA. *Proceedings of the Sixth Biennial Convention . . . 1924.* n.p., n.d.

AMERICAN FEDERATION OF LABOR. *Reports of Proceedings of the Annual Conventions, 1887–1930.* New York: American Federation of Labor, 1887–1930.

ANDREANO, RALPH, ed. *The Economic Impact of the American Civil War.* Cambridge: Schenkman, 1962.

————., ed. *New Views on American Economic Development.* Cambridge: Schenkman, 1965.

ARONOWITZ, STANLEY. *False Promises: The Shaping of American Working Class Consciousness.* New York: McGraw-Hill, 1973.

ATCHISON, RENA MICHAELS. *Un-American Immigration: Its Present Effects and Future Perils.* Chicago: Charles H. Kerr, 1894.

AURAND, HAROLD W. *From the Molly Maguires to the United Mine Workers: The Social Ecology of an Industrial Union, 1869–1897.* Philadelphia: Temple University Press, 1971.

BAILEY, THOMAS A. *Theodore Roosevelt and the Japanese-American Crisis: An Account of the International Complications Arising from the Race Problem on the Pacific Coast.* 1934 Reprint. Gloucester, Mass.: Peter Smith, 1964.

BALCH, EMILY GREENE. *Our Slavic Fellow Citizens.* 1910. Reprint. New York: Arno Press and The New York Times, 1969.

BANCROFT, HUBERT HOWE. *History of California.* 7 vols. San Francinsco: History Co., 1884-1890.

BARNES, CHARLES B. *The Longshoremen.* New York: Survey Associates, 1915.

BARTH, GUNTHER. *Bitter Strength: A History of the Chinese in the United States.* Cambridge: Harvard University Press, 1964.

BARTON JOSEF. *Peasants and Strangers: Italians, Rumanians and Slovaks in an American City, 1890-1950.* Cambridge: Harvard University Press, 1975.

BEAN, WALTON. *Boss Ruef's San Francisco: The Story of the Union Labor Party, Big Business, and the Graft Prosecution.* Berkeley: University of California Press, 1967.

BEDFORD, HENRY F. *Socialism and the Workers in Massachusetts, 1886-1912.* Amherst: University of Massachusetts Press, 1966.

BENNETT, MARION T. *American Immigration Policies: A History.* Washington: Public Affairs Press, 1963.

BERNARD, WILLIAM S. ed. *American Immigration Policy: A Reappraisal.* New York: Harper and Brothers, 1950.

BERNHEIMER, CHARLES S., ed. *The Russian Jew in the United States.* Philadelphia: John C. Winston, 1905.

———. *The Shirt Waist Strike.* New York: University Settlement, 1910.

BERNSTEIN, IRVING. *The Lean Years: A History of the American Worker, 1920–1933.* 1960. Reprint. Baltimore: Penguin Books, 1966.

———. *Turbulent Years: A History of the American Worker, 1933-1941.* Boston: Houghton Mifflin Company, 1969.

BERTHOFF, ROWLAND TAPPAN. *British Imigrants in Industrial America. 1790–1950.* Cambridge: Harvard University Press, 1953.

BEST, HARRY. *The Men's Garment Industry of New York and the Strike of 1913.* New York: University Settlement Society, [1914].

BILLINGTON, RAY ALLEN. *The Protestant Crusade, 1880–1860: A Study of the Origins of American Nativism,* New York: Macmillan, 1938.

BLUM, JOHN MORTON. *V Was for Victory: American Politics and Culture During World War II.* New York: Harcourt Brace Jovanovich, 1976.

BODNAR, JOHN E., ed. *The Ethnic Experience in Pennsylvania.* Lewisburg, Pa.: Bucknell University Press, 1973.

———. *Immigration and Industrialization: Ethnicity in an American Mill Town, 1870–1940.* Pittsburgh: University of Pittsburgh Press, 1977.

BOGEN, JULES I. *The Anthracite Railroads: A Study in American Railroad Enterprise.* New York: Ronald Press, 1927.

BOHME, FREDERICK G. *A History of the Italians in New Mexico.* New York: Arno Press, 1975.

BOONE, GLADYS. *The Women's Trade Union Leagues in Great Britain and The United States of America.* New York: Columbia University Press, 1942.

BRIGGS, JOHN W. *An Italian Passage: Immigrants to Three American Cities, 1890–1930.* New Haven: Yale University Press, 1978.

BRISSENDEN, PAUL F. *The I.W.W.: A Study of American Syndicalism.* 1919. Reprint. New York: Russell and Russell, 1957.

BRODY, DAVID. *Labor in Crisis: The Steel Strike of 1919.* Philadelphia: J. B. Lippincott, 1965.

———. *Steelworkers in America: The Nonunion Era.* 1960 Reprint. New York: Harper Torchbooks, 1969.

BROEHL, WAYNE G., JR. *The Molly Maguires.* Cambridge: Harvard University Press, 1964.

BROOKS, JOHN GRAHAM. *American Syndicalism: The I.W.W.* 1913 Reprint. New York: Arno and The New York Times, 1969.

BROPHY, JOHN. *A Miner's Life.* Edited and supplemented by John O. P. Hall. Madison: University of Wisconsin Press, 1964.

BRUCE, ROBERT V. *1877: Year of Violence.* 1959 Reprint. Chicago: Quadrangle Books, 1970.

BUDISH, J. M., and SOULE, GEORGE, *The New Unionism in the Clothing Industry.* New York: Harcourt, Brace and Howe, 1920.

BURNER, DAVID. *The Politics of Provincialism: The Democratic Party in Transition, 1918–1932.* New York: Alfred A. Knopf, 1970.

BYINGTON, MARGRET F. *Homestead: The Households of a Mill Town.* New York: Charities Publication Committee, 1910.

CALIFORNIA CHINESE EXCLUSION CONVENTION. *Proceedings and List of Delegates.* San Francisco: Star Press, 1901.

CALIFORNIA: STATE BOARD OF CONTROL. *California and the Oriental: Japanese, Chinese, and Hindus.* Sacramento: California State Printing Office, 1922.

CAREY, H. C. "Capital and Labor." In Report of the Committee on Industrial Interests and Labor, Constitutional Convention of Pennsylvania [1872–1873]. Philadelphia: Collins, 1873.

CAROLI, BETTY BOYD. *Italian Repatriation from the United States, 1900–1914.* New York: Center for Migration Studies, 1973.

CARPENTER, NILES. *Immigrants and Their Children.* Washington: Government Printing Office, 1927.

———. *Nationality, Color and Economic Opportunity in the City of Buffalo.* Buffalo, N.Y.: University of Buffalo, 1927.

CARR, JOHN FOSTER. *Guide for the Immigrant Italian in The United States of America.* Garden City, N.Y.: Doubleday, Page, 1911.

CARROLL, MOLLIE RAY. *Labor and Politics.* 1923. Reprint. New York: Arno and The New York Times, 1969.

CARSEL, WILFRED. *A History of the Chicago Ladies' Garment Workers' Union.* Chicago: Normandie House, 1940.

CELLER, EMANUEL. *You Never Leave Brooklyn.* New York: John Day, 1953.

CHIU, PING. *Chinese Labor in California, 1850–1880: An Economic Study.* Madison: State Historical Society of Wisconsin, 1963.

CHRISTIE, ROBERT A. *Empire in Wood: A History of the Carpenters' Union.* Ithaca, N.Y.: Cornell University Press, 1956.

CHURCHILL, CHARLES W[ESLEY]. *The Italians of Newark: A Community Study.* New York: Arno Press, 1975.

THE CLOAK MAKERS' STRIKE. *New* York: Cloak, Suit and Skirt Manufacturers' Protective Association, 1910.

COBEN, STANLEY. *A. Mitchell Palmer: Politician.* New York Columbia University Press, 1963.

COHEN, NAOMI W. *A Dual Heritage: The Public Career of Oscar S. Straus.* Philadelphia: Jewish Publication Society of America, 1969.

———. *Not Free to Desist: The American Jewish Committee, 1906–1966.* Philadelphia: Jewish Publication Society of America, 1972.

COLE, DONALD B. *Immigrant City: Lawrence, Massachusetss, 1845–1921.* Chapel Hill: University of North Carolina Press, 1963.

COLEMAN, MCALISTER. *Men and Coal.* 1943. Reprint. New York: Arno and The New York Times, 1969.

COMMITTEE OF THE SENATE OF CALIFORNIA. *Chinese Immigration.* Sacramento: State Printing Office, 1877.

COMMONS, JOHN R. *Labor and Administration.* New York: Macmillan, 1913.

———. *Races and Immigrants in America.* 2d ed. New York: Macmillan, 1920.

———, and ASSOCIATES. *History of Labour in the United States.* 4 vols. New York: Macmillan, 1918–1935.

COOLIDGE, MARY ROBERTS. *Chinese Immigration.* 1909. Reprint. New York: Arno Press and The New York Times, 1969.

CORNELL, ROBERT J. *The Anthracite Coal Strike of 1902.* Washington: Catholic University of America Press, 1957.

CROSS, IRA B. *A History of the Labor Movement in California.* 1935. Reprint. New York: Johnson Reprint Corporation, 1966.

CURRAN, THOMAS J. *Xenophobia and Immigration, 1820–1930.* Boston: Twayne Publishers, 1975.

D'ANGELO, PASCAL. *Son of Italy.* 1924. Reprint. New York: Arno Press, 1975.

DANIEL, PETE. *The Shadow of Slavery: Peonage in the South, 1901–1969.* Urbana: University of Illinois Press, 1972.

DANIELS, ROGER. *The Politics of Prejudice: The Anti-Japanese Movement in California and the Struggle for Japanese Exclusion.* Berkeley: University of California Press, 1962.

DANISH, MAX D. *The World of David Dubinsky.* Cleveland: World Publishing Company, 1957.

DAVIS, MOSHE, and MEYER, ISIDORE S. eds. "The Writing of American Jewish History," *Publication of the American Jewish Historical Society,* 46 (March, 1957).

DECONDE, ALEXANDER. *Half Bitter, Half Sweet: An Excursion into Italian-American History.* New York: Charles Scribner's Sons, 1971.

DICK, WILLIAM. *Labor and Socialism in America: The Gompers era.* Port Washington, N.Y.: Kennikat Press, 1972.

DILLON, RICHARD. *Humbugs and Heroes: A Gallery of California Pioneers.* Garden City, N.Y.: Doubleday, 1970.

DINNERSTEIN, LEONARD, and DAVID M. REIMERS. *Ethnic Americans: A History of Immigration and Assimilation.* New York: Dodd, Mead, 1975.

DIVINE, ROBERT A. *American Immigration Policy, 1924–1952.* New Haven: Yale University Press, 1957.

DUBINSKY, DAVID, and RASKIN, A. H. *David Dubinsky: A Life with Labor.* New York: Simon and Schuster, 1977.

DUBOFSKY, MELVYN. *Industrialim and the American Worker, 1865–1920.* New York: Thomas Y. Crowell, 1975.

———. *We Shall Be All: A History of the Industrial Workers of the World.* Chicago: Quadrangle Books, 1969.

———. *When Workers Organize: New York City in the Progressive Era.* Amherst: University of Massachusetts Press, 1968.

DUBOFSKY, MELVYN, and WARREN VAN TYNE. *John L. Lewis: A Biography.* New York: Quadrangle, 1977.

DULLES, FOSTER RHEA. *Labor in America: A History.* 3d ed. Northbrook, Ill.: AHM Publishing Corporation, 1966.

EHRLICH, RICHARD L., ed. *Immigrants in Industrial America, 1850–1920.* Charlottesville: University Press of Virginia, 1977.

ELY, RICHARD T. *The Labor Movement in America.* New York: Thomas Y. Crowell, 1886.

EPSTEIN, MELECH. *Jewish Labor in America.* 2 vols. New York: Ktav Publishing House, 1969.

————. *Profiles of Eleven*. Detroit: Wayne State University Press, 1965.

ERICKSON, CHARLOTTE. *American Industry and the European Immigrant, 1860–1885*. Cambridge: Harvard University Press, 1957.

————. *Invisible Immigrants: The Adaptation of English and Scottish Immigrants in Nineteenth-Century America*. Coral Gables, Fla.: University of Miami Press, 1972.

ERNST, ROBERT. *Immigrant Life in New York City, 1825–1863*. New York: King's Crown Press, 1949.

ESTHUS, RAYMOND A. *Theodore Roosevelt and Japan*. Seattle: University of Washington Press, 1966.

EVANS, CHRIS. *History of United Mine Workers of America, 1860–1900*. 2 vols. [Indianapolis: United Mine Workers of America, 1918.]

FALZONE, VINCENT J. *Terence V. Powderly: Middle Class Reformer*. Washington: University Press of America, 1978.

FEDERATION OF ORGANIZED TRADES AND LABOR UNIONS OF THE UNITED STATES AND CANADA. *Reports of the Annual Sessions*. Cincinnati: Federation of Organized Trades and Labor Unions, 1882–1886.

FEINGOLD, HENRY L. *The Politics of Rescue: The Roosevelt Administration and the Holocaust, 1938–1945*. New Brunswick, N.J.: Rutgers University Press, 1970.

FELDMAN, HERMAN. *Racial Factors in American Industry*. New York: Harper and Brothers, 1931.

FELS, RENDIGS. *American Business Cycles, 1865–1897*. Chapel Hill: University of North Carolina Press, 1959.

FENTON, EDWIN. *Immigrants and Unions, A Case Study: Italians and American Labor, 1870–1920*. New York: Arno Press, 1975.

FETHERLING, DALE. *Mother Jones, The Miners' Angel*. Carbondale: Illinois University Press, 1974.

FITCH, JOHN A. *The Causes of Industrial Unrest*. New York: Harper and Brothers, 1924.

————. *The Steel Workers*. New York: Charities Publication Committee, 1910.

FOERSTER, ROBERT F. *The Italian Emigration of Our Times*. Cambridge: Harvard University Press, 1919.

FONER, PHILIP S. *The Fur and Leather Workers Union: A Study of Dramatic Struggles and Achievements*. Newark: Nordan Press, 1950.

————. *History of the Labor Movement in the United States*. 5 vols. New York: International Publishers, 1947–1980.

————. *Women and the American Labor Movement: From Colonial Times to the Eve of World War I.* New York: Free Press, 1979.

FOSTER, WILLIAM Z. *The Great Steel Strike.* 1920. Reprint. New York: Arno Press and The New York Times, 1969.

FOX, PAUL. *The Poles in America.* New York: George H. Doran, 1922.

FRICKY, EDWIN. *Production in the United States, 1860–1914.* Cambridge: Harvard University Press, 1947.

FRIEDHEIM, ROBERT L. *The Seattle General Strike.* Seattle: University of Washington Press, 1964.

GAMBINO, RICHARD. *Blood of My Blood: The Dilemma of the Italian-Americans.* Garden City, N.Y.: Doubleday, 1974.

————. *Vendetta.* Garden City, N.Y.: Doubleday, 1977.

GAMIO, MANUEL. *Mexican Immigration to the United States: A Study of Human Migration and Adjustment.* Chicago: University of Chicago Press, 1930.

GANS, HERBERT J. *The Urban Villagers: Group and Class in the Life of Italian-Americans.* New York: Free Press of Glencoe, 1962.

GARIS, ROY L. *Immigration Restriction.* New York: Macmillan, 1927.

GARRATY, JOHN A. *Henry Cabot Lodge: A Biography.* New York: Alfred A. Knopf, 1953.

GAVETT, THOMAS W. *Development of the Labor Movement in Milwaukee.* Madison: University of Wisconsin Press, 1965.

GINGER, RAY. *This Bending Cross: A Biography of Eugene Victor Debs.* New Brunswick, N.J.: Rutgers University Press, 1949.

GINZBERG, ELI, and BERMAN, HYMAN, eds. *The American Worker in the Twentieth Century.* New York: Free Press of Glencoe, 1963.

GLANZ, RUDOLF. *Jew and Irish: Historic Group Relations and Immigration.* New York: Waldron Press, 1966.

————. *Jew and Italian: Historic Group Relations and the New Immigration (1881–1924).* New York: Shulsinger Bros., 1970.

————. *The Jewish Woman in America: Two Female Immigrant Generations, 1820–1929.* Vol. 1. *The Eastern European Jewish Woman.* New York: Ktav Publishing House and National Council of Jewish Women, 1976.

GLAZER, NATHAN, and DANIEL P. MOYNIHAN. *Behind the Melting Pot: The Negroes, Puerto Ricans, Jews, Italians, and Irish of New York City.* 2d ed. Cambridge: M.I.T. Press, 1970.

GLÜCK, ELSIE. *John Mitchell: Labor's Bargain with the Gilded Age.* New York: John Day, 1929.

GOLAB, CAROLINE. *Immigrant Destinations.* Philadelphia: Temple University Press: 1977.

GOMPERS, SAMUEL. *Labor and Common Welfare*. Compiled and edited by Hayes Robbins. New York: E. P. Dutton, 1919.
———. *Labor in Europe and America*. New York: Harper and Brothers, 1910.
———. *Seventy Years of Life and Labor*. 2 vols. New York: E. P. Dutton, 1925.
[———, and GUTSTADT, HERMAN.] *Some Reasons for Chinese Exclusion: Meat vs. Rice. . . .* Washington: American Federation of Labor, 1902.
GOODRICH, CARTER. *The Miner's Freedom: A Study of the Working Life in a Changing Industry*. Boston: Marshall Jones, 1925.
GRANT, MADISON. *The Passing of the Great Race*. New York: Charles Scribner's Sons. 1916.
GREEN, CHARLES H. *The Headwear Workers: A Century of Trade Unionism*. New York: United Hatters, Cap and Millinery Workers International Union, 1944.
GREEN, MARGUERITE. *The National Civic Federation and the American Labor Movement, 1900–1925*. 1956 Reprint. Westport, Conn.: Greenwood Press, 1973.
GREENE, VICTOR R. *For God and Country: The Rise of Polish and Lithuanian Ethnic Consciousness in America, 1860–1910*. Madison: State Historical Society of Wisconsin, 1975.
———. *The Slavic Community on Strike: Immigrant Labor in Pennsylvania Anthracite*. Notre Dame: University of Notre Dame Press, 1961.
GROB, GERALD N. *Workers and Utopia: A Study of Ideological Conflict in the American Labor Movement, 1865–1900*. Evanston, Ill.: Northwestern University Press, 1961.
GROSSMAN, JONATHAN. *William Sylvis, Pioneer of American Labor*. New York: Columbia University Press, 1945.
GRUBBS, FRANK L., JR. *The Struggle for Labor Loyalty: Gompers, the A. F. of L., and the Pacifists, 1917–1920*. Durham, N.C.: Duke University Press, 1968.
GUTMAN, HERBERT G., *Work, Culture and Society in Industrializing America: Essays in Working-Class and Social History*. New York: Alfred A. Knopf, 1976.
HALL, PRESCOTT F. *Immigration: And Its Effects Upon the United States*. New York: Henry Holt, 1907.
HANDLIN, OSCAR. *Boston's Immigrants: A Study in Acculturation*. Rev. and enlarged ed. Cambridge: Harvard University Press, 1959.

————. *Race and Nationality in American Life*. Boston: Little, Brown, 1957.

————. *The Uprooted*. Boston: Little, Brown, 1951.

HARBAUGH, WILLIAM HENRY. *Power and Responsibility: The Life and Times of Theodore Roosevelt*. New York: Farrar, Straus and Cudahy, 1961.

HARDMAN, J. B. S. *American Labor Dynamics*. 1928. Reprint. New York: Arno and The New York Times, 1969.

HARTMANN, EDWARD GEORGE. *The Movement to Americanize the Immigrant*. New York: Columbia University Press, 1948.

HARVEY, KATHERINE A. *The Best-Dressed Miners: Life and Labor in the Maryland Coal Region, 1835–1910*. Ithaca, N.Y.: Cornell University Press, 1969.

HARVEY, ROWLAND HILL. *Samuel Gompers: Champion of the Toiling Masses*. Stanford: Stanford University Press, 1935.

HASKEL, HARRY. *A Leader of the Garment Workers: The Biography of Isidore Nagler*. New York: Amalgamated Ladies' Garment Cutters' Union Local 10, I.L.G.W.U., 1950.

HEIZER, ROBERT F., and ALMQUIST, ALAN F. *The Other Californians: Prejudice and Discrimination Under Spain, Mexico and the United States to 1920*. Berkeley: University of California Press, 1971.

HIGHAM, JOHN, ed. *Ethnic Leadership in America*. Baltimore: Johns Hopkins University Press, 1978.

————. *Send These to Me: Jews and Other Immigrants in Urban America*. New York: Atheneum, 1975.

————. *Strangers in the Land: Patterns of American Nativism, 1860–1925*. New Brunswick, N.J.: Rutgers University Press, 1955.

HILQUIT, MORRIS. *Loose Leaves From a Busy Book*. 1934. Reprint. New York: Da Capo Press, 1971.

HOROWITZ, DANIEL L. *The Italian Labor Movement*. Cambridge: Harvard University Press, 1963.

HOURWICH, ISAAC A. *Immigration and Labor: The Economic Aspects of European Immigration to the United States*. 2d ed. rev. New York: B. W. Huebsch, 1922.

HOWE, IRVING, and GREENBERG, ELIEZER, eds. *Voices From the Yiddish: Essays, Memoirs, Diaries*. Ann Arbor: University of Michigan Press, 1972.

HOWE, IRVING, with KENNETH LIBO. *World of Our Fathers*. New York: Harcourt Brace Jovanovich, 1976.

HURWITZ, HOWARD LAWRENCE. *Theodore Roosevelt and Labor in New York State*. 1943 Reprint. New York: AMS Press, 1968.

HUTCHINSON, E. P. *Immigrants and Their Children: 1850–1950*. New York: John Wiley and Sons, 1956.

HUTHMACHER, J. JOSEPH. *Senator Robert Wagner and the Rise of Urban Liberalism*. New York: Atheneum, 1968.

ICHIHASHI, YAMATO. *Japanese in the United States*. 1932. Reprint. New York: Arno Press and The New York Times, 1969.

IMMIGRATION RESTRICTION LEAGUE. *Report of the Executive Committee for the period from May 16, 1901, to June 30, 1902*. n.p., n.d.

INTERNATIONAL LADIES' GARMENT WORKERS' UNION. *Reports and Proceedings of the Annual Convention, First to Twentieth Conventions (1900–1929)*.

IORIZZO, LUCIANO, J., and MONDELLO, SALVATORE. *The Italian-Americans*. New York: Twayne Publishers, 1971.

ISAACS, HAROLD R. *Images of Asia: American Views of China and India*. 1958. Reprint. New York: Harper Torchbooks, 1972.

ISRAEL, FRED L., ed. *The War Diary of Breckinridge Long*. Lincoln: University of Nebraska Press, 1966.

ISRAEL, JERRY. *Progressivism and the Open Door: America and China, 1905–1921*. Pittsburgh: University of Pittsburgh Press, 1971.

JAHER, FREDERIC C., ed. *The Age of Industrialism: Essays in Social Structure and Cultural Values*. New York: Free Press, 1968.

JELLEY, S. M. *The Voice of Labor*. Chicago: A. .B Gehman, 1887.

JENKS, JEREMIAH W., and LAUCK, W. JETT. *The Immigration Problem: A Study of American Conditions and Needs*. 6th ed. New York: Funk and Wagnalls, 1926.

JENSEN, VERNON H. *Heritage of Conflict: Labor Relations in the Nonferrous Metals Industry up to 1930*. 1950. Reprint. New York: Greenwood Press, 1968.

JEROME, HARRY. *Migration and Business Cycles*. New York: National Bureau of Economic Research, 1926.

JONES, MALDWYN ALLEN. *American Immigration*. Chicago: University of Chicago Press, 1960.

JOSEPH, SAMUEL. *Jewish Immigration to the United States from 1881 to 1910*. 1914. Reprint. New York: Arno Press and The New York Times, 1969.

JOSEPHSON, MATTHEW. *Sidney Hillman: Statesman of American Labor*. Garden City, N.Y.: Doubleday, 1952.

KARSON, MARC. *American Labor Unions and Politics, 1900–1918*. Carbondale: Southern Illinois University Press, 1958.

KAUFMAN, STUART BRUCE. *Samuel Gompers and the Origins of the American Federation of Labor, 1848–1896*. Westport, Conn.: Greenwood Press, 1973.

KELSEY, CARL., ed. "Present Day Immigration, With Special Reference to the Japanese." *Annals of the American Academy of Political and Social Science* 93 (January 1921).

KESSNER, THOMAS. *The Golden Door: Italian and Jewish Immigrant Mobility in New York City, 1880–1915.* New York: Oxford University Press, 1977.

KIPNIS, IRA. *The American Socialist Movement. 1897–1912.* 1952 Reprint. New York: Greenwood Press, 1968.

KIRKLAND, EDWARD C. *Industry Comes of Age: Business, Labor and Public Policy, 1860–1897.* New York: Holt, Rinehart and Winston, 1961.

KNIGHT, ROBERT EDWARD LEE. *Industrial Relations in the San Francisco Bay Area, 1900–1918.* Berkeley: University of California Press, 1960.

KNIGHTS OF LABOR. *Proceedings of the General Assembly.* 1878–1902.

KOLKO, GABRIEL. *Main Currents in Modern American History.* New York: Harper and Row, 1976.

KOREN, JOHN. "The Padrone System and Padrone Ranks." *Bulletin of the Department of Labor,* no. 9 (March, 1897), pp. 113–29.

KORMAN, GERD. *Industrialization, Immigrants and Americanizers: The View From Milwaukee, 1866–1921.* Madison: State Historical Society of Wisconsin, 1967.

KUZNETS, SIMON, and RUBIN, ERNEST. *Immigration and the Foreign Born.* Occasional Paper no. 46. New York: Natinal Bureau of Economic Research, 1954.

LARSON, SIMEON. *Labor and Foreign Policy: Gompers, the AFL, and the First World War, 1914–1918.* Rutherford, N.J.: Fairleigh Dickinson University Press, 1975.

LASLETT, JOHN. *Labor and the Left: A Study of Socialist and Radical Influences in the American Labor Movement, 1881–1924.* New York: Basic Books, 1970.

LAUCK, W. JETT, and SYDENSTRICKER, EDGAR. *Conditions of Labor in American Industries.* 1917. Reprint. New York: Arno and The New York Times, 1969.

LEISERSON, WILLIAM M. *Adjusting Immigrant and Industry.* New York: Harper and Brothers, 1924.

LEONARD, IRA M., and PARMET, ROBERT D. *American Nativism, 1830–1860.* 1971. Reprint. Huntington, N.Y.: Robert E. Krieger, 1979.

LESCOHIER, DON D. *The Knights of St. Crispin, 1867–1874.* 1910 Reprint. New York: Arno and The New York Times, 1969.

LEVASSEUR, E. *The American Workman.* Translated by Thomas S. Adams and edited by Theodore Marburg. Baltimore: Johns Hopkins Press, 1910.

LEVENSTEIN, HARVEY A. *Labor Organizations in the United States and Mexico: A History of Their Relations.* Westport, Conn.: Greenwood Press, 1971.

LEVIN, NORA. *While Messiah Tarried: Jewish Socialist Movements, 1871–1917.* New York: Schocken Books, 1977.

LEVINE, LOUIS (pseud. LOUIS LORWIN). *The Women's Garment Workers.* 1924 Reprint. New York: Arno and The New York Times, 1969.

LI, TIEN-LU. *Congressional Policy of Chinese Immigration or Legislation Relating to Chinese Immigration to the United States.* Nashville, Tenn.: Publishing House of the Methodist Episcopal Church South, 1916.

LINGENFELTER, RICHARD E. *The Hardrock Miners: A History of the Mining Labor Movement in the American West, 1863–1893.* Berkeley: University of California Press, 1974.

LINK, ARTHUR S. *Wilson: Campaigns for Progreesivism and Peace, 1916–1917.* Princeton, N.J.: Princeton University Press, 1965.

———. *Wilson: The New Freedom.* Princeton, N.J.: Princeton University Press, 1956.

LINKH, RICHARD M. *American Catholicism and European Immigrants.* Staten Island, N.Y.: Center for Migration Studies, 1975.

LIVESAY, HAROLD C. *Samuel Gompers and Organized Labor in America.* Boston: Little, Brown and Company, 1978.

[LODGE, HENRY CABOT, ed.] *Selections from the Correspondence of Theodore Roosevelt and Henry Cabot Lodge, 1848–1918.* 2 vols. New York: Charles Scribner's Sons, 1925.

LONDON, MEYER. "Immigration: Speech of Hon. Meyer London of New York in the House of Representatives March 24, 1916." Washington: Government Printing Office, 1916.

LOPREATO, JOSEPH. *Italian Americans.* New York: Random House, 1970.

LORD, ELIOT, TRENOR, JOHN J. D., and BARROWS, SAMUEL J. *The Italian in America.* New York: B. F. Buck, 1905.

LORWIN, LEWIS L., with the assistance of Jean Atherton Flexner. *The American Federation of Labor: History, Policies, and Prospects.* 1933. Reprint. New York: AMS Press, 1970.

LYMAN, STANFORD M. *Chinese Americans.* New York: Random House, 1974.

MCBRIDE, PAUL W. *Culture Clash: Immigrants and Reformers, 1880–1920.* San Francisco: R and E Research Associates, 1975.

MCGOVERN, GEORGE S., and GUTTRIDGE, LEONARD F. *The Great Coalfield War.* Boston: Houghton Mifflin, 1972.

MCKEE, DELBER L. *Chinese Exclusion versus the Open Door Policy,*

1900–1906: Clashes Over China Policy in the Roosevelt Era. Detroit: Wayne State University Press, 1977.

McLEOD, ALEXANDER. *Pigtails and Gold Dust: A Panorama of Chinese Life in Early California.* Caldwell, Ida.: Caxton Printers, 1947.

McMURRY, DONALD L. *Coxey's Army: A Study of the Industrial Army Movement of 1894.* 1929 Reprint. New York: AMS Press, 1970.

McNEILL, GEORGE E., ed. *The Labor Movement: The Problem of To-Day.* Boston: A. M. Bridgman, 1887.

McWILLIAMS, CAREY. *Brothers Under the Skin.* Rev. ed. Boston: Little, Brown, 1964.

———. *Factories in the Field: The Story of Migratory Farm Labor in California.* Boston: Little, Brown, 1939.

———. *A Mask for Privilege: Anti-Semitism in America.* Boston: Little, Brown, 1948.

———. *North from Mexico: The Spanish-Speaking People of the United States.* 1949. Reprint. New York: Greenwood Press, 1968.

———. *Prejudice: Japanese-Americans: Symbol of Racial Intolerance.* Boston: Little, Brown, 1944.

MALKIEL, THERESA SERBER. *The Diary of a Shirtwaist Striker.* New York: Co-operative Press, 1910.

MANDEL, BERNARD. *Samuel Gompers: A Biography.* Yellow Springs, Ohio: Antioch Press, 1963.

MANGANO, ANTONIO. "The Italian Colonies of New York City." In *Italians in the City: Health and Related Social Needs.* New York: Arno Press, 1975.

———. *Sons of Italy.* New York: Missionary Education Movement of the United States and Canada, 1917.

MARTIN, GEORGE. *Madam Secretary: Frances Perkins.* Boston: Houghton Mifflin, 1976.

MASSACHUSETTS LABOR AND INDUSTRIES DEPARTMENT. *Thirty-First Annual Report of the Bureau of Statistics of Labor, March, 1901.* Boston: Wright and Potter Printing Co., 1901.

MEARNS, ELIOT GRINNELL. *Resident Orientals on the American Pacific Coast: Their Legal and Economic Status.* New York: American Group, Institute of Pacific Relations, 1927.

MELENDY, H. BRETT. *The Oriental Americans.* New York: Twayne Publishers, 1971.

MILLER, RANDALL M., and MARZIK, THOMAS D., eds. *Immigrants and Religion in Urban America.* Philadelphia: Temple University Press, 1977.

MILLER, SALLY M. *Victor Berger and the Promise of Constructive Socialism 1910–1920.* Westport, Conn.: Greenwood Press, 1973.

MILLER, STUART CREIGHTON. *The Unwelcome Immigrant: The American Image of the Chinese, 1785–1882*. Berkeley: University of California Press, 1969.

MITCHELL, JOHN. *Organized Labor*. Philadelphia: American Book and Bible House, 1903.

MONTGOMERY, DAVID. *Beyond Equality: Labor and the Radical Republicans, 1862–1872*. New York: Alfred A. Knopf, 1967.

———. *Workers' Control in America: Studies in the History of Work, Technology, and Labor Struggles*. New York: Cambridge University Press, 1979.

MORISON, SAMUEL ELIOT. *"Old Bruin": Commodore Matthew C. Perry, 1794–1858* Boston: Little, Brown, 1967.

MORRIS, JAMES O. *Conflict Within the AFL: A Study of Craft versus Industrial Unionism, 1901–1938*. Ithaca, N.Y.. Cornell University Press, 1958.

MORSE, ARTHUR D. *While Six Million Died*. New York: Random House, 1967.

MURRAY, ROBERT K. *Red Scare: A Study in National Hysteria, 1919–1920*. New York: McGraw-Hill, 1955.

NATIONAL BOARD OF TRADE. *Proceedings of the Eighteenth Annual Meeting*. Boston: Geo. E. Crosby, 1888.

NATIONAL CIVIC FEDERATION. *Facts About Immigration*, n.p., 1907.

NEIDLE, CECYLE S. *America's Immigrant Women*. Boston: Twayne Publishers, 1975.

NEILL, CHAS P. *Report on Strike of Textile Workers in Lawrence, Mass in 1912*. U.S. Senate Document no. 870, 62d Congress, 2d session. Washington: Government Printing Office, 1912.

NELLI, HUMBERT S. *The Italians in Chicago, 1880–1930: A Study in Ethnic Mobility*. New York: Oxford University Press, 1970.

NEU, CHARLES E. *An Uncertain Friendship: Theodore Roosevelt and Japan, 1906–1909*. Cambridge: Harvard University Press, 1967.

NEWCOMB, SIMON. *A Plain Man's Talk on The Labor Question*. New York: Harper and Brothers, 1886.

NOVAK, MICHAEL. *The Guns of Lattimer*. New York: Basic Books, 1978.

ODENCRANTZ, LOUISE C. *Italian Women in Industry: A Study of Conditions in New York City*. New York: Russell Sage Foundation, 1919.

OLIN, SPENCER C., JR. *California's Prodigal Sons: Hiram Johnson and the Progressives, 1911–1917*. Berkeley: University of California Press, 1968.

ONEAL, JAMES. *A History of the Amalgamated Ladies' Garment Cutters' Union Local 10*. New York: Local 10, 1927.

O'NEAL, MARY T. *Those Damn Foreigners*. Hollywood, Calif.: Minerva Printing, 1971.

PARK, ROBERT E., and MILLER, HERBERT A. *Old World Traits Transplanted*. New York: Harper and Brothers, 1921.

PAUL RODMAN, W. *The Abrogation of the Gentlemen's Agreement*. Cambridge: Harvard University Press, 1936.

PERLMAN, SELIG. *A History of Trade Unionism in the United States*. 1922. Reprint. New York: Augustus M. Kelley, 1950.

PERRY LOUIS B., AND PERRY, RICHARD S. *A History of the Los Angeles Labor Movement, 1911–1941*. Berkeley: University of California Press, 1963.

PESOTTA, ROSE. *Bread Upon the Waters*. Edited by John Nicholas Beffel. New York: Dodd, Mead, 1944.

PESSEN, EDWARD. *Most Uncommon Jacksonians: The Radical Leaders of the Early Labor Movement*. Albany: State University of New York Press, 1967.

PETERSEN, H. C., AND FITE, GILBERT C., *Opponents of War, 1917–1918*. Seattle: University of Washington Press, 1957.

POMEROY, SARAH GERTRUDE. *The Italians*. New York: Fleming H. Revell, 1914.

POPE, JESSE ELIPHALET. *The Clothing Industry in New York*. Columbia: University of Missouri, 1905.

PORTER, KIRK H. AND JOHNSON, DONALD BRUCE, eds. *National Party Platforms, 1840–1956*. Urbana: University of Illinois Press, 1956.

POWDERLY, TERENCE V. *The Path I Trod*. Edited by Harry J. Carman et al. New York: Columbia University Press, 1940.

————. *Thirty Years of Labor, 1859–1889*. Columbus, Ohio: Excelsior Publishing House, 1889.

PRATT, NORMA FAIN. *Morris Hillquit: A Political History of an American Jewish Socialist*. Westport, Conn.: Greenwood Press, 1979.

PRESTON, WILLIAM, JR. *Aliens and Dissenters: Federal Suppression of Radicals, 1903–1933*. Cambridge: Harvard University Press, 1963.

RADOSH, RONALD. *American Labor and United States Foreign Policy*. New York: Random House, 1969.

RAYBACK, JOSEPH G. *A History of American Labor*. Rev. ed. New York: Free Press, 1966.

REED, LOUIS S. *The Labor Philosophy of Samuel Gompers*. New York: Columbia University Press, 1930.

REISLER, MARK. *By the Sweat of Their Brow: Mexian Immigrant La-*

bor in the United States, 1900–1940. Westport, Conn.: Greenwood Press, 1976.

RIGGS, FRED W. *Pressure on Congress: A Study of the Repeal of Chinese Exclusion*. New York: King's Crown Press, 1950.

RISCHIN, MOSES. *The Promised City: New York's Jews, 1870–1914*. Cambridge: Harvard University Press, 1962.

ROBERTS, KENNETH L. *Why Europe Leaves Home*. Indianapolis: Bobbs-Merrill, 1922.

ROBERTS, PETER. *Anthracite Coal Communities*. New York: Macmillan, 1904.

———. *The Anthracite Coal Industry*. New York: Macmillian, 1901.

———. *The New Immigration*. 1912. Reprint. Arno Press and The York Times, 1970.

ROBINSON, DONALD B. *Spotlight on a Union: The Story of the United Hatters Cap and Millinery Workers International Union*. New York: Dial Press, 1948.

RODGERS, DANIEL T. *The Work Ethic in Industrial America, 1850–1920*. Chicago: University of Chicago Press, 1978.

ROGOFF, ABRAHAM W. *Formative Years of the Jewish Labor Movement in the United States (1890–1900)*. New York: n.p., 1945.

ROGOFF, HARRY [HILLEL]. *An East Side Epic: The Life and Work of Meyer London*. New York: Vanguard Press, 1930.

ROLLE, ANDREW F. *The Immigrant Upraised: Italian Adventurers and Colonists in an Expanding America*. Norman: University of Oklahoma Press, 1968.

RONEY, FRANK. *Frank Roney, Irish Rebel and California Labor Leader: An Autobiography*. Edited by Ira B. Cross. Berkeley: University of California Press, 1931.

ROSENBLUM, GERALD. *Immigrant Workers: Their Impact on American Labor Radicalism*. New York: Basic Books, 1973.

SALOUTOS, THEODORE. *The Greeks in the United States*. Cambridge: Harvard University Press, 1964.

SANDERS, RONALD. *The Downtown Jews: Portraits of an Immigrant Generation*. New York: Harper and Row, 1969.

SANDMEYER, ELMER CLARENCE. *The Anti-Chinese Movement in California*. Urbana: University of Illinois Press, 1939.

SANIEL, J. M., ed. *The Filipino Exclusion Movement, 1927–1935*. Quezon City, Philippines: Institute of Asian Studies, University of the Philippines, 1967.

SAPOSS, DAVID J. *Left Wing Unionism: A Study of Radical Policies and Tactics*. New York: International Publishers, 1926.

SAXTON, ALEXANDER. *The Indispensable Enemy: Labor and the Anti-*

Chinese Movement in California. Berkeley: University of California Press, 1971.

SCHIAVO, GIOVANNI ERMENEGILDO. *Italian-American History.* 2 vols. New York: Vigo Press, 1947–1949.

———. *The Italians in America Before the Civil War.* New York: Vigo Press, [1934].

———. *The Italians in Chicago.* 1928. Reprint. New York: Arno Press, 1975.

[SCHLOSSBERG, JOSEPH, ed.] *Documentary History of the Amalgamated Clothing Workers of America, 1914–1920.* 3 vols. N.p., n.d.

———. "Problems of Labor Organization." Amalgamated Educational Series, Pamphlet no. 2. New York: n.p., 1921.

SEIDMAN, JOEL. *The Needle Trades.* New York: Farrar and Rinehart, 1942.

SERETAN, L. GLEN. *Daniel DeLeon: The Odyssey of an American Marxist.* Cambridge: Harvard University Press, 1979.

SHERIDAN, FRANK J. "Italian, Slavic, and Hungarian Unskilled Immigrant Laborers in the United States," *Bulletin of the Bureau of Labor,* no. 72 (September 1907), pp. 403–86.

SOLOMON, BARBARA MILLER. *Ancestors and Immigrants: A Changing New England Tradition.* Cambridge: Harvard University Press, 1956.

SOULE, GEORGE. *Sidney Hillman: Labor Statesman.* New York: Macmillan Company, 1939.

SPERANZA, GINO. *Race or Nation: A Conflict of Divided Loyalties.* Indianapolis: Bobbs-Merrill, 1923.

STEIN, LEON ed. *Out of the Sweatshop: The Struggle for Industrial Democracy.* New York: Quadrangle, 1977.

———. *The Triangle Fire.* Philadelphia: J. B. Lippincott, 1962.

STEINER, STAN. *Fusang: The Chinese Who Built America.* New York: Harper and Row, 1979.

STELLA, ANTONIO. *Some Aspects of Italian Immigration to the United States.* New York: G. P. Putnam's Sons, 1924.

STIMSON, GRACE HEILMAN. *Rise of the Labor Movement in Los Angeles.* Berkeley: University of California Press, 1955.

STODDARD, LOTHROP. *The Revolt Against Civilization.* New York: Charles Scribner's Sons, 1922.

———. *The Rising Tide of Color Against White World-Supremacy.* New York: Charles Scribner's Sons, 1920.

STOLBERG, BENJAMIN. *Tailor's Progress: The Story of a Famous Union and the Men Who Made It.* Garden City, N.Y.: Doubleday, Doran, 1944.

STONE, ALFRED HOLT. *Studies in the American Race Problem.* 1908. Reprint. New York: Negro Universities Press, 1969.

STRONG, EARL D. *The Amalgamated Clothing Workers of America.* Grinnell, Iowa: Herald Register Publishing Co., 1940.

SULLIVAN, WILLIAM A. *The Industrial Worker in Pennsylvania, 1800–1840.* Harrisburg: Pennsylvania Historical and Museum Commission, 1955.

SUNG, BETTY LEE. *Mountains of Gold: The Story of the Chinese in America.* New York: Macmillan, 1967.

SYLVIS, JAMES C. *The Life, Speeches, Labors and Essays of William H. Sylvis.* Philadelphia: Claxton, Remsen and Haffelfinger, 1872.

SZAJKOWSKI, ZOSA. *Jews, Wars, and Communism.* 3 vols. New York: Ktav Publishing House, 1972–19777.

TAFT, PHILLIP. *The A.F. of L. in the Time of Gompers.* New York: Harper and Brothers, 1957.

———. *The A. F. of L. from the Death of Gompers to the Merger.* New York: Harper and Brothers, 1959.

———. *Labor Politics American Style: The California State Federation of Labor.* Harvard University Press, 1968.

———. *Organized Labor in American History.* New York: Harper and Row, 1964.

TANNENBAUM, FRANK. *The Labor Movement: Its Conservative Functions and Social Consequences.* 1921. Reprint. New York: Arno and The New York Times, 1969.

TAYLOR, GEORGE ROGERS. *The Transportation Revolution, 1815–1860.* New York: Holt, Rinehart and Winston, 1951.

TAYLOR, PAUL S. *Mexican Labor in the United States.* 3 vols. Berkeley: University of California Press, 1930–1934.

TAYLOR, PHILIP. *The Distant Magnet: European Emigration to the U.S.A.* New York: Harper Torchbooks, 1972.

TCHERIKOWER, ELIAS, ed. *The Early Jewish Labor Movement in the United States.* Translated and edited by Aaron Antonovsky. New York: YIVO Institute for Jewish Research, 1961.

TELLER, JUDD L. *Strangers and Natives: The Evolution of the American Jew from 1921 to the Present.* New York: Delacorte Press, 1968.

THERNSTROM, STEPHAN. *The Other Bostonians: Poverty and Progress in the American Metropolis, 1880–1970.* Cambridge: Harvard University Press, 1973.

———. AND SENNETT, RICHARD, eds. *Nineteenth-Century Cities: Essays in the New Urban History.* New Haven: Yale University Press, 1973.

THOMAS, WILLIAM I., AND ZNANIECKI, FLORIAN. *The Polish Peasant in Europe and America.* 2 vols. 2d ed. 1927. Reprint. New York: Dover Publications, 1958.

TINKHAM, GEORGE H. *California Men and Events: Time 1769–1890.* Stockton, Calif.: Record Publishing Company, 1915.

TODES, CHARLOTTE. *William H. Sylvis and the National Labor Union.* 1942. Reprint. Westport, Conn.: Hyperion Press, 1975.

TOMASI, LYDIO F. ed. *The Italian in America: The Progressive View, 1891–1914.* Staten Island, N.Y.: Center for Migration Studies, 1972.

TOMASI, S[ILVANO] M., ed. *Perspectives in Italian Immigration and Ethnicity: Proceedings of the Symposium held at Casa Italiana, Columbia University, May 21–23, 1976.* New York: Center for Migration Studies, 1977.

———. *Piety and Power: The Role of the Italian Parishes in the New York Metropolitan Area, 1880–1930.* Staten Island, N.Y.: Center for Migration Studies, 1975.

Truth versus Fiction, Justice versus Prejudice: Meat for All, Not for a Few; A Plain and Unvarnished Statement Why Exclusion Laws against the Chinese Should NOT be Re-enacted; Respect Treaties, and Make General Not Special, Laws. N.p., n.d. [1902?].

UNITED MINE WORKERS OF AMERICA. *Proceedings of the Annaul Conventions, 1891–1908.* Columbus, Ohio: 1891–1908.

UNITED STATES, ANTHRACITE COAL COMMISSION. *Report to the President on the Anthracite Coal Strike of May-October, 1902.* Washington: Government Printing Office, 1903.

———. BUREAU OF THE CENSUS. *The Statistical History of the United States from Colonial Times to the Present.* Stamford, Conn.: Fairfield Publishers, 1965.

———. BUREAU OF LABOR. *First Annual Report of the Commissioner of Labor, March, 1886.* Washington: Government Printing Office, 1886.

———. "The Italians in Chicago: A Social and Economic Study," In *Ninth Special Report of the Commissioner of Labor.* Washington: Government Printing Office, 1897.

———. *The Miners' Strike in the Bituminous Coal Field in Westmoreland County, Pa.* Washington: Government Printing Office, 1912.

———. *A Report on Labor Disturbances in the State of Colorado, from 1880 to 1904, Inclusive.* Washington: Government Printing Office, 1905.

———. *Report on Conditions of Employment in the Iron and Steel*

Industry. 4 vols. Washington: Government Printing Office, 1911-1913.

———. CONGRESS, HOUSE, COMMITTEE ON IMMIGRATION. *Hearings: Biological Aspects of Immigration.* 66th Congress., 2d session. Washington: Governement Printing Office, 1921.

———. *Hearings: Immigration and Labor.* 67th Congress, 4th session. Washington: Government Printing Office, 1923.

———. SENATE, COMMITTEE ON IMMIGRATION. *Hearings: Emergency Immigration Legislation,* 66th Congress, 3d session. Washington: Government Printing Office, 1921.

———. DEPARTMENT OF LABOR. *Proceedings of the First Citizenship Convention.* Washington: Government Printing Office, 1917.

———. IMMIGRATION COMMISSION. *Reports of the Immigration Commission.* 41 vols. 1911. Reprint. New York: Arno Press and The New York Times, 1970.

———. INDUSTRIAL COMMISSION. *Reports of the Industrial Commission on Immigration: Including Testimony with Review and Digest.* New York: Arno Press and The New York Times, 1970.

VALLETTA, CLEMENT LAWRENCE. *A Study of Americanization in Carneta: Italian-American Identity Through Three Generations.* New York: Arno Press, 1975.

VAN KLEECK, MARY. *Artificial Flower Makers.* New York: Survey Associates, 1913.

VIRTUE, G. O. "The Anthracite Mine Laborers." *Bulletin of the Department of Labor,* no. 13 (November 1897), pp. 728–774.

WALKOWITZ, DANIEL J. *Worker City, Company Town: Iron and Cotton-Worker Protest in Troy and Cohoes, New York, 1855-84.* Urbana: University of Illinois Press, 1978.

WALL, JOSEPH FRAZIER. *Andrew Carnegie.* New York: Oxford University Press, 1970.

WANG, PETER H. *Legislating Normalcy: The Immigration Act of 1924.* San Francisco: R and E Research Associates, 1975.

WARE, NORMAN. *The Industrial Worker, 1840–1860.* 1924. Reprint. Gloucester, Mass.: Peter Smith, 1959.

———. *The Labor Movement in the United States, 1860–1895.* 1929. Reprint. Gloucester, Mass.: Peter Smith, 1959.

WARNE, FRANK JULIAN. *The Coal-Mine Workers: A Study in Labor Organization.* New York: Longmans, Green, 1905.

———. *The Slav Invasion and The Mine Workers: A study in Immigration.* Philadelphia: J. B. Lippincott, 1904.

———. *The Tide of Immigration.* New York: D. Appleton, 1916.

————. "The Union Movement Among Coal Mine Workers," *Bulletin of the Bureau of Labor*, no. 51 (March, 1904), pp. 380–414.

WEINSTEIN, GREGORY. *The Ardent Eighties and After: Reminiscences of a Busy Life*. 3d ed. New York: International Press, 1947.

WEINSTEIN, JAMES. *The Corporate Ideal in the Liberal State: 1900–1918*. Boston: Beacon Press, 1968.

WEINTRAUB, HYMAN. *Andrew Furuseth: Emancipator of the Seamen*. Berkeley: University of California Press, 1959.

WELCH, RICHARD E., *George Frisbie Hoar and the Half-Breed Republicans*. Cambridge: Harvard University Press, 1971.

WERTHEIMER, BARBARA MAYER. *We Were There: The Story of Working Women in America*. New York: Pantheon Books, 1977.

WEYFORTH, WILLIAM O. *The Organizability of Labor*. Baltimore: Johns Hopkins University Press, 1917.

WILLETT, MABEL HURD. *The Employment of Women in the Clothing Trade*. New York: Columbia University Press, 1902.

WILLIAMS, PHYLLIS H. *South Italian Folkways in Europe and America*. New Haven: Yale University Press, 1938.

WISCHNITZER, MARK. *To Dwell in Safety: The Story of Jewish Migration Since 1800*. Philadelphia: Jewish Publication Society of America, 1948.

WISCONSIN BUREAU OF LABOR AND INDUSTRIAL STATISTICS. *Second Biennial Report, 1885–1886*. Madison: Democratic Printing Company, 1886.

WOLFF, LEON. *Lockout: The Story of the Homestead Strike of 1892: A Study of Violence, Unionism, and the Carnegie Steel Empire*. New York: Harper and Row, 1965.

WOODS, ROBERT A., and KENNEDY, ALBERT J. *The Zone of Emergence: Observations of the Lower Middle and Upper Working Class Communities of Boston, 1905–1914*. Abridged and edited by Sam Bass Warner, Jr. 2d ed. Cambridge: M.I.T. Press, 1969.

WRIGHT, CARROLL D. "Influence of Trade Unions on Immigrants." *Bulletin of Bureau of Labor*, no. 56 (January 1905), pp. 1–8.

WYMAN, DAVID S. *Paper Walls: America and the Refugee Crisis, 1938–1941*. Amherst: University of Massachusetts Press, 1968.

YANS-MCLAUGHLIN, VIRGINIA. *Family and Community: Italian Immigrants in Buffalo, 1880–1930*. Ithaca, N.Y.: Cornell University Press, 1977.

YEARLEY, CLIFTON K. *Britons in American Labor: A History of the Influence of the United Kingdom Immigrants on American Labor, 1820–1914*. Baltimore: Johns Hopkins Press, 1957.

————. *Enterprise and Anthracite: Economics and Democracy in*

Schuykill County, 1820–1875. Baltimore: Johns Hopkins Press, 1961.

YELLEN, SAMUEL. *American Labor Struggles.* New York: Harcourt, Brace, 1936.

YELLOWITZ, IRWIN. *Industrialization and the American Labor Movement, 1850–1900.* Port Washington, N.Y.: Kennikat Press, 1977.

ZARETZ, CHARLES ELBERT. *The Amalgamated Clothing Workers of America: A Study in Progressive Trades-Unionism.* New York: Ancon Publishing Company, 1934.

ZIEGER, ROBERT H. *Republicans and Labor, 1919–1929.* Lexington: University of Kentucky Press, 1969.

ZINN, HOWARD. *LaGuardia in Congress.* Ithaca, N.Y.: Cornell University Press, 1959.

Index